DENISON'S ICE ROAD

DENISON'S

Edith Iglauer

ICE ROAD

HARBOUR PUBLISHING

Reprinted in 2009

First Harbour Publishing edition copyright © 1991 by Edith Iglauer
First edition copyright © 1974 by Edith Iglauer, published: New York: E.P.
Dutton; Toronto: Clarke Irwin
First paperback edition published Vancouver: Douglas & McIntyre, 1982

Harbour Publishing
P.O. Box 219
Madeira Park, BC
V0N 2H0
www.harbourpublishing.com

Cover design by Roger Handling
Cover background photograph by Dr. A. Farquhar / Image Finders,
Vancouver
Cover inset photographs by Edith Iglauer
Printed and bound in Canada

Harbour Publishing acknowledges financial support from the Government
of Canada, through the Book Publishing Industry Development Program
and the Canada Council for the Arts, and from the Province of British
Columbia through the British Columbia Arts Council and the Book
Publisher's Tax Credit through the Ministry of Provincial Revenue.

THE CANADA COUNCIL | LE CONSEIL DES ARTS
FOR THE ARTS | DU CANADA
SINCE 1957 | DEPUIS 1957

BRITISH
COLUMBIA
ARTS COUNCIL
Supported by the Province of British Columbia

National Library of Canada Cataloguing in Publication Data

Iglauer, Edith
  Denison's ice road

  ISBN 1-55017-041-4

  1. Northwest Territories—Description and travel—1951–1980.
2. Roads, Ice—Northwest Territories. I. Title
FC4167.3.I33 1991   917.1´93   C91-091333-1   F1060.92.I33 1991

To my sons,
Jay and Richard Hamburger

ACKNOWLEDGMENT

This adventure started, as all my trips before to the Northwest Territories in Arctic Canada have done, as an assignment for *The New Yorker*. The full story became a book. I am grateful to the editor, William Shawn, for sending me to the North, and to *The New Yorker* for permission to include in this book certain material that first appeared in the magazine.

CONTENTS

I dream
of space and sky
the whiteness of snow
the ice stretching limitless
across a lake.
As I once saw it.

Chapter One

There is a road made of snow and ice that exists only in winter, in a marvelous part of Canada so strange, so far north that hardly anybody lives there. The road forges an overland link in the Northwest Territories between two of the world's largest inland seas: Great Slave Lake, near the southern border above Alberta province, and Great Bear Lake, on the Arctic Circle. The length of the road changes each winter with all the troubles encountered during construction, but it usually runs for about 325 miles, some of them a little rugged.

The creator of this road of snow and ice is a lanky, laconic, sometimes humorous Canadian in his fifties named John

Denison, whose family motto is the Latin word, *Perseverando*. Perseverance was Denison's outstanding trait during the ten years he was engaged in his eccentric specialty of building winter roads where no one else dared to make them. The Denison family crest, engraved on a gold ring which he rarely wears because it annoys him when he is working, is a hand, its index finger pointing towards a star. For John Denison, that star is the North Star.

The bright twinkle of the North Star securely located above the North Pole is the one dependable feature for the small band of adventurers who annually have braved the savage cold, blinding snow, wild winds and perilous terrain to build the Ice Road. Their ostensible purpose has been economic: to double the period for shipping freight cheaply in and out of one particular silver mine during the year. The road, which melts each spring, and is rebuilt each winter, has made travel possible for the three to four cold months, using the icy surface provided by nature on the lakes as a highway. These frozen lakes lace the region between Yellowknife, capital of the Northwest Territories, on the 11,000-square-mile Great Slave Lake, and a tiny point of human habitation called Port Radium, on Great Bear Lake, which is a thousand square miles larger and 1,356 feet down at its deepest point.

Port Radium is one of two places on the entire shoreline around the 12,000 square miles of Great Bear Lake where people stay throughout the year. They dwell in frail wooden houses that cling precariously to the sides of a steep hill on a small inlet, Echo Bay. The hundred or so inhabitants of this small outpost do not live there because they like the scenery, which is beautiful, but to dig minerals from the surrounding ground. Uranium gave Port Radium its name. The famous Eldorado Mine, opened there in the 1930s, provided the raw material for the first atomic bombs. Eldorado closed in 1960, but five years later another company, Echo Bay Mines Limited, began extracting exceptionally high-grade silver ore at the same location, using the old mine buildings and adding a few of their own. The birth, life and death of a northern mine, no matter how great its mineral wealth, are governed by the cost of reaching it to bring in freight—heavy equipment and ordinary supplies—and carry out the tons of ore that must compete with products of more accessible mines to the south. During brief ice-free summers that begin in July and end in early fall, freight barges call at Port Radium, and all year small costly backup shipments come and go by air. The Ice Road, besides adding three winter months for freighting economically, has provided quick door-to-door delivery of cumbersome objects. A prefabricated building for the Echo Bay Mine that included a cookhouse, dining room, recreation hall and several bathrooms arrived by road on trailer trucks over February ice, delivered directly to its permanent site at the top of the hill. It came from Edmonton, in Alberta province, on four huge vehicles that rumbled over the Mackenzie Highway and its extensions into the Territories for almost a thousand miles; crossing the great Mackenzie River when it was frozen, over an ice bridge; turning left off the highway onto Denison's Road, for the final third of the journey that ended at Port Radium.

Before the Mackenzie Highway was extended all the way to Yellowknife in 1962, bulk freight going to Yellowknife and beyond—buildings, cars, furniture, liquor, food, mining equipment—arrived across Great Slave Lake by barge. Pools were formed to take bets on what day the first barge would come and everyone in Yellowknife turned out to celebrate its arrival. Nobody notices any more. Even the haul of an entire building through the Northwest Territories by truck has become a routine venture up to the point seventy miles west of Yellowknife on the Mackenzie-Yellowknife Highway where the Ice Road begins. At the turnoff to Port Radium John Denison put up a garage, and adorned it with fuel storage tanks and a trailer containing bunks, a kitchen and a telephone that occasionally works. The garage replaced one that burned down, in Yellowknife, and its new location saves truckers a seventy-mile trip into the capital for rest, fuel and repairs, and another seventy miles backtracking out again. Just for fun, Denison named his new highway stop Fort Byers, in honor of the freighting concern, Byers Transport Limited, of which he was part owner when he was pioneering his northern operations. At Fort Byers, his base camp, drivers going to Port Radium pause to fix broken equipment, reload or switch trailers, and to get food, sleep and the late news on colleagues ahead of them. Then they climb back into their trucks, turn north off the gravel highway, and plunge straight through the scrub bush onto the Ice Road, known locally as the Echo Bay Road, the Denison Trail, or sometimes simply as Denison's Road.

Denison's Road. The North grips a man; the space, the quiet, the feeling of being a pioneer gets to him. The men who began driving for Denison still come back year after year to make the dangerous run he carved out for them. Their oversized trailer trucks carry everything from tractors to peanuts; refrigerators, mine machinery, cribbage boards, heavy steel beams, small pickup trucks, groceries, beer, propane gas, lumber, fuel drums, crude ore in dull grey bags, or a million and a half dollars worth of "jig," silver ore so high grade it is shipped out rough-crushed in a sealed van. A lonely, hazardous trip, even in convoy. A driver usually can see the truck behind him in his side mirror or watch the massive vehicle ahead move safely across a lake and fight its way up the incline of the next portage, but something in his own truck may snap any time in the brittle cold; or he can misjudge a curve in the road or a snowbank and overturn; or on the lake that the truck ahead just crossed safely, he can plunge to the bottom. On the Ice Road, especially when crossing the lakes, a driver keeps one hand on the steering wheel and the other on the handle of the door nearest him, which he may already have left ajar on the second latch. When a driver and his truck run out of ice it's time to jump and every second counts.

Very few of Yellowknife's 8,000 inhabitants venture into the wild open country beyond the city limits in winter; only the prospectors, miners, pilots, game wardens, hunters and trappers who have business there. Yellowknife residents, many of whom make a living from the two gold mines in town and from servicing mines in the bush beyond, have often referred to the annual opening of the Echo Bay Ice Road in the dark month of January, with its subzero temperatures, as "a crazy thing to be doing." No one has agreed with this evaluation more than John Denison. "If you make any sense out of this crazy outfit at all," he once said, "well then, you have to look at it just as a job. I specialize in winter roads where nobody else wants to go, when the ice is frozen." He was sitting in a camper truck, deathly ill, drinking coffee, halfway up his unfinished road, surrounded by broken equipment, several days behind schedule, with the temperature outside sixty degrees below zero. He waved a long arm at the frosted window whose inside edge was caked with snow and through which the headlights of one of his other trucks glowed dimly in the mid-afternoon darkness. With a shrug that dismissed the sequence of mishaps pursuing him he added, "None of this amuses me particularly, but it suits me. I'm my own boss here. Nobody else wanted to do the job so I said, 'Why not?' Ennaway, I like doin' it and if I lie down and quit, I might as well never have started."

Denison began his career in transportation in 1947, when he left the Royal Canadian Mounted Police force eleven months after he was posted to Yellowknife to start freighting with a barge on Great Slave Lake. A legal resident now of British Columbia, he has spent so much time in Yellowknife that townspeople think of him as an Early Settler. His arrival there coincided with the gold-mining boom that eventually transformed Yellowknife from a bush camp around a bay that served as a float-plane base at the north end of the lake, into a lively metropolis with hotels, Chinese restaurants and high-rise apartment buildings. Although only 38,000 people live in the Northwest Territories and it is almost unknown Outside, it is a third of Canada, extending from the borders of the Yukon Territory in the west to the Atlantic Ocean in the east, and north to the Pole. Yellowknife, the seat of the Territorial Government, is also the biggest community and only city, but with 7,000 inhabitants it is still small enough to find someone by driving around until you see his car, by stopping at the post office, where everyone picks up mail, or by making periodic checks of the leading coffee shop and bar, in the oldest hotel, the Yellowknife Inn. Very little goes on, especially in connection with mining, that old residents don't know about. Denison's unnerving experiences in the bush and in the Barrens, the treeless desert in the Territories east and north of Yellowknife, have been followed with pride and the laughter that northerners reserve for their own people who thumb their noses at the cold and survive.

It was taken for granted that when John Denison and his road crews went out on the Ice Road they wouldn't freeze, and their adventures there became instant northern legends. Denison's reputation for going any place to make a road and hauling over it any freight that could be fastened on the back of a lowboy trailer truck, even a two-story house thirty feet wide hanging eleven feet out over each side, inspired assorted characterizations. He has been called an awful man for work, a gambler, an incredible optimist, a determined, stubborn, bull-headed, reckless man in a hurry, a straight go-ahead truck driver, a true northerner, and the kind of a man who gives the North greatness in the eyes of other northerners, who think the North is the greatest place on earth and wouldn't live any place else.

Chapter Two

FIRST TRIP OUT:
ICE AND FIRE

Why did I go up the Ice Road while it was being built, on a journey from which I knew I might not return? I had no way of foreseeing, because John Denison did not know himself, that it would be the last year he would build the Echo Bay Road. He and his partners sold their whole trucking business to an airline late that spring, and younger men who worked for Denison have now taken over the active construction of the Ice Road. But when the north wind rises to a screaming pitch and snow settles in a thick white covering over the sparse trees, the rocks, the rolling land and the smooth lake surfaces, when the temperature sinks below the lower limit of most thermometers and darkness reigns through the greater part of the day as well as all of the night, Denison still returns to travel his road in a consultative role with his successors. There are people who say —and the truckers who know him and love him believe—that so long as there is a road to Echo Bay the spirit of John Denison will be driving up and down it in his camper, gliding through the bush and over the lakes on his oversized balloon tires as lightly as if he were dancing, peering out his side window in the mirror to see what is behind, looking ahead for holes and bumps that need levelling. A tough, hard, impatient, worried man; joking, cajoling, laughing, caring; travelling with a single-minded passion, to make this long white strip of road in ice as if his life depended on its completion. North. Always a little further north.

I was working in Yellowknife when I first saw John Denison, the previous winter. He was recuperating from an operation for ulcers in a manner that would not gain any doctor's approval: by going almost directly from an Edmonton hospital to build the Ice Road. When we met he had just returned from Port Radium to Yellowknife after completing the road and opening it for the season. His health seemed precarious, even to a stranger. He was painfully thin for his height, six feet four, and his clothes drooped from his big frame as if in mourning for seventy missing pounds they had once covered, his brown cardigan sweater falling slack from his broad shoulders. His face, its melancholy enhanced by sunken cheeks and deep circles around his large blue eyes, was transformed when he talked, which was with animation and a breezy humor that erupted in frequent bursts of laughter.

"How do you build an ice road?" I asked him.

"Easy. It's a piece of cake," he said. "Ninety percent of the road is over hard water." I must have looked puzzled because he added, "There's lots of hard water up here," and laughed. "Well, not hard, a little stiff. We stay on the lakes as much as we can and pack the snow to make a portage on land between lake and lake. We've been making the winter road to Port Radium every year since nineteen sixty-four, so it's routine. We usually start the day after Christmas, on Boxing Day, if we can, as soon as there's ten inches of ice. I won't haul a load over ice, though, until it's eighteen inches thick and we ought to have thirty-six for a hundred-ton load. The lakes are easy, but the knack is to find the portage on the other side. Come back at the New Year when we are building the Echo Bay Road again and see how it's done."

I did return at the New Year, checking into the Yellowknife Inn, and at six-thirty in the evening on January second we left Yellowknife for Port Radium. I would not arrive at the Echo Bay Mine until the Ice Road was finished and I would be travelling with Denison and his construction crew all the time they were making it.

The air was cold and clear, the ground white with snow, the sky a deep navy blue studded with stars. I threw my sleeping bag and a small black overnight case, packed with only the most essential changes of clothing and toilet articles, into the back of the camper before I climbed into the front seat of the truck. Denison introduced me to a man already sitting there named Romeo Dusseault, who had been hired as the new cook for the two or three men who stayed at Fort Byers to service the vehicles.

We drove off down the empty highway. The darkness was broken twice on our seventy-mile ride by the bright lights of trailer trucks roaring past us into town. Each time Denison remarked that the truck was his, but otherwise he was remote and preoccupied. He still looked ill, his large eyes even larger when his brown-grey hair was hidden by a green-visored cap he was wearing. The John Denison surfacing here was quite different from the easygoing cheerful man I had met last year. His face was so still and expressionless that his features looked as if they had been carved from stone.

The new cook, Dusseault, told me he had just come from

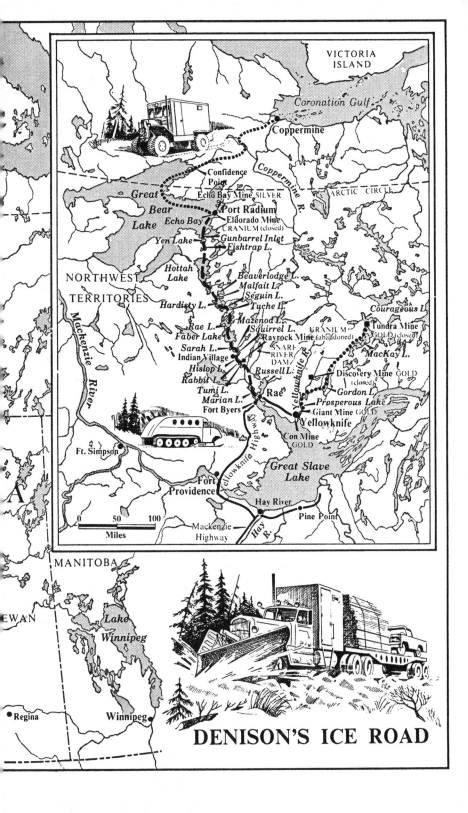

DENISON'S ICE ROAD

Edmonton and would not be returning there until May. I said I was going to accompany the construction crew all the way to Port Radium, to record how they built an ice road. "Well!" he exclaimed, and turned sideways in the seat to get a better look at me. "Pretty cold up there," he said. I explained that I was wearing long underwear and my heaviest ski pants, a shirt and a heavy sweater under my Eskimo-made parka, which had a hood trimmed with wolverine; the parka a two-piece combination of thick white duffle, a very warm heavy Arctic wool cloth, covered by a nylon windbreaker. I held up a foot so he could see my caribou-skin mukluk Eskimo boot and I showed him my deerskin mitts with sheep's wool liners. He nodded approvingly, then sat back, lit a cigarette and puffed on it a few times. "I wouldn't want to change places with you, anyway," he finally said.

After an hour we came to a lighted clearing beside the highway, turned in and stopped. We had arrived at Fort Byers, where the approach to the Ice Road began. A fort? A funny kind of a fort: three large upright fuel tanks, a fourth cylinder lying flat on the snow, and a big tin shed, everything silvery in the electric glare. A tan metal trailer with a wooden, windowed vestibule. Several bare poles supporting overhead wires. A tree, a joke of a tree, a tropical punctuation mark. Was I looking at a palm tree? I reminded myself of where I was. The tree was an evergreen, probably a spruce, but its long trunk was bare, with a pyramid of broad green boughs drooping from the very top.

We pulled in between two trucks that dwarfed our vehicle and engulfed us in clouds of steam from the exhausts of their idling motors. "Leave your things where they are, in the camper," Denison said. "You'll be sleeping in the garage tonight." He and Dusseault went into the tan trailer and I hurried after them. I pulled the door to the vestibule shut behind me in a tug-of-war with the wind and entered a narrow kitchen with a small bathroom at one end and a bunkroom at the other. Several men at a table eating dinner looked up in obvious surprise when I came in. I knew three of them from my previous stay in Yellowknife: a truck driver named Bobby Fry; Henry Ford, the taciturn mechanic in charge of the garage; and Jimmy Watson, Denison's nephew, a bright-eyed, handsome young man in his early twenties with a short black beard.

I was not imagining the hesitation in their welcome; I had braced myself for it. The very few outsiders who had travelled all the way to Port Radium over the Ice Road were men, and they came only after the road was in. There had never been a passenger during the road-building process before me. "You might as well come, if you are going to ask all those dumb questions. There is no way I can tell you what it's like," Denison had said when he suggested that I see it for myself; but I had had no idea then of accepting his offer.

The night after our meeting the year before I had dined at the home of the Commissioner of the Northwest Territories, Stuart Hodgson, executive head of the Territorial Government. When I casually mentioned Denison's invitation and that I had no intention of taking him up on it, Hodgson had shouted at me, "You've *got* to go!" and begun pacing up and down in his living room in excitement, waving his arms. Hodgson, a tall, jolly man with a walrus moustache, was speaking in his favorite role, supersalesman for the North, and when he does that he always talks in exclamation marks. "John never takes anyone on that Ice Road! *I* have never been on it! Practically *nobody* around here has been on it! A chance to travel with the construction crew while it builds an ice road so far north! You, a woman! Think of it! A pioneering endeavour! The hardships! The danger! Wonderful! A great northern story! You can't turn down such an opportunity to record history! I want to see the mystery taken out of the North!"

So here I was. Jimmy offered me a cup of coffee and the men moved around at the table to make a place for me. Denison walked over to a two-way radiotelephone in the corner, flicked a button on the receiver and began calling into the microphone,

"SX One-five-two-one-three. SX One-five-two-one-four. Do you read me, Tom? Over." He paused, flicked the button again and waited beside the black box. He repeated his chant several times but there was no response to his call letters at the other end of the phone. I asked Jimmy what he was doing.

"The men began work on the Ice Road a week ago and are sixty miles up, around the second lake, Tumi," Jimmy said. "They have radiophones—radios hooked into the telephone system—in their trucks same as this one here, and John's trying to get in touch with them. He's been away, lining things up, flying between Edmonton and Yellowknife until now. The men are supposed to call in at regular hours during the day and evening, but reception's been very bad. I sure am surprised to see you," he added. "John never tells anybody anything, you know that, so nobody knew you were coming!"

Denison slammed down the phone and went out to the garage with Henry Ford. The others soon followed, and I, feeling a bit uncertain where to go, stayed to watch Dusseault make bread. He shaped the dough into neat square loaves which he set on the counter to rise overnight. At ten I put on my parka and went out to the garage myself. The temperature was a cold thirty below and there was still a sharp wind, so I put my head down and ran the few hundred feet to the small door in the side of the shed. I pulled hard against the wind and the door opened suddenly, slamming shut behind me. I was standing inside a long, half-heated shed that was saturated with gasoline and oil fumes, gazing through a forest of trucks, tires, automotive parts, welding machines, heaters, nuts, bolts and black grease. I hesitantly started walking and recognized the rectangular box form of a Herman Nelson heater, a compressor-type machine weighing about 150 pounds and mounted on skids for moving around, with a powerful gasoline motor, that is used for warming up frozen machinery outdoors in the North. The black arms of an overhead crane loomed at me under the slanting metal roof. Then I spied the cab end of a trailer truck over a repair pit. Across the cab's open radiator hood I saw the green visor of Denison's cap and the greying top of Henry Ford's head.

I walked around the truck and looked up at the two men who were perched on a fender several feet above me peering down into the motor. Two physicians in consultation over a sick patient. Trucks have a sameness only until you know them. I would have recognized this Colossus, this gigantic red truck any place, even without the numerals "36" painted in gold letters on its door. It was the largest truck I had ever seen when I drove in it the winter before; my first, amazing ride in one of John Denison's big vehicles. The trucks were customarily referred to by their identifying numbers in the company's books, but someone had named this truck, Number 36, *The African Queen*, and the name suited her. Her size was queenly, thirteen feet high and eight feet wide, and she moved with heavy, stately dignity. Riding in the African Queen was uncomfortable, because only a makeshift seat alongside the driver had been provided, on the wooden box that held the batteries, but the view from her great height, at least eight feet above the snow and ice, was superb. She was an old-fashioned, square-sided, unstreamlined shape, and had six-wheel drive with dual tires on the rear and singles on the front that were three feet high. From the front of her stubby firetruck red radiator, to which Denison had attached a two-ton snowplow of his own concoction with wings like an angel, to the back end of her long flat trailer, she was thirty-four feet, easily carrying on her back a huge tractor or a serpentine roadgrader, a two-ton pickup truck or a house. Travelling empty she weighed just 39,000 pounds, or about twenty tons, but fully loaded she could weigh up to 100,000 pounds or fifty tons, a sizable matriarch and overweight for any place but a private road or pretty thick ice. She started life as a Mack truck, was rebuilt by the Canadian Army for use on the Alaska Highway; and finally Denison bought her for $6,000. A new truck anything like her would have cost him at least $50,000, and then

Denison would not have been satisfied until he had reconstructed her as he did all his trucks, to meet the peculiar needs of his road. The only parts of 36 that were still Mack were the transmission and rear-end mechanism that drove the wheels.

I had been instructed that the camper would be my home on the Ice Road, but I had a special affection for 36. Denison's drivers, assigned for the whole winter to one vehicle in which they lived for days, became deeply attached to that special truck. The man and his machine formed a close partnership of mutual dependency that evoked strong emotions: grief when the truck broke down; intense jealousy when another driver took the wheel; pride if the truck performed well and brought them both smoothly through a bad trip. The driver knew his truck inside out. He must. He had to be able to diagnose correctly any erratic behaviour and repair breakdowns, even weld parts together, out in the open on the Ice Road day or night, sometimes in sixty-below cold while a thirty-mile-an-hour wind was blowing. All radios in the North have an unhappy habit of conking out when needed, but even when truck radios worked, help or spare parts arrived after a long wait, on another truck or by chartered plane. The alternative to self-help was to sit down in an ailing truck with the motor still running, if it still *could* run, and hope someone would come past in another truck to attach a towline before the fuel supply ran out.

I once asked Denison if I interpreted correctly how the men felt about their trucks. "I try never to change trucks and guys around if I can help it," he said. "If someone gets sick we have to use their truck, but the longer you give a man the same truck, the more pride he takes in it, and if you start switching the men around, they lose interest."

"Have you ever had a favorite truck?" I asked. He looked astonished. "What the hell for?" he snapped. "Most of them are a pile of junk ennaway." He paused. "No, most of them are pretty good," he said. "We've had some beautiful trucks, we've had some that were *really* beautiful."

At the far end of the garage I found the camper, which had been driven inside so I could sleep in a warm place. I walked around it. The three-quarter-ton red pickup truck looked solid enough and the silvery metal house mounted on its back bore the reassuring name, *Security Traveler*. A tiny silver sheet-metal house, ten feet long, eight feet wide and seven high, with curtained windows to give it a cosy appearance and an overhang that fitted neatly above the driver's cab. I mounted three steps attached to the rear, opened a glass-and-steel door set between two windows, and entered a charming living-dining room panelled in beige plywood, with dainty yellow-and-white tieback drapes at the windows and yellow-and-green floralled upholstery on the seat cushions. My sleeping bag and case were on a long bench at one side of the door and across the narrow carpeted aisle was a table set on a chrome metal pole with a bench on three sides. A sliding door opened into a miniature brown and yellow kitchen with a wall refrigerator, cupboards and a four-burner yellow enamel stove with an oven underneath, a little steel double sink and a scrap of counter space. In the overhang beyond, at the level of my chin when I stood in the kitchen, was a large double bunk, piled now with more sleeping bags.

I hung my parka in a closet beside the refrigerator, sat down and pulled off my boots, dazzled by my comfortable surroundings. I had assumed that my living quarters would be primitive. A knock on the door, and when I opened it, Denison and Jimmy Watson were standing outside. They came in, Denison bending his head to enter. When I told him that this was my first time travelling in a camper and how nice it was, he beamed and said, "Like it, eh? Without my camper on the road I'd be lost, as if I was without feet. It's quick transportation, a place to sleep and for the men to eat in. I allus say, I make my wages cooking their breakfast and they sure don't mind someone cooking for them; but what I mean is, I get 'em up and on the road at five in the morning, a couple of hours ahead of what they would do if I wasn't there." He was his easy self again. "I rented this camper because it has a furnace that I want to try out," he added. "In the camper I own I have to have an open propane heater going all the time to keep it warm. The only things I own on *this* outfit are the wheels, and flotation tires. They cost me six hundred dollars."

Jimmy removed the table pole and dropped the tabletop to the level of the bench to form a neat, square bunk for me, with the seat cushions laid flat as a mattress. Henry Ford was leaving the garage and Denison and Jimmy stepped out of the camper onto the garage floor and joined him. "So long," Jimmy called back. "Have a good sleep." Someone snapped off the garage lights and I heard the outer door slam shut.

I was alone with the big truck shadows, the reaching arms of the black crane, the wind beating against the tin garage walls. I pulled off a sweater, one pair of socks, unrolled my sleeping bag on the new bunk, turned off the camper lights and got into bed. In the darkness, I inhaled gasoline and oil fumes, and meditated.

Until now I had been busy just getting here with no time to think about what came next. I stared into the darkness inside the camper, which was a separate darkness from the darkness outside in the garage, and I said to reassure myself, "This is only a journey from Point A to Point B. If I can stay out of everyone's way and make myself useful, I'll be all right. I'll take each day as it comes."

I did not dare to imagine what travelling with the construction crew on the Ice Road would be like, but I knew what to expect when we arrived at Port Radium. I had made a two-hour flight in a small plane up to Echo Bay Mine last year, and stayed overnight in the spare bedroom in the mine manager's house. Port Radium proved to be not a town or a village, but a cluster of old-fashioned white frame buildings with green trim, scattered along the narrow shore of Echo Bay, at the foot of a hill and on top of its precipitous slope; perhaps thirty buildings in all, for the mine is a small one, with about a hundred employees. We had landed on an airstrip plowed out by one of Denison's trucks on the frozen bay, close to the docks where the summer boats and barges were locked into the ice for the winter. The Ice Road had been open then for two months, and Denison's trucks were parked at the bottom of the hill, standing among the squares and rectangles of buildings that were garages and warehouses, a bunkhouse, machine shop, power plant and mill, the latter distinguished by a long chute that ran out to the bay on narrow girders and partially screened the fuel-tank farm beyond. When I got out of the plane, someone pointed out the house of the mine manager, John Zigarlik, on top of the hill. To reach it, I climbed 128 steps on a wooden scaffolding to the wooden catwalks connecting the mine offices with mine officials' houses. One of these narrow plank paths led to the Zigarliks', a red-roofed, white frame house with a broad view across the bay to low undulating hills speckled with trees that hid the head frame and shaft of the silver mine. From the Zigarliks' living-room window, an admirable observation post, you could see all the way to the mouth of Echo Bay and beyond. In the distance, clearly visible and ablaze with light on the sunny day of that first visit, was the windswept open space of The Big Lake: Great Bear Lake.

All that was a year ago. Now I was trying to fall asleep in a truck parked in an Arctic garage 300 and some miles south of Great Bear Lake, surrounded by vehicles the size of dinosaurs, wind pummelling pounding the thin layer of tin that protected me from minus-thirty-degree cold. If I called out, no one would hear me. I longed for sleep, but I was awake, staring at the ceiling of the camper, with memories racing through my mind; a film running backwards. It stopped in March of the year before when I was standing with the mine manager's wife, Olga Zigarlik, at the window in her house at Port Radium, admiring the stunning view of Great Bear Lake in the setting sun, long salmon streaks in a fawn-grey sky. Mrs. Zigarlik is an alert, vital, plain-looking woman; thinning brown hair, sharp eyes behind steel-rimmed spectacles, with a capacious mind that eagerly absorbs and catalogues every detail of the mine operation. "The breaking of the Ice Road is something we look forward to each year," she had said. "The men make bets on the day when the first truck will come through and the women begin watching every day for a week beforehand. I get out my field glasses and then I can see a great distance." She had gone to a desk drawer, returning to the window carrying a handsome pair of binoculars. "A professor of botany from the States sent these to me after he had been at the mine," she said proudly, and raised them to her eyes, scanning the lake. Handing the glasses to me, she had pointed to a minute black speck, miles away. In the binoculars it became a truck surrounded by puffy clouds, the only moving thing in the whole panorama of outspread lake ice beyond the entrance to the bay. I had told Mrs. Zigarlik that I hoped to return the following January to record the building of the Ice Road. "If you come back next year with the trucks, we'll be watching for you, just like this," she said. "The trucks don't look very big when they are first sighted and they disappear from time to time behind obstructions, or the height of the land will hide them. But when they are six miles away, from then on they are coming straight towards us on The Big Lake. This year, the trucks broke the road into the mine at eleven o'clock in the evening. If you arrive after dark, the trucks will look like a whole lot of little lights and we'll know when you hit a piece of rough ice, because they'll flicker. We'll be able to see your lights, twinkling, moving closer all the time, for an hour and a half before you come in."

The truck we had watched approaching that afternoon was the great snowplow, 36, the African Queen, driven by Jimmy Watson, whom I met then for the first time. He was driving in with a load of groceries for the mine, and the plow of his truck threw up a snowy froth against the canvas sheet that kept the drifting snow he was clearing off the Ice Road from clouding his view through the windshield. Two trucks came in several hours behind him, four sparkling dots of light in the far-away darkness, twin pairs of eyes, one behind the other, edging slowly towards the mine. When the trucks crossed the airstrip below, we saw the clumsy burdens that had kept them back to a pace of less than fifteen miles an hour. The trucks' yellow clearance lights outlined the swaying, oversized buildings, the new cookhouse and dining room, each hanging thirteen feet over the back of the trailer to which it was chained.

Now I was wide awake in my new strange bedroom in the garage. What kept me from sleeping? My neighbors? Truck 36 was alongside me in the garage at this moment, standing next to the camper. A presence, to focus the backward-moving film in my memory on a brief trip I had made in 36 on Great Bear Lake the year before. I was the passenger on the makeshift battery box seat; John Denison, the driver. He had spent the evening before at Port Radium talking to John Zigarlik about cutting a new truck route another 300 or so miles farther north into the Arctic, beyond Great Bear Lake to Coppermine, a small Eskimo settlement on the north shore of the mainland, and from there across Coronation Gulf onto the High Arctic Islands, to deliver government supplies to a remote communications station. "Ennaway, I want to prove it can be done," I heard him say. Early the next morning, while Jimmy was still asleep at the mine after driving for more than thirty-five hours from Yellowknife, Denison and I went out on Great Bear Lake in Truck 36 to start a new road to Coppermine; plowing a nine-foot-wide highway for approximately 150 miles from Echo Bay across to the other end of The Big Lake, and from there overland another 150 miles to the north coast and beyond. John wanted to use the four or five daylight hours of this particularly beautiful, golden day, to get as much of the road marked out as he could, and then to go back to Echo Bay and "get the rest of it going," as he casually explained. Jimmy was to join us, following in the faster camper when he woke up.

I had flown to Port Radium, so this was my introduction to ice-road travel. I was thoroughly relaxed, enjoying the spectacular view on this perfect day, of flat snow and endless ice all the way to the horizon, bordered at the distant shore on both sides by black pencil marks that must be trees. My seat on the hard wooden top of the battery box had been improved by the addition as padding of sleeping bags, essential items for any Arctic venture even five minutes away from a settlement. Thirty miles out on that frozen sea the front wheels of 36 dropped with a thud and we came to an abrupt halt. The sunny scene through the windshield, a peaceful empty landscape of blue sky, white clouds, glittering ice and far-off shoreline, suddenly shifted to a red radiator hood heading downwards. The loose wooden lid of the battery box slid forward and I was sitting on the knobby top of an exposed battery. "What's happened?" I asked. But I knew.

"We just fell into Great Bear Lake," Denison said. He removed his sunglasses and leaned back in the driver's seat, chewing on an earpiece. He turned to look at me. "Are you scared?" he asked.

I heard myself say, truthfully, "No. Should I be?"

He laughed and pulled up his parka hood, put on his mitts and got out of the truck. I followed him to where the truck wheels had dropped into a crack about two feet wide in the ice. Fresh water bubbled up through the ice around the massive three-foot-high front wheels. I removed a glove and stuck my finger into the crack. It was wet there, and very very cold. I turned and looked back at the truck. Ninety percent of the African Queen still rested majestically on the ice. Denison said, "The ice will probably hold until help comes. I never travel alone. Jimmy will be here in an hour in the camper." He pushed back his parka hood, scratched his head and swore. "I saw this crack but I thought we could make it across," he said. "I would never be here if I didn't take chances."

We climbed back in 36 and waited. There was no place else

to go, and the outdoor temperature on Great Bear Lake had dropped to forty below zero. The floor heater in the cab blew hot air at our knees and the idling motor made a comfortable chug-chug sound. Jimmy Watson showed up exactly an hour later in the camper, which had a chain winch on its front bumper, fastened into the frame of the truck; the winch, a drum powered by the truck's engine that turns at very low gear, winding up a cable with a short chain at its end to lift heavy objects, with luck in this case the front wheels of 36 from under the ice. Denison took a small pot from the camper's kitchen, scooped water from the open crack where the truck wheels were resting, and handed the pot to me. "Make tea for us while we try to pull Thirty-six out before its wheels freeze in," he said.

The two men attached the winch to 36 and I hurried inside the camper to heat water. I had the pot on the propane stove and had lit the burner when the camper began swinging furiously in a wide arc. Grabbing the pan, I braced myself against the stove, holding the pot of water down over the flame to heat while the floor I was standing on skated in circles on the ice. The camper and I flew around, but 36 never budged. When we stopped swinging, Denison and Jimmy came in for tea. Then we abandoned 36 with her motor running, helpless giantess with her front feet caught in the ice. All three of us drove back over the road we had plowed to Port Radium, and Denison and I flew back to Yellowknife the same day. Jimmy returned to 36 late that night with another driver and truck. The African Queen's motor was still running when he came to fetch her. He used her own rear axle as a "dead man" or anchor, which he disconnected and placed in a hole he drilled down through the ice the axle's length, about four feet, twenty feet behind 36. He connected the winch on the back of 36 to her own detached axle anchored in the ice, and then, as he later described it, "I just went back and sat down inside Thirty-six, looked in her mirror and watched while she pulled herself out." When her front wheels were up from the crack Jimmy hauled her back to safety with the other truck. Then he replaced her axle in its rear wheel slot and drove 36 back to Port Radium.

Two weeks later, almost a hundred miles farther along in the direction we were heading that day, a Bombardier, a tracked vehicle with skis on the front that looked like a small bus, and weighed only two tons, went through the ice and sank. It was new and belonged to Toronto promoters planning to establish a copper mine along Denison's future northern road. Its driver, an Indian named Al Frost, managed to jump clear, but he was alone in sub-zero weather without shelter on Great Bear Lake for more than a week before he was found. I could see Denison's words when he told me this news, like a big red neon sign in my camper bedroom, now, a year later. "If we had gotten that far in Thirty-six the day we were heading down Great Bear Lake we would have gone in, instead of Frost," he had said. "I thought there was more ice there."

I fell asleep finally and awoke in the morning to the rat-a-tat of a welding machine, the clink of tools, the sound of voices outside. It was after seven when I stepped from the camper onto the garage floor. Henry Ford and Jimmy were installing a new starter in 36, Denison was patching the gas pump on the camper pickup, and someone was putting studs, hub bolts, in the giant wheel of another truck. Outside in the black Arctic morning air, Bobby Fry, the truck driver, was leaving for Edmonton. "See you on the Ice Road," he called to me out his truck window. "I got a load of dynamite for the mine waiting to go in on the first trip." He waved, rolled up his window, and pulled out into the highway, heading south.

In Romeo's warm kitchen there was the wonderful smell of baking bread. "Take your time," he said when I sat down to eat the eggs, bacon and pancakes he put before me. "You won't leave for two hours." John came in to try the phone, without success, and departed with an armload of canned goods from stores in the vestibule. I hurried through breakfast and went out to the garage with a second load of cans. Denison and Jimmy were kneeling on the benches inside the camper, sealing window and door frames with heavy plastic. The dainty yellow curtains and the strip of rug had vanished. The floor was covered instead with brown corrugated box sections. "For warmth," John said. "They absorb moisture and when they get dirty, we throw them out and get some more." I made several trips to the food stores and Denison filled the drawers and cupboards with the cans and boxes: tins of butter, jams, fruits, vegetables, soups, stews and fish; boxes of macaroni, dehydrated milk and potatoes; cheese, bread, sausage, bacon, fresh eggs, coffee, tea, and a dozen rolls of paper towelling, which Denison stuffed wherever there was an empty space, including the twin sections of the sink. "Can't use the sink ennaway," he said. "Pipes would freeze." When he had packed everything away he opened the garage doors and drove the camper outside to the fuel tanks. While he was transferring 150 gallons of gasoline into the camper's regular and extra tanks, Jimmy removed the camper steps, placed them in a special rack underneath the camper floor outside, and attached a battered blue Bombardier to a trailer hitch where the steps had been. "You'll need the Bug," he said. "It's good for scouting, because it goes quickly over any terrain." He got in, started the motor of the driverless Bombardier which we were going to be pulling behind us, and returned to the garage. Denison was in the driver's seat of the camper, ready to go. I asked why Jimmy had started the Bombardier's motor and he said, "If we didn't start it now we wouldn't be able to when it gets *really* cold. We never know when we will want to use it, so it's easier to leave it running and then it'll be ready to go when it's needed."

One more stop. We drove over to the kitchen and John picked up several packages of fresh meat, and two loaves of newly baked bread which he threw into the back of the camper. He tossed the meat boxes into the space between the front bumper and radiator of the truck. I had heard of meat being roasted on the engine manifold, but had never seen a bumper used as a refrigerator. "Fridge, hell," John said. "It's the best deep-freeze I know of at this time of year."

It was an hour after dawn, eleven o'clock in the morning. A grey windless day, and exhaust smoke from idling truck motors hung in the dry cold air at Fort Byers as if it had been pinned there. We crossed the highway onto a rough road wide enough for two trucks to pass.

"This is the old road to Rayrock, a uranium mine that has been closed for about ten years," Denison said. "You'll be able to see the mine from the road when we get about sixty miles up the line. I brought my tractor in by barge last summer to fix up this road, so it's a lot better than it was."

We leapt over bumps, dropped into ruts, and I wondered as I braced myself to keep from hitting the windshield, the ceiling, and Denison's $2,000 two-way mobile radio, what the road was like before it was fixed up. After two miles we arrived at Marian Lake, the first of the chain of lakes serving as the highway for the Ice Road. The air was so grey that I didn't see the lake until we dropped from the road to its flatness. The other end was somewhere twenty-five miles distant and the shoreline on both sides was marked by low spruce trees and willow bushes. "I never feel I'm on the Ice Road until I get here, at Marian Lake," Denison said. "That little two-mile stretch we just went through doesn't matter." We were driving at forty miles an hour down the middle of the lake on a smooth white road bordered by two-foot-high snow drifts. Denison inserted an old Guy Lombardo dance recording, "Golden Medleys," into the stereo and the silky tones of the music blended with the cosy hum the tires made on the ice. "Want to dance?" he said suddenly. We both laughed.

"Do you ever think about falling through the ice?" I asked. I was looking straight ahead but I couldn't see the end of this lake. The wind had come up with a fury that made the camper shudder.

"Funny you should mention that. I was talking with an old

friend, Del Curry, about ice just three days ago, on New Year's Eve," John said. "If it hadn't been for guys like Del I could never have got going. He would go on trips with me to look at the road, and he never told me I couldn't go, or couldn't make it. He always backed me up and his men and equipment worked with me all the time. Del has a construction business now in Yellowknife, but when he came north in forty-three he freighted with Cat trains on Great Slave Lake. Cat trains are four or five sleighs hooked together and hauled by tractors, and we call all tractors Cats, although in the beginning they were just the ones made by the Caterpillar Tractor Company. Cat trains just walked right through the bush, they didn't bother packin' the snow, or makin' a road; they'd just pull the sleighs through behind them. But they were so slow. Their top speed was four miles an hour, and the trucks can go thirty or forty, up to sixty sometimes now. Del said he knew he had to get out of the business of hauling winter freight across lake ice when he was afraid to send one of his men in a lead Cat and drove it himself instead. One particular trip, he was doing the same thing he had been doing for maybe ten, twelve winters and he realized he had lost the confidence to make that snap decision to tell his men, 'That ice is safe. Go across.' He says the only fellow who knows ennathing about ice is in his first or second year working on it, because he still has some confidence left. The longer you stay with it, the less you know."

We passed an Indian family, a man, woman and child riding in a boxlike carry-all with canvas sides built up about one foot, on a toboggan drawn by five dogs. "The Mackenzie Highway first opened between Edmonton and Yellowknife in winter and we had a heavy Diesel Mack truck with a full load of freight waiting to cross the Mackenzie River on the ice bridge," Denison said, turning the driver's wheel back and forth in an easy rhythm while he talked. "The ice bridge over the river is the same as our road on the lakes, a track where the snow has been cleaned off, which has made the ice go down further, and get thicker. The government marks a place as a crossing and keeps the ice depth tested for safety, but sometimes we flood it ourselves and put water on top to increase the thickness of the ice so it's sure to be safe for us. I was in Yellowknife, but I was in touch with the engineer at the ice bridge, which is at Fort Providence, two hundred miles south of Yellowknife by road. He sent word that the minimum depth of the ice was seventeen-and-a-half inches. I knew that was enough for our truck. I phoned my partner on the other side, at our freight terminal at Hay River, a small town on the south shore of Great Slave Lake, and said 'Bring the truck over.' But somebody at Hay River had also telephoned, telling him how bad it was on the ice bridge, so he said, 'If you want the truck over there, come and get it yourself.' I jumped right on a plane and went over to Hay River and got in that truck and started driving it towards Yellowknife, with my partner following in a pickup truck, which was empty, besides being much lighter ennaway. Meanwhile, our competitor from Yellowknife was also there on the ice bridge, with a hose, trying to flood it and make more ice. I didn't pay any attention to him, because I knew I had enough ice, although I wasn't easy. We only owned about three trucks then, so if we lost that truck, we'd lose the load, and would have been damned near out of business. I was willing to take the gamble, so I crossed on the bridge, going north, back to Yellowknife, while everybody else watched, hopin' I'd lose, with my partner sweatin' behind in the light pickup truck. I drove about five miles an hour in third gear and I was plenty nervous. I knew this was a no-return deal. I could never go back once I started." He skidded into a drift and stopped talking, while he gently backed away.

"Did you drive with the door open?" I asked.

"You're damned right!" he exclaimed as he resumed the road again. "I drove with the door open and one foot outside on the fender. Watchin' for cracks, lookin' for cracks, listenin' for cracks. When the ice cracks you're safe. It makes you more nervous, but it's safer."

"Why?"

"I don't know," he replied. "We think it is, ennaway. My competitor was sittin' in his truck on the south side of the bridge and after he watched us go across he cranked up his trucks and crossed after us, and had to follow us to Yellowknife. It was the first time anyone had taken a van over the Mackenzie Highway all the way to Yellowknife. The first regular load of freight was mine, and a delegation from the Chamber of Commerce met me at the edge of town out by the airport. There was Del Curry; another oldtimer, Ivor Johnson, and someone else I forget, with a bottle of whiskey, and they got out of their car and drove in my truck with me into town."

"That's a very nice story," I said.

"Well, I wouldn't do it again," Denison said. "I know too much about ice now. It's not safe." He looked at me. ". . . You cold?" he asked.

Yes. I was shivering. The fierce wind shrilled through an open space on the floor cut to make room for the winch lever. In this kind of rough, off-road travel, a winch is an essential piece of equipment and most of the vehicles on the Ice Road had one. Ours was mounted on the front, but on the big trucks it was behind the cab. Truckers like to say that a winch triples the power of their engines, because it supplies them with leverage to pull themselves out of a hole without using their wheels, if they are stuck. A button on the dashboard put the winch into gear; letting the clutch out with your foot wound up the cable.

When I looked down through the opening I could see the white road underneath. A thin layer of snow had blown in and was building up around the base of the gear shift and my feet. John turned the heat up a little and said, "Wind is our worst enemy. It's always colder on the lakes, especially a big open one like this, because of the wind. More snow. More plowing to keep the road from blowing in. That's about a twenty-five-mile-an-hour wind blowing now. When the wind's over thirty miles an hour we've about had it, and it can get up to a hundred. It'll be warmer in among the trees."

We rode for miles without talking. The orchestra music and wind harmonized, high-decibel violins and shrieking wind. Denison appeared to be pushing our vehicle through the violent gusts that shook the truck body. He was hunched forward with both hands on the wheel, which he twisted and turned to the wild wind rhythm. During a lull he relaxed, dropping a hand to the gear shift and humming off-key. When the music stopped he removed the cartridge from the stereo and put it away in an open box of tapes on the floor. "Ennathing can happen on ice, ennathing," he said. "I'll probably pull out like Del Curry did. Maybe in a couple of years. No two years are the same and your ice conditions change hourly. You can have six inches of ice and get across and have the thirty-six inches we think we need to cross in the ten-ton trucks and go through. As a rule, it's the second guy who goes through and the first man over who cracks the ice. It all depends on how the cracks are formed and where they are. It's smart to go slow when you're not sure, about six miles an hour, so as not to bend the ice when you are coming near the shore. Because if you make a wave, it has no place to go, and will snap back and break the ice. The heavier the load the more ice you need, so I don't take contracts after April first and I like to get off the roads by April fifteenth. It's pretty mushy after that. I usually go on, but I'm not happy about it, even though mostly just a wheel or two goes through." He shrugged. "Almost everyone who works with ice has had a pretty narrow escape. Del Curry was telling me that Hughie Arden, one of the most experienced men around here on ice, once rode his Cat down because his overshoe got caught in a gear. He had to tear his shoe off under thirty-five foot of water in Yellowknife Bay to save himself."

"Did you ever go through?" I asked.

Denison laughed. "Couple of years ago I was driving a Bug —a Bombardier—of mine across Prosperous Lake, twelve miles from Yellowknife, and I didn't see the ice crack. That stupid Bug went in, but it floated six or eight minutes, so I climbed out of my seat and jumped out the door. A Bug has a hull like a boat, except that it's full of holes, with windows and openings, and not watertight. A Cat, now that's something else again. It's solid iron and drops like a rock through water."

I asked what happened to the Bombardier he dropped into Prosperous Lake. "Oh, I left it there and walked the twelve miles home," he said. "I sent a man to find out how deep the water was and he probed two hundred and fifty feet and couldn't touch bottom. I said, 'I've got to have it, it's the only thing I have to make a road with. Probe to five hundred.' Well, we found it at three hundred and fifty, in a spot where the gas had discolored the ice. We drilled a hole every six feet through the ice until we found it, dropped an iron on a string, made a big heavy grappling hook, hooked that Bug eight times, and lifted it with a winch on an A-frame through a little hole we cut in the ice with a chainsaw, and set the Bug over on a ten-foot-square pad made of timbers frozen into the ice. The gas tanks had collapsed but we had brought along extra ones which we installed, and then we dried the Bug out with a Herman Nelson heater and drove it home. The same Bug is now at the bottom of Hardisty Lake, in a narrows where the fast water is, almost a hundred miles farther north on this road, and I haven't had time to go and get the stupid thing, so it's still there. It'll be a tough job, because that's open running water, too deep, and hard to get to because of thin ice," he said. "It's the only one we've lost but I don't think of it as really lost, just in cold storage. A machine doesn't deteriorate under water, only when the air hits it. Not much damage done if the engine is turned off before the machine hits the water. I've dropped five machines in the lakes around here in seven years, but it's the only one I've lost. I'm more likely to put a piece through than my men are because I'll go where they don't dare. These men have spent their lives on ice and dropped more Cats through than I have, so they are more scared than I am; men who scout for me, like Hughie Arden and Jim Magrum. We work a lot together and it would be real tough without them, but they are more cautious than I am. I'll go where they won't go. Do you remember Magrum?" I did. He was Denison's chief guide the year before, an all-around man, and a long-time Yellowknife resident. Jim and his wife, June, were friends of mine.

"Maybe I'll get time to go back and pull up that Bombardier this year," Denison said. "I allus say, you got to make up your mind to get it or not when somethin' falls through. There are no half measures." He slowed down. A white, scrawny Arctic hare was sitting in the middle of the road. It stared at us as if paralyzed before it leapt across the road to safety. John veered to let it pass, and picked up speed again. "Talkin' about my Bug in Hardisty reminds me of the time they were salvaging some Cats that had fallen into Great Slave Lake," he said. "They worked for months in the summer to find this Cat. Divers fastened a cable to it, and a rope attached to an empty barrel for a float, as a marker. In the winter they went out and lifted the Cat out with gin poles and winches. A Cat weighs about twenty tons, and is worth fifteen to twenty thousand dollars, ennaway, and they worked for weeks to get it out. They got it up on the ice and running, and ran it away from the hole a little bit, while they went into a caboose on the ice to get coffee. They heard a crackin' noise, and they ran outside. There was the Cat, goin' chug, chug, chug, and then clunk! It was gone again. Disappearin' right through the ice and they couldn't do ennathing about it! All that work for nothing! I think what happened, when they blasted the ice they must have fractured it, and the vibration of the motor running shook down through. If they had driven just a little further away it would have been all right." He opened the window to look back at the Bug we were hauling, then rolled the window up again. "I don't mind ennathing else, but I do mind the cold," he said. "When the temperature hits forty below zero, about what it is now, nothing but trouble! Air lines freeze and you just don't have any brakes."

The portage at the end of Marian Lake was the longest on the Ice Road, forty miles, and terribly rough. A "portage" on the Ice Road, is the land between two lakes which has to be crossed because either there is no water or there are rapids or currents that make it impossible to stay on ice. We were crawling at four miles an hour around a very narrow curve in the portage when Denison said, "It was right here that one of my drivers, Shannon O'Reilly, rolled his truck last season." I must have looked puzzled; this was a new language to me. "Rolling a truck is laying it on its side," Denison explained, "and when a driver says he has rhubarbed, that means he went off the road in the ditch but stayed on his tires. Well, Shannon had a real heavy load—Johnny Zigarlik's new four-wheel drive pickup truck, an electric engine, and a couple of thousand feet of lumber—on his lowboy. A lowboy is a trailer only three feet off the ground, the kind we use on our trucks for carrying heavy equipment, tractors, trucks, houses, drag lines for hauling, that sort of thing. We use highboys, which are four and a half feet off the ground, for general freight. Ennaway, Shannon didn't see this narrow place because of the snow and dropped right over the edge. When the truck rolled over, a bottle of the propane gas we carry for our heaters exploded, so he didn't bother opening the door, he went through the windshield. When he saw that everything was fine he went back to the truck and turned the engine off. The cab and trailer were on their sides with their wheels in the air, so the oil was on top and couldn't lubricate the bearings to run the motor ennaway. Normally, we keep all our engines going on the road night and day. If they stop, we can't be sure we can start them up again in this cold, and the temperature was forty below."

He cut his speed as we came to a series of humps in the road, frowned, drove carefully through this rough spot, and resumed his cruising speed. "Luckily, Shannon had two other trucks travelling with him," Denison continued. "I never like to see the men go out alone because of this kind of thing. Our Cat was working just ahead too, and came back with a winch, and another truck happened by then on its way back to Yellowknife, with a second winch. I was right behind Shannon in my camper with *my* winch, so we put all three winch cables over the top of the cab and trailer and after three or four hours managed to pull them right side up again. The truck that was going to Yellowknife hauled Shannon's truck with Shannon riding in his cab home for repairs, and Jimmy Watson came along in Thirty-six, hooked onto Shannon's trailer and took it up to Port Radium. So Zigarlik's truck reached Echo Bay a little dented, but we were sure lucky. We rarely have that much equipment at the scene of an accident."

Another rough place, and this time he did not slow down. I held onto the door with one hand, and the seat with the other. "Do you have many accidents yourself?"

"Lots of times a guy goes off the road in the ditch if you're going to be driving, and I drove lots of miles," Denison said, "but the only time I ever had a real accident was when I upset a load of whitefish and trout I was taking from Great Slave Lake to Edmonton in nineteen forty-nine. I had this D. and S. Trucking Service, and my partner, Bob Seddon, and I had been in business about a year. The truck I was driving was brand new, the first new one we bought, a KB-8. It was the first semi-trailer on the road, and this was our first effort. I was one of the very few trucks on the road that day and I was goin' uphill and it was icy and I spun out. . . ." He glanced at me. "Know what that means?" I shook my head. "No traction. I started sliding back and tried to put the truck in reverse but the engine stalled. When an engine doesn't run with vacuum brakes, that means there *are* no brakes, and I was goin' back for a long time, eh? So my truck went across the road and laid on its right side across the road, blocking it. About half an hour later another truck came and put a chain over my deck and managed to put me back on my wheels but all those fish—they weighed ten to forty pounds each—had come sliding out on the road. Luckily, some Indians were in the neighbourhood and I hired them to load the trailer up again, but I had knocked a hole in my radiator and had to be towed back to the little town I had just left. I worked on that truck most of the night, and I was in Edmonton by the next day.

"I turned over my camper once too, but I don't hardly count that," he said. "Winter before last, I was going home in a real whiteout, and I couldn't see. I was on the lake we'll be coming to next, Tumi, and there were high banks on each side of the road. My wheel caught in the snow on one side and pulled me up on the bank and laid my camper on its side. Right in the road, on the lake! I tried to get the camper on its feet and I could have done it if I had had to, with a jack and poles, but it was a hard job for me alone, so I thought I'd wait until the trucks came. I knew they were behind me a couple of hours. All the damned stuff in the cupboards went splat against the walls, especially the catsup and jam, but the worst was a catsup bottle that busted and went all over every place. The wall was my floor and the bed was standing on end, eh? So there was no place to lie down. I laid down standing up in a corner and had a sleep until the trucks came along. I sure got the razzberries from the boys. They wanted to know what the hell I was doing, and I said, 'Resting, what do you think?' " He laughed. "They pulled me on my feet and I took off for home, and when I got there I had that mess to clean up. Jeez!"

A flock of ptarmigan, white snow birds—Arctic grouse about the size of chickens—flew off to the side, just missing our radiator with their slow ascent. "That same year up on Hottah Lake my exhaust pipe broke," Denison went on. "I inhaled a lot of gas and that carbon monoxide made me pretty sick. I managed to call for a pilot on my radio, and when the plane came to pick me up I crawled into the back of that goddamned plane and laid down. Pretty soon it was getting dark and pretty late, and I knew the pilot was way off course. I looked out the window and said, 'Straighten out and go home!' He did, but he only made two trips up north after that. They run him off."

We went over a large bump, my head hit the ceiling, and the camper stopped. We were stuck. John was cursing softly. "I should have known that bump was there," he said, and began shifting gears to make the camper rock gently back and forth. Forward, back. Forward, back.

"When you rock a vehicle, you just keep it moving enough so the wheels won't skid, and pack a track. Once you pack a track you've got enough room to move on," he explained. We were still stuck. "It's that damned stupid Bug on the back," he said. He got out and unhitched the Bombardier, brought a shovel from the camper, tore limbs off the trees by the road and filled the deep holes around the wheels with snow and branches. He got back in the camper, more gentle rocking and we moved ahead out of the ruts. He stopped, went back for the Bombardier where he had left it with its motor chugging softly, drove it easily on its tracks and skis over the treacherous spot, connected it again to the camper and we continued our journey. "We may fall through the damned Emile River next," he said.

No time to see if he is joking, we are at the river, broad, ominously dark, black sparkling rushing water, a barely wide enough rickety bridge the only crossing. Open hilly land down to the river bed, restful beauty here except for the menace of that swift-currented deepness to be crossed; that strip of bubbling black water, swirling whirling pool, lovely song, the open flowing river rumbling through its rocky bed, the only sound except for us; ours the droning motor, grinding gears to shatter this quiet world. I am caught in the white freeze, the black running sound, as we cross the frail bridge that complains with creaks and a loose rattling of boards.

We had been heading for a group of low buildings nestled into the snow on a mountainside. A picturesque Alpine resort, closed for the winter? Once again I had forgotten where I was! We were looking at the empty shells of buildings, the skeleton of the closed Rayrock Mine. "Most of Rayrock is sitting where I moved it, at a gold mine called Tundra that opened in the Barrens after Rayrock closed," John said. Past the abandoned mine, the road narrowed to a single eight-foot-wide track. Low willow bushes and graceful spruce trees brushed against us on both sides. "Here's the real beginning of my road," Denison said. "We should be meeting up with my men any time now."

I did not see until we stopped. We had come up behind another great red snowplow truck like 36, only bigger, parked at the top of a hill.

John got out and walked over to the strange truck, climbed into its cab and emerged shortly with two men I had met the previous year at Port Radium: Al Frost, the young Indian who had fallen into Great Bear Lake in the Bombardier last year, and Tom Berry. Brown-bearded, powerful, quick-witted Tom Berry; in the coldest weather he never wore a parka, and half the time he travelled without a sleeping bag because he had hocked it for a bottle of whiskey. "He's the best man I've got when he leaves booze alone," Denison once said. "He's a *really* good man with equipment." The only concession Tom had made now to the cold was a wool cap pulled over his balding head. Otherwise he was dressed just as when I met him before, in khaki pants and a red-and-black checked wool shirt suitable for a brisk run in the country on a fall day. Away from Yellowknife's temptations, Tom was a master mechanic, truck driver and road-builder. A loner who accepted people slowly, he surprised me now by greeting me as a friend, throwing back his head and welcoming me with a hearty laugh that echoed through the quiet woods and revealed wide gaps between his teeth.

Tom returned to his truck; Al Frost unhooked the Bug from the camper and got into it, and our vehicles crossed a little river single file. We climbed the bank on the other side by a half-cleared deeply rutted road, and at the top met a large red tractor slowly advancing towards us, crushing trees and bushes in its path on the overgrown portage road. A black-bearded man's head protruded grotesquely above a canvas sheet stretched high across the open front of the Cat for a windbreaker. We stopped and John got out again, this time climbing up on the tread of the tractor to shout over the clattering noise of the Cat motor to the black beard, who nodded vigorously. When John returned and we drove on past the tractor, he said crossly, "I've been seeing piles of snow in the woods all the way from Ray-rock. I told that fool to stop wasting valuable snow and to put it back on the road where it belongs and pack it down. When you are making an ice road you don't take snow off the road, you use it, because it's like cement and you've *got* to mix it as if that's what it is. You've got to beat the goddamned air out of it right away so it will freeze hard. Take the two feet of snow that we have around here now. Well, we'll keep dragging it, take all the air out until we have only two inches of snow left, and when the weather is cold like this it'll freeze right away. Once the ice is packed down it goes on making more ice, about two inches a day, and there's your ice road! There's a science to making ice roads. If I had my books with me I could show you how the Russians and Swedes have been studying it." He grimaced. "But those guys write in such technical terms that even when it's translated into English I don't understand. So I make my roads my own way."

"How do you start building a road?"

He navigated the camper to avoid deep ruts, keeping to a steady speed of thirty miles an hour. "First I go by plane over the area where I am planning to make my road to see if it's possible," he said. "Then I scout the ground between the lakes —the portages, to find the best routes across the land, and sometimes there aren't any. Magrum has a sure instinct in this country for scouting, and has trained Jimmy Watson, too. First I use the Bug we brought with us now to mark out the route; it's the fastest, lightest vehicle over ice, when it runs. Then the

Cat clears the trees and stumps and rocks away so we can get the other equipment through, and the third step is to knock the snow down from two feet to two or three inches with special steel drags I've designed to pack it that we hook on behind the Cat, and behind the trucks later. We try to save all the snow we can to fill the holes and make a more level road. We pack the snow down into the holes to freeze, with Cats and drags and the wheels of heavy trucks like Thirty-six and Tom's Thirty-four and a couple more trucks you haven't met up with yet that go back and forth over it at least a half-dozen times. We try to camp ahead of the working crew so we can be gone first in the morning and make more tracks for them. After the road's packed down it's left to freeze for twenty-four hours without any traffic if possible; it's rough and if you walk on it before it's set you leave a mark, just like wet cement. Temperature makes a difference; the road takes less time to set at fifty below than at ten below, because the colder the weather the quicker it freezes hard, just like putting something in a deepfreeze. When the road's made, you have to keep at it. After every snowfall we have to drag it; otherwise fresh soft snow would insulate the road like a down comforter, pulling the frost out from below so the snow underneath would lose its hardness. We get six inches of soft snow packed down to half an inch that has no air holes, and then the frost just keeps going down and down through the packed snow turning to ice, to make the Ice Road thicker and thicker. The portage and lake roads, of course, are two different kinds. On the lakes, we just go across with a snowplow truck and open a road. Depending on how much ice there is, we have to decide how heavy a vehicle we can put on it to begin with, eh? Once the road is in on the lake we keep plowing off excess snow all season, so the frost can go down. We've had roads on the lakes where the ice is only eighteen inches thick along the sides, but three feet deep where we plowed it. The more it's plowed, and the more traffic there is, the thicker the ice gets, sometimes so thick that it will have deep cracks and tend to raise up. Our trouble comes the odd time when we arrive at a small pothole, a real small lake with very little ice and lots of snow, where the ice isn't thick enough to hold the plow truck, so we can't plow the ice. When that happens, we pack it down with a Bombardier like this Bug behind us, and go through with a vehicle I've got I call the Beaver. It's real light and will float, and even runs in water. I bought it just for this kind of thing."

Denison's eyes were fastened on the road; hardly a road, a half-broken trail so rough I gripped the seat and the door so I wouldn't hit the mobile radio. We were rocking from side to side in our bucking steel bronco and the ruts were a foot deep. One final leap: we slapped down on a small lake.

I unclenched my jaws, which had been clamped together until they ached. "When we bang down on ice like that, how do you know we won't go through?" I asked.

"We've got to go over the lake ennaway, so what's the difference?" Denison replied.

I consulted a mining map I had bought in Yellowknife. "This is Tumi Lake," I said.

"The next will be Rabbit," John said. "You might as well learn the names of the lakes that make up the Ice Road. Not counting potholes, there are nineteen." I fished paper and pencil from my pocket and he ticked off the lake names while I wrote them down. "Marian, Tumi, Rabbit, Hislop, Squirrel, Mazenod, Sarah, Faber, Rae, Tuche," he said in one breath and it sounded like a chant. "Séguin, Hardisty, Malfait, Beaverlodge, Hottah, Fishtrap, Yen, Gunbarrel Inlet. Great Bear Lake."

Another rough portage. Denison kept his eyes on the road but he was relaxed and talkative. "Today is January third. We should have the road open to Echo Bay by the fifteenth, but as to when we really get it done, I won't know until we get there," he said.

"I allus try to get farther than what I know I am going to make. I might as well shoot for the maximum and sometimes I'm lucky enough to make lots of miles, but I never can plan ahead on the damned thing. I don't even know what I'm doing tomorrow! Tomorrow morning the weather might blow in and we might have to stay wherever we are for a week! I make my money on the freight loads, so the sooner I get my road in, the better. The government and the mine each put up fifteen thousand dollars every year, and by the time I clear portages, drag them and blast a few rocks it costs me around a hundred dollars a mile to make my road. Every year we improve the old portages or make new ones. Did you know you can see our road from the air in summer?" I said I didn't know this. "It takes years for a portage to grow over," he said. "You might be able to find it eighty years from now. It takes trees so long to grow up here. Once a road is cut we can allus find it again from the air, but on the ground we have a lot of trouble in winter sometimes finding a twelve-foot hole among the trees where it starts, and we can go all around a lake trying to remember where the bloody thing came off last year. In summer from the air our road is a lighter strip along the bottom of the lakes, a kind of light green with everything dark brown around it, the color depending on the kind of vegetation there is in that particular lake. Since the ice on the road is so much thicker than the lake ice around it, the road takes much longer to melt than the rest of the ice on the lakes, and so the growth of vegetation directly underneath is retarded. Sometimes sections of the road take so long to melt that pieces seven feet long float around on the lake most of the summer! In the spring, while we are still travelling our road, snow melts on top of the ice and it looks like there is water all over even though there is plenty of ice underneath. The road is pushed down a bit by then and where the sun beats down in the warm weather on bare ice, the road melts. Water runs in the tracks, so we have to build another road where it's dryer. The ice is safe enough because by then you can have as much as a seven-foot thickness, but it sure feels dangerous. You can hardly get from the shore to the ice because the lakes melt from the shore out first. You just have to take the chance and drive across. The odd time, the trucks drop through, and maybe go down a couple of feet. Then we drag 'em out with a Cat or a winch truck, or make a bridge with logs, and if it's bad enough, send a boat out. The portages are so damned rough too that you mostly are travelling over muskeg, because snow melts on land before it does on ice."

We came around a sharp bend in the road and directly ahead of us were four dogs pulling an Indian sled that appeared to be driverless. Denison pressed the camper horn but it didn't work, so when we were right behind the sleigh he shifted gears into neutral and raced the motor. An Indian popped up in the carry-all and pulled over to the side of the road so we could get by. "He's from the Dogrib Tribe at Fort Rae, a couple of miles from Fort Byers," Denison said. "The Indians go hunting on this road as soon as it's in. They travel right down the middle, wrap themselves in their caribou hides and fall asleep in their carry-alls, and the dogs wander all over the place. They're a terrible hazard because you can't see them in the big trucks until you're right on top of them and when it's forty below you don't have any brakes. Last year one of our men accidentally pitched an Indian and his dog team over the bank with the snowplow. Nobody hurt. Another driver ran down a sleeping Indian, and to avoid hitting him turned the truck into a ditch. Fifty-six hundred dollars' damage to the truck. When we first started making the Ice Road the Indians made their camps in the middle of the road. Their campfires melted the snow and left big holes, so I went to the Indian chief at Fort Rae and asked him if he'd tell his fellows not to build fires on our road, but get off in the bushes. By the time we come back through here, the Indians will have their platforms at the side of the road stacked with caribou for us to haul back in the trucks to Fort Rae for meat for them to eat. We must have hauled fifty ton last year, always free. It's a damned nuisance."

"Have you ever travelled by dog sled?" I asked.

"One trip, when I was in the R.C.M.P., and it was one too

many for me," Denison said. "It was December 1946 and we had gotten a report that a trapper was missing in the Barrens. I was a lowly constable and I was assigned to the case. I had just come from Saskatchewan, and didn't know north from south, so as a guide I took along a guy named Norm Burgess, who had been around here a long time. A Canadian Pacific Airline pilot named Sandy Tweed agreed to fly us up to a place called Gordon Lake to pick up five dogs from an Indian there, because we didn't have any, and when Sandy was trying to get one of the dogs who was fighting and biting, into the plane, that dog lifted his leg and went on Sandy's old boot. Oh, was Sandy mad! Then we had to go back to Yellowknife because of the weather and sit down and wait, with six dogs in the plane stinkin' it up. God, what a mess! Ernie Boffa, CP Air's chief pilot, took us back out and we managed to get into a camp buried in the snow at Courageous Lake, three miles north of what became Tundra Mine. It was *really* cold up there, well, not really cold, only fifty below, and in December there's not much goddamn daylight. Ernie was one of the best bush pilots the North ever had, and I remember that before he took off the next morning he sent his engineer out to warm up the plane. Ernie looked out the window and the blowpot was goin' *under* the plane and the guy was pouring gasoline in the plane, with the pot burning right underneath! He was just a young fella learning the business, but Ernie really ate him up. They took off and left us alone. This was my first time in the Barrens, my first time with a dog team, and when that plane took off, I felt very lonesome. The partner of the lost trapper, a fellow named Carl Holme, was there with another dog team, and George Magrum, Jim's father, was there too. George was quite a man to be out in the bush with. If there were three peas left over he would put them in a bag and save them, because he'd figure he might need them. That's an old northern saying, but it *really* describes old George. Ennaway, we went out with our two teams and followed the trapper's tracks along his line, which ran east and west from his main camp for about eight miles. He had a peculiar walk, straddling like a duck, and we followed his tracks straight east to the end of his line and half-way back, when all of a sudden they turned straight south. He was obviously off his rocker."

"How would you know that?" I asked.

"Well, wouldn't ennabody be, who was up at the Arctic Circle and started for California?" Denison replied. "Ennaway, we followed his tracks again for twenty miles right out on Courageous Lake and he never veered off from goin' straight south. Then we got on glare ice—no snow—and couldn't find his tracks at all, and by then it was ten or twelve days since he hadn't come home so we abandoned the search. This was at Christmas time, and we only had two or three hours of daylight every day. I went back to the base camp with Carl, and Norm and old George camped out in the bush for the night. It was a nice bright night with the wind blowing, and one of Norm's dogs, an old white one, started caterwauling, so he walked out in his long underwear and boots to give him a good kick. He found himself looking at two white dogs except that he only had one, so he hollered, 'George, there's a wolf here!' George said, 'Don't be foolish. A wolf doesn't attack a dog,' but Norm said he didn't wait to see if the wolf had read the same book George had. Norm swears he jumped thirty-five feet back into his tent to get his gun, without leaving a track. He grabbed the first thing he saw, the stovepipe, and cracked it over the wolf's head but the wolf just took it in his teeth, and away went the pipe. So Norm grabbed his gun, but it was froze up tighter'n hell, and there were the two of them, George and Norm, inside the tent trying to thaw that gun out with their hands, with the wolf sittin' staring at them. Norm shot that wolf ten feet in front of their tent and brought home the evidence. We reported to Yellow-knife by radio that we couldn't find the lost trapper and the R.C.M.P. said, 'Drive the dogs home.' We said, 'In no goddamn way, send the plane back,' which they did. That's the way I spent my first Christmas in the North, in the Barren Lands, and I was glad I was there. Know why? If I had been in Yellowknife, they had a real bad fire in the Negus Mine—that's a gold mine that only produced in Yellowknife for a very short time—and if I had been there I would have had to spend my time pickin' up bodies. It was one of the coldest goddamn winters anyone ever spent in Yellowknife and some of the corpses froze. The police were the undertakers at that time, and when I came home we had to saw one man up and put him in a box. He was all brown and his legs and arms stuck out. I bought the rum and my partner did it, because he was a butcher, ennaway."

I shuddered.

Denison glanced quickly at me, sideways. He said quietly, "You got to remember there is nothin' left then. Chase the person out and all we are is nothin'. Our bodies are nothin'. Our minds are the only things living, really."

"I was going to tell you," he said abruptly, "on that same trip, Norm and I were lookin' hard one day and we let the dogs drift off and were hopelessly lost. But Norm had a staking map with him, and when we found a numbered stake we were able to orient ourselves and get back. So you learn something. If you are in mining country, take a staking map with you because the claims are all numbered, recorded, and put on a map."

"How did you know how to drive a dog team, if you had never had one before?" I asked.

"Oh, Norm knew how. But you just holler low and clear. Holler at 'em, kick 'em, beat 'em."

We came to a steep place and stopped, our wheels spinning. Denison moved back cautiously, then put his foot down hard on the gas. We sprang forward and went on. "This is all open country and belongs to the government, or the people, eh?" he said. "This is a tote road and ennabody can go on it. Whoever uses it has to maintain it and get himself out if he gets stuck, but we worry even if we have no responsibility. I combine road plowing with hauling freight so snow won't drift in on the road every time there's a blow. Sometimes on the lakes it's easier to plow a new road but wherever it is, you always have to keep plowing. After the road's built, and in good weather, and if nothin' breaks down, the trip takes twenty-four to thirty-six hours to Port Radium in the trucks, but it can take three or four days in bad weather. I average twelve to fourteen in the camper when the road is good. I've divided my road into three parts, with stops approximately every hundred miles where the men can get rest and food without having to cook their own meals. One is at Sarah Lake, about a hundred miles from Fort Byers, and the other is a hundred miles farther along at Hottah Lake, which is about a hundred miles from Great Bear Lake."

We drove for what seemed like a long time in silence. The sun was slowly sinking, lingering at tree level. We were travelling a narrow corridor, snow banked on either side, shafts of faltering light streaking through the trees. "I wonder what you are thinking about," I said lazily. I was watching the rays from the setting sun play around the treetops and not thinking about anything, myself.

Denison didn't reply, and I had an eerie feeling that he was coming back from a great distance. Finally he said crossly, "When someone asks me a question like that it makes me forget what I'm thinking about. I allus have been that way. I can remember years ago when my nephew Dave was a little boy. After we had been drivin' a couple of hours he said to me, 'Uncle John, why don't you say something?'" He sighed. "It really bugs me to be interrupted like this. I just don't get organized in a few minutes. I have no other choice, there's an urgency to get everything done before the ice melts. It's not like a highway where if you don't do it now you can do it next week. No way. It's all got to be *now*." We rolled over a big bump, and he frowned, stopped, got out and went back into the camper. He returned with a long red stake, which he placed at the far side of the bump by the road. "So the men'll know that's a bad place, when they come by," he explained when he got back in the driver's seat, and started off again. "They'll smooth that bump down, and when we come back it'll be gone."

He was in a much better humor now. "You asked what I was thinkin' about," he said. "When I'm drivin' along I'm thinkin' about equipment. I'm allus tryin' to remember where everything is, whether a vehicle is runnin', where I can get another if it isn't, what kind of fellow I have on each truck, especially the snowplows, and remembering that all the time my men at Yellowknife and Hay River want to know when they can start sending the trucks. It's all got to be tied together or it's clumsy, and if one piece isn't working, it may hold us all up."

He reached for a digestive wheat biscuit in a package on the dashboard, and continued talking while he munched. "I like to have six pieces of equipment when I'm breaking the road in," he said. "I can do without ennathing *but* my snowplow trucks, if I have to. First, there's the Bug. I keep this old blue Bombardier, hooked on behind now, just for this one week a year when I need it to go out in front and scout the way, because it travels fast and can go ennawhere. It was built for fishermen and running on lakes, and it's got an escape hatch out the top, so if it went through the ice a guy could jump through the roof. Then there's my TD-14 International Harvester, the same size Cat as a D-6 made by the Caterpillar Company which Hughie Arden owns and we sometimes use if we need a second Cat. The TD-14 is always red, which is Byers Transport Company's color too; all our big trucks like Thirty-six and Thirty-four are red. Hughie's D-6 is yellow because that's the Caterpillar color, but it weighs the same as mine, twelve tons, and both have winches on the back. The Beaver: we paid twelve thousand dollars for that clumsy silly thing, but it's amphibious. I got it basically to go over thin ice, but it's a kitchen too, and does a wonderful job packin' snow on the portages with those big wide flotation tires. The big trucks: I need them to snowplow the lakes. A heavy-duty snowplow truck like Thirty-six, with a trailer, hauls the Cat across hard water, and Thirty-four, Tom's truck, has a caboose that sleeps four and is carrying eight-hundred-and-fifty gallon of gas and the same of Diesel fuel. As for this camper, it's a place to eat and sleep, and quick transportation. One extra piece along now. Fud. Twenty years old and the engine's not even the one that came with it. I use Fud for snowplowing and dragging, just in winter, and Fud hardly even runs in winter for sure, but it's real handy to have around. It's got one of my V snowplows, nine feet wide with a hydraulic lift on the front. It packs the road down *really* good. The eight-by-eight caboose on its back has two bunks, and hot water from the engine to heat it. Most of the time Fud carries our extra gas, our emergency supply."

"Are any of the trucks new?" I asked.

"The only new truck we've ever had is Thirty-seven, which is so new we haven't had a chance to use it yet, but I may bring it up if we need another snowplow," he replied. "It's a six-wheel-drive, ten-ton cabover model—the cab's over the motor —that we had specially built for this northern operation by a Vancouver firm, and we paid forty-five thousand dollars for it. It's a White Freightliner, with its own shack we built that has two bunks, a propane cook stove and hot water heaters off the engine to give heat in the back. It sure is a beautiful truck but how do you pay for a forty-five-thousand-dollar truck? It takes a *long* time to make forty-five thousand dollars. We bought it new after we lost some of our big trucks in the fire last year that burned down our garage in Yellowknife, and it's a little heavier than the other trucks, and capable of running on a highway. But it's not that fast and has a lot more moving parts to break. I don't really think such an expensive unit can earn enough in these few months to make it pay. When we were a small outfit tryin' to get along we didn't have the money to buy new trucks so we had junk to start with and not too much money in equipment, and that's how we made money. Those little trucks, the ones that cost from forty-five hundred to six thousand dollars, are what's made us our money."

The sun slipped lower and lower, until it was behind the trees. The last rosy light disappeared when we came out in the open on Hislop Lake. Total darkness. Our headlights shone on the smooth white unplowed lake. The crusty snow crackled when our wheels crushed it down. We made our own road for a few feet and stopped. "We'll spend the night here," John said. "The others'll be along any minute, wanting coffee." Night so soon? My watch said four o'clock. Outside, bright yellow-white stars twinkled in a black velvet sky. At the shoreline a border of snow-laden trees, their branches white shadowy arms, reaching into the night air.

The absolute darkness was broken by the glittering beamed eyes of the Bombardier as it dropped off the shore to the lake, and behind and above it, by the large yellow eyes of Tom Berry's big truck. Lumbering far behind, the one-eyed torch of the tractor split the night with a single shaft of light. The vehicles clustered around us in a half-circle, facing inwards. The men left their trucks with motors idling, stopping to test the ice around us while I hurried into the camper to make coffee. No water, so I rushed outside and scooped up snow at the door, heaping it into the bottom of the percolator, adding coffee in the top. I set the pot on a burner, lighted it, and waited for the coffee to percolate, but nothing happened. I looked inside. Tiny bubbles of air but no water! I was still staring into the pot when the men arrived for coffee. Snow to make coffee! They shook their heads; how come I am so dumb that I don't know that snow is mostly air?

Denison departed with a pail and an ice auger, a long-handled drill with a sharp cutting edge shaped like a spoon to slice through the ice, and returned with a supply of glistening lake water. On my second attempt to make coffee, I filled the percolator with water. Tom Berry walked over to the stove and poured half the water out into an open pan, and placed it on a second burner. "Cuts the boiling time in half and the coffee perks twice as fast," he said. "How come you didn't know *that?*" My cold-weather cooking lesson wasn't over. As if I wasn't confused enough already, the store bread I had put away in a cupboard was frozen stiff, but the fresh-baked bread that Denison had cached in the refrigerator was ready to eat. What a topsy-turvy world! The cupboards were a deepfreeze and the insulated refrigerator by comparison was warm. From then on, the last thing I did before I went to bed each night was to remove a package of frozen bacon from a cupboard and put it in the refrigerator so that it would be soft for breakfast.

Although it was after dark, it was still afternoon. Tom and Denison left in the Bug to scout the entrance to the next portage, at the north end of Hislop Lake, eight miles away. The black beard who drove the Cat, Gilles Chartrand, went to sleep on the bunk in the overhang, and Al Frost settled down comfortably against the flowered cushions on the bench to drink his coffee. He put his feet up and lit a cigarette.

"I've been wondering what it was like when you fell into Great Bear Lake last year in the Bug," I said. (*I was remembering Denison's remark: "If we had gotten that far in Thirty-six the day we were heading down the lake we would have gone in instead of Frost . . . I thought there was more ice there . . ."*)

"I fell in at a place called Confidence Point," Frost said. "I started from Echo Bay two days before, and had made maybe a hundred miles, stoppin' to check the ice now and then by choppin' a hole about a foot deep. If I didn't see water, I'd figure it's okay. When I was tired, I'd just stop for the night, gas up the Bug, cook me a couple of steaks and a vegetable on my primus stove, put my eiderdown across the seats, read a mystery, and go to sleep. The third day just before daylight I had gone about ten miles at my average speed, only ten or twelve miles an hour, and I was goin' through this narrows and that's where I felt my rear end come down. I just felt somethin' wasn't quite right in the machine so I looked back and saw it was sinkin' backwards. The driver's seat in a Bug is in the middle, and all I could think about was gettin' out and not gettin' wet. I knew the right door didn't work, so it would have to be the left one. The front end was up in the air so I shoved the door open and jumped. Luckily, the ice was thick enough where I landed to hold me, but my left leg got wet. I watched the Bug goin' down fast, with a few bubbles. The first thing to come up was a barrel with about fifteen gallons of gas. In the little thin sports jacket I was wearin', I had two boxes of matches I always carry, expectin' something like this to happen, so I made a big fire and dried my socks and waited to see what else would come up."

(Could I have jumped clear? Could I have done that?)

"Could you see the Bug?" I asked.

(I am still asking myself: Could I have jumped? No.)

"Well, I got a long dry tree branch and brushed the snow off the ice and then I could see the Bug down about fifteen feet," Frost replied. "It was restin' on a rock. The first thing I did was to fish out the junk beginnin' to float up. Like, a case of pork chops. That's all I had to eat, about thirty pork chops, and I made a hook with some wire in my pocket and fished out my teapot and that's what I used to cook my pork chops."

(Down fifteen feet. Two more feet of water than the height of Truck 36.)

"What else did you get?"

"See, when I jumped, all my food and blanket and gun was in the cab in the front and slid out the door under water," Frost said. "I just had whatever gear I was wearing, a summer jacket, winter underwear, pants, work boots, a knitted hat but no mitts, and the temperature was thirty below. I did fish out my blanket four days later, only then it took me two days to dry it. I had plenty of water to drink but I got mighty tired of pork. Hell, I had five or six chops the first day. I began to ration them, and even had three or four left when I was picked up. My gun went down in the Bug and I wished I had it for all the caribou and foxes and wolves that were passin' by me every day. Especially the wolves that were always kind of hangin' around. I don't know what they were waitin' for, but it looked suspicious."

Frost got up, poured himself fresh coffee and sat down again. "I worked every day tryin' to fish somethin' out of the

Bug but the big idea was never to let my fire go out," he continued. "If it got too low I would freeze to death in my sleep, so I didn't sleep for about four or five days. Just a little now and then. I had used all the gas to get a fire started so for the first two days all I did was to bring wood and make a big shelter so I could keep warm. I was playin' Tarzan all the time, breakin' down spruce trees for markings on the lake too. I piled a huge bunch together so you could see them from the air, in two lines so if you didn't see one you would see the other. I did that in my spare time, which I had lots of."

Frost cut himself a slice of bread, buttered it and spread jam on it, then slowly ate it. "I was there seven nights and eight days alone and I was startin' to answer myself," he said. "I figured I'd get picked up sooner or later and the second day I heard a plane. The pilot, Smoky Hornby, was supposed to be comin' to check on me, but he did a pass and went on. The next day, I hear another plane that passes on and then for three or four days you can't see for the fog. If I hadn't been picked up soon it was my intention to walk back but I figured I'd be runnin' to keep warm. It would take at least three days and my only rest would be to make the kind of half-assed camp I already had in the nearest bush, warm up and sleep for a half hour and keep goin'."

(Walk home? My God!)

"On the eighth day I heard a plane circlin' where I was supposed to have been goin' and then Smoky must have seen my markers," Frost went on. "He wandered a bit and finally saw my trees and circled there. I had trees all around so nobody would land where I went through, where the ice was thin, four or five inches. I ran out on the lake and started jiggin' around, about four hundred feet from where the Bug went under. When Smoky landed I was so glad to see him I even opened the door for him and said somethin' goofy, I don't know what, but it made him laugh. I remember his first words were, 'My God, you're lookin' healthy!' I had lost a few pounds but I did feel pretty healthy."

He leaned across the table almost confidentially and said to me, "I'll tell you somethin'. I was just lucky to have a couple of boxes of matches in my pocket, just lucky. Because I never would have survived without 'em. I've been in the bush all my life and I used this," he said, tapping his head. "I made sure I had plenty of wood, made markers, and a shelter, all that sort of thing. I got tired doin' the same old thing, lookin' at the same old grub, and I missed a wash in the worst way, more than food. But take a white man in those circumstances. He'd have been dead."

(*"We just fell into Great Bear Lake. . . . Are you scared?" . . . Yes. Now I am.*)

"Does it scare you now to travel on ice?" I asked cautiously.

Frost shrugged. "The next time I'll be a little more alert, you might say, and make sure both doors are workin' before I leave the garage and that my little match bottle is on me and not in my packsack where it should never have been."

Sitting completely relaxed with his cap perched on the back of his head, Al Frost looked like a schoolboy, but he was twenty-six. He was from Old Crow, a well-established Indian community on the Porcupine River in the Yukon Territory, where his father, now dead, was with the Mounted Police until he married and settled down there as a storekeeper, trapping on the side. His mother was a full-blooded Cree Indian and was still living in Old Crow, which is famous for its skiers. Frost's brothers and sisters were fine skiers and his own skiing career had looked promising until it was cut off by a jump in which he lost his balance, fainted, and came to with his leg facing the wrong way. He was still in high school then, training for races in Alaska, and he finished school by correspondence from a hospital bed. Now he worked as an operator of a Cat, which, in trucking lingo, is a Cat skinner.

"I'm happy with what I'm doin', I guess," Frost said, removing his cap and scratching his head, "but I got no future." He looked puzzled. "I got through high school and I have a good education, like my mum. She likes to read detective stories and mysteries, just like me."

The trucks worked back and forth over the previous portage between Rabbit Lake, which was behind us, and Hislop, where we were camped, all night. The men took off only an hour to sleep before they came to breakfast in the camper. Afterwards, Denison tried the radio at the regular call hour, and reached Jimmy Watson, thirty miles behind us on the Rayrock Road, in 36, where he had spent the night. "I'm at the south side of Hislop, south side of Hislop," John said, speaking into the small microphone cupped in his large hand. "We'll wait for you here. Wait for you here."

A crackling sound, then Jimmy's voice repeated the message, "Wait for me there, wait for me there. Roger." John replaced the microphone on the hook on the phone box. "Jimmy won't be here for another two and a half hours," he said. "When he comes, he can carry the Cat across the lake on his lowboy, it'll save fuel and time. On its own, the Cat walks four or five miles an hour and Jimmy goes fifteen or twenty. We only need that Cat for clearing portages and the less it walks across the lake ice the better. It's cold driving in the open, but nobody should *ever* drive on a lake in a Cat with a covered cab, because you can get trapped in it. When a Cat goes down it sinks so fast there's no time to open a door before you jump." He looked out at the sky and scowled. "It's a hell of a day," he said. It had begun to snow.

The men slept until Jimmy came and by the time he arrived the snow was falling so thickly that twenty feet away the African Queen was a shadowy bulk with fuzzy orange spheres for headlights. It was ten in the morning, and as soon as Jimmy had had breakfast we started across Hislop Lake. I was in the first truck with Tom Berry, who was plowing the road. His truck, 34, was another six-wheel-drive Mammoth, only bigger and newer than 36. I was sitting comfortably on an upholstered leather seat, almost eight feet above the snowy lake, beside Tom. I had an irrational sense of power and participation as he slowly, slowly broke eight miles of new road. The plow was casting snow in a white cloud to either side as Tom peered through his windshield, trying to find yesterday's fading tracks that he and John had made scouting in the Bug. We were at the head of a convoy; directly behind us, John was impatiently treading on our rear, followed by Al Frost in the Bug and, finally, Jimmy carrying the Cat on the trailer of his truck, with black-bearded Gilles inside on top of the battery box beside him.

This was a whiteout, the weather northerners dread most, when strong winds combine with heavy snowfall to create a thick white swirl that reduces visibility to zero. The whole world in front of me had suddenly become a blank and I couldn't see a thing, as if we had gone into a cloud. Travellers caught in a whiteout sit down wherever they are and wait, and truckers frequently take advantage of a whiteout to sleep until it is dark. Then, with their lights on they can see enough at least to keep going. Tom was travelling with his headlights on but several times he stopped, got out of the truck and walked in front, looking for the road. Most of the time he said he was guided by the way the truck felt when it met the bank on either side. Geographical features that marked the way simply dissolved into this white opacity—whiteness that eddied and blew; a whiteout whiteinwhiteout day. Occasionally the snow parted to expose glinty steel, a corner of the wing of the great snowplow at the front of the truck, scooping up the lake's surface of snow and tossing it away to either side, to form the continuous strip of snowbank that marked off the corridor for travel.

Tom dons yellow goggles to cut the glare. Slowly. Slowly. He is feeling his way. His window is open and he brushes snow off the outside mirror so he can see the trucks behind, and the road. An occasional gust lifts the snowy screen and reveals a long white strip, the road of ice we have just plowed behind us on the lake.

The interior of Tom's cab gleamed. The dashboard had as many dials as a small plane; instant reporting on fuel, speed, air, batteries, temperatures; switches for the plow, which operated on a hydraulic lift, the motor-powered winch, the lights, the windshield wipers. His two-way radio, the duplicate of John's, was mounted just below the windshield in front of me. Directly behind the cab we were in, but accessible only by going outside and in again by its own door, was his caboose, a seven-by-eight foot custom-made shack with two bunks, stove, lamps, and a food box. This was where Tom lived while he was assigned to Truck 34. The African Queen had no such luxurious accommodations, no caboose. Jimmy had to bed down for the night in 36 in his sleeping bag on the front seat in the cab, and ate cold food from his box, but whenever he could, he caught up with the camper and stayed there. Every truck, even the old Bug, carried emergency food rations and was supposed to have a propane gas heater; but if all else failed, including the motor, the life saver was a sleeping bag until rescue arrived.

I watched Tom shift gears. There were two gear boxes, with twenty forward gears and four reverse, permitting so many variations that a diagram was pasted on the inside cab wall to keep them straight. I complimented Tom on his housekeeping. He patted the truck's steering wheel affectionately. "I can tell all about a man the minute I see the inside of his cab," Tom said. "This is *my* truck. Jimmy had it for a few days and frankly, I was a bit provoked about that but it's okay, because Thirty-four is back with *me* now. Last year, I near quit when a man working for Echo Bay went down The Big Lake on the road-grader I was driving then. That's a machine that looks something like a giant grasshopper. The first time the operator who had it before me took it out he was goin' downhill on one of those steep grades at the mine and got so scared that he jumped off and let her go. When I got that grader the roof and door were smashed, the plow was off and the windows were all broke out. I put in new plywood to make a roof and door, and new windows, lights, a heater and my little cookstove so I could live right in the cab." His laugh reverberated inside the truck; an outdoor laugh that made the cab feel crowded. "When that man drove my grader away, I took off for Yellowknife and got loaded," Tom added, "but after a while I come back and so did the grader."

We were creeping along at three miles an hour and Tom stopped three times to get out and test the ice with an ice auger. The depth of the ice ranged from twenty to thirty inches thick. The slow pace got to Denison. He suddenly swung out and around us and ran along ahead in the lighter, faster camper, making tire tracks in the snow. Tom shook his head. "I'd do anything for John but if I owned any trucks I'd hate to see him drive off in one, he's so hard on machines," Tom said. "He's the worst driver of all, very reckless. John's a straight, go-ahead driver. You don't make any money backing up, though, and if it wasn't for him some of the mines around here wouldn't have opened. The Cat trains were so slow, and you had to take the sleighs over the portages one at a time; besides, Cats drop in these lakes for sure."

The back lights on the camper were small red blurs, scarlet dots disappearing into the snowy cloud. "John's proved that freighting with standard trucks right up into the Arctic is feasible. Take a load of lumber straight from Vancouver to Port Radium! Why not? This kind of operation is making this country," Tom continued. "He builds and maintains the roads, operates and repairs his own equipment, everything. John's road is part and parcel of the growth of the North. He's not more experienced than a lot of oldtimers around Yellowknife with ice, but he's willing to take more chances. When he started hauling freight in trucks successfully this far north, even into the Barren Lands, he was the only man in the Territories doing it. Everybody said he was nuts. Everybody." He stopped again, and got out with the auger and checked the ice. When he came back, he stamped his feet on the running board, shook himself clean of the film of fresh snow that had settled already on his shirt and the top of his bald head, sat down and resumed driving. "Don't tell Dad, but after he and I went scoutin' I went out again last night plowin' in the truck and was easin' along and easin' along and thought I was following the track we had made. What do you think it was?" He threw back his head, laughing. "Caribou tracks!" He brushed the remaining snowflakes out of his beard and said to me, "Say, I sure was surprised to see you come out of the camper yesterday. I'd have thought you'd had enough after you fell into Great Bear Lake in Thirty-six last year."

"Well, I guess I didn't," I said.

"You're probably hooked like the rest of us," he said. "Some of us leave for a while, maybe two or three months or a couple of years, but we always come back. I don't know what it is about the North. Maybe it's these spaces. But you ought to see some of the drivers when they first come. You wouldn't believe it! One driver was wearing oxfords and didn't have a sleeping bag. No nothing, when sometimes you can't move five minutes away from shelter without carrying your sleeping bag right along with you in case you get caught in a storm and can't find your way back. That happens. Ordinarily, trucking's a cut-throat business, but up here it's built in to be nice to each other. Everybody's *got* to get along. You *have* to use your head and help each other, not like down south where if an oldtimer doesn't like his second driver he just won't truck. You can't pull into a garage here when something busts, and below forty-five degrees, metal crystallizes and the machines are *always* breaking down. A three-quarter-inch chain snaps like the stem of a wine glass, and if you hit a rock almost anything is liable to go. Every man has to look out for hisself because, mostly, nobody's around to tell you what to do. You have to have your own little toolbox along and you have to know your engine and be able to do *anything*."

The camper had disappeared but we were following in its

freshly made tracks. We drove in silence while Tom smoked a cigarette. He threw the butt out the window, closed it and said, "I was with John ten years ago on the first road he made this far north, to Tundra, a gold mine two hundred and fifteen miles north of Yellowknife in the Barrens. No trees, only tundra, and rocks, big as trucks. It was fifty-eight degrees below zero for six weeks." He peered out the side window. It had stopped snowing and he could see the Bug in his mirror. "Did you know that I went out and got the Bug that Frost dropped in The Big Lake last year?" Tom asked. I said no, I didn't know that. "Well, one of the trucks took me and a Cat, a Herman Nelson heater and a tent to where it was," Tom said. "I dug a hole at the shore, put a twelve-foot plank through it with the Cat's winch-line cable laid on top of the plank, dug another hole every eight feet for three hundred and fifty feet and pushed the plank and winch line under the ice, between the holes straight to the Bug. I don't weigh more than about a hundred and eighty, a lot less than a Bug, so I could walk around on that ice, no trouble; you can walk on less ice than I can, because you're lighter than me. At the hole where the Bug went through, I dropped the winch line under until I hooked the frame, and started windin'. I drug the Bug underneath the ice to shore but I pulled it too close and had to chop the ice there to get her out. When I got it up on shore I put the tent over it quick so she wouldn't freeze up, because it was about fifty below, put the Herman Nelson underneath to warm it and drained out all the oil. I had to strip the engine and take the head off but I put it back together again and drove the Bug home. I was seven days on the lake getting the Bug running again, and three days getting it home, and when I returned it to the fellow who owned it, what do you think he did? He gave me hell because the roof was hurt. 'That's a brand new Bug,' he said, so I said, 'That's too bad. I should have left it down there.' "

Denison had turned the camper around up ahead and was flashing his lights on and off to signal the entrance to the next portage. It was noon, and we had gone just eight miles, to the north end of Hislop. We parked and made our camp there. A dozen small log cabins and wooden houses were situated a half mile away, in the curve of the shore and up from the beach that slanted to the lake's edge, where a pile of red fuel drums and a line of overturned canoes lay beside a small dock. Tom pointed to the nearby meat caches, frozen caribou carcasses stored on open wooden platforms on stilts to prevent dogs and wolves from getting at them. We were camped beside an old Indian village inhabited by members of the Dogrib Tribe, originally from Fort Rae.

I stood up, turned around and carefully climbed down from Tom's high truck; left foot on the cab floor for a starter, right foot on a footrest out into the fender, left foot stretching stretching until my toe touched solid ice and then both feet were down on the Ice Road. Just in time to see a strange truck entering our circle, spluttering like a percolator; a mangy orange one with a snowplow in front and a silver shack on its back. Number 43 on Denison's truck roster, a twenty-year-old, United States-made, F.W.D. 4 (for Four Wheel Drive), which everyone referred to affectionately as "Fud." Its driver joined our lunch table in the camper, a cheerful, stocky young man with thinning reddish hair and very blue eyes, who was introduced to me as Billy Mukluk. His last name was the same as the word for a sealskin waterproof Eskimo boot, and this puzzled me when he told me that he was of Ukrainian descent, from a large White Russian settlement in Alberta. Although Canadian-born, he spoke Russian at home and his English had a slight accent. I did not find out for several days that his name was really Billy Michalchuk, but by that time I was calling him "Mukluk" as everyone else did.

Back in the camper, I counted seven people to be fed — Mukluk, Jimmy Watson, Chartrand, Tom Berry, Al Frost, Denison and myself. Everyone had settled down expectantly as if I knew what I was doing. I hastily heated soup, got out the bread, salami, and cheese, opened canned fruit, and made coffee by the double-pot method I had so recently learned. I hadn't planned ahead, and the salami was frozen. I had to use a saw to slice it. Before the men started eating, Mukluk, who belonged to the Pentecostal Church, bowed his head and murmured grace. His religion made Mukluk different than the other truck drivers. He never swore. He also didn't like to work on Sundays, but like the others, he took a lot of pride in his work and equipment, and it always bothered him terribly when something broke down. He explained to me once that he liked coming North because there was nothing else to do but work, so he could come home to his wife and children with his whole paycheck, and also because Denison gave him responsibility and left him alone to figure things out. "I was workin' around the Byers terminal in Edmonton, and I went up to John and told him I wanted to go North," he said. "If I stay all winter, I'll get a bonus."

The wind had died down. Outside our small house the thermometer read thirty-two below zero, but inside it was so warm that I took off a sweater. The furnace in the camper wasn't working and apparently never had worked. Now something mysterious seemed to have happened to the camper's electricity, because there were no lights. I was much too scared of being labelled "dumb" again to ask what had happened. Denison had installed a powerful infra-red heater, called variously a Silent Sue and a Lazy Susan, in the living-room area. Its small red-hot grill, banded by silvery metal reflectors that gave off a rosy glow, was attached by a vertical pipe to a fat tank of propane gas that sat from then on in the aisle by the door so that we had to step around it to go in or out. With so many people in such close quarters, the heater was an added, exceedingly dangerous drain on our oxygen supply, and John had chipped the ice from a skylight in the center of the kitchen roof and opened it, untaped a small side window and opened that too. A warning popped from a corner of my memory to nag me;

an Arctic administrator whom I had met one winter in the North went out the following spring on a small fishing boat in Hudson Bay with two Eskimos. They went to sleep on a cold night in the craft's tiny cabin with just such a propane heater to keep them warm, and they never woke up again.

We were still eating lunch when three Indian men and a young boy came across the ice on their sleds from the village and knocked on our door. John invited them to lunch, and asked them how the ice was. The men turned to the boy, who talked to them in their own language. Then the boy said to John in English, "Pretty good."

"Hunting much?" John asked. The boy shook his head. "Fishing?"

"Not much," the boy said. The men talked to the boy again, in the Dogrib language, and he asked John, in English, speaking slowly, "Did you see a dog team? We are expecting the chief to come from Fort Rae."

"No," said John, "but we'll have the road plowed up to here by tomorrow, so he'll probably come then."

The boy spoke again with the older Indians, who had finished eating and were staring at me. Then they got up and departed, as quietly as they had come.

Everyone but Denison left shortly in the trucks; they were going back eight miles to work over the newly broken portage. I washed dishes: one inch of lake water heated in a dishpan on the stove for washing, paper towels for drying. John seemed to be waiting for something, which proved to be the drone of an airplane motor overhead. He opened the door and watched a small red-and-white Cessna 180 land on the lake ice and glide smoothly to a stop on its skis. Denison went out in the Bug to bring the pilot and his passenger who had alighted from the plane back to the camper, and I put a fresh pot of coffee on the stove. Like most things that happened, the plane's arrival was a surprise to me. Denison had summoned the pilot, Bill Hettrick, through the mobile radiotelephone in the cab of our camper, to come out and take its generator back to Yellowknife to be repaired, and the plane would also take back Al Frost, who had another job commitment. Hettrick became one of the constants of our life on the Ice Road; a sure sign of catastrophe, each time he appeared at whatever lake we happened to be on, at a cost of at least two hundred dollars per visit, depending on time and distance. He would come down from the sky, materializing like a large red-and-white bird from the world of people, to remove a vitally needed piece of equipment for repair, or bring us essential parts or an expert on the salvaging of submerged vehicles. This time he had brought Hughie Arden, a dark-haired, husky man, to consult with John.

I watched the men nursing their mugs of coffee between their hands. I thought, coffee is the ceremonial drink of the North; no meeting of two or more people is complete without it. Tea is sometimes served as well, but coffee is the obligatory offering. We had brought more bags of coffee in our stores than any other commodity, not excepting the rolls of paper towelling that Denison used for everything and had stuffed into every empty cranny. John told Hughie that he hoped to move ahead three lakes during the night and arrive at Faber, but he was uncertain of the portage there. "I'd ruther go at night because I can see better by the moon and stars," John said, "but I still can't find my way to that portage, although I've been over it, must be a hundred times. I even tried putting up colored markers, but the Indians take them."

"Why don't you take an Indian guide from the village here?" Hughie suggested.

Denison shook his head. "I have to learn some time, and I've always done the big ones, Hardisty and Hottah lakes, myself, so I guess I can do Faber too," he said.

"Well then, watch for an island and a long line of hills," Hughie said.

The air was clear and cold, and we stood at the door of the camper when Hettrick, Al Frost and Hughie Arden left, and watched their plane until it was a speck in a sky that at three was already turning pink for a lovely sunset. Hettrick's arrivals always occurred in late morning or early afternoon and his visits were of short duration because of the necessity of getting home in daylight; there were no emergency landing fields between us and his home air base in Yellowknife; no lights to guide him after sunset. Like all Arctic bush pilots, his flying day in winter was constricted to about six hours, when the sun was up.

"The pilot I used before Hettrick was one of the guys that made this operation work," Denison said. He sat down at the table and buttered himself a piece of homemade bread and slowly ate it. "His name was Chuck McAvoy, and he was a hell of a good guy, about a dozen or so years younger than me, and he'd do ennathing for you. We would never have made our roads without him. He did all my flying as long as he was alive, in an old Fairchild high-winged monoplane from about nineteen thirty-seven. Once I was flying with McAvoy in that old clunker of his, lookin' for my trucks, and he was short of fuel," Denison continued. "It was a terribly noisy plane, with an engine that roared, and all of a sudden everything was very very quiet. Just like *nothin'*. It was only a second or two that the engine cut out but I just about *died*, and I would have been even more scared if there had been time, but then it started up again. Turned out Chuck had waited to switch tanks until the first one was dry, because he said how else would he know there was nothin' left, and he didn't want to waste any gas when we were so short. The dangerous part of that is it might not catch when you switch tanks. You have to be awfully sure of yourself."

"What happened to him?"

"It was in the spring when the ice was melting," Denison said. "He went north a couple of years ago in the spring and he was never found, not hide nor hair of him or that old plane of his. Most of us think the tail fell off or something and that Chuck must have gone down in a lake somewhere."

The pattern of Denison's road-building operation was quite simple, and after the first confusion I could see it. His goal —it was an obsession with him—was to break new road forward every day as many miles as possible, and we moved ahead daily to make a new camp along raw road that had just been cleared. From there each morning the trucks went back with the Cat to clean and smooth down the portage road just opened while the Bug moved forward to scout a new section, marking out the route ahead for the Cat and trucks to work on at night after supper. Going across the lakes was amazingly simple—an easy matter of sweeping a path on the ice with the plow, of clearing snow away; but the snow drifted or blew back on the lake roads so fast that a plow truck had to be provided with each convoy of regular freight. The portages were the hard part of the construction; the land must be cleared and levelled. Yet only one-tenth of the area covered by the Ice Road was over land. Ironically, rough as the portages often were to traverse, and as difficult as they were to break through, they were the safer portion of the Ice Road; the lakes that underlay nine-tenths of the road were the potential death traps.

Tom Berry returned from the road, and since it was still light, he and Denison set off in the Bug to scout ahead. Blissfully alone, I heated water, washed clothes, took a sponge bath, baked a whole box of macaroni and cheese in a casserole in the oven. It was lovely and quiet on the lake beside the Indian village. A peaceful, remembered hour of solitude, the only one I ever had on the Ice Road. I was just settling down to read when there was a timid knock on the door and when I opened it an Indian man, woman and child were standing outside. I invited them into the camper, they drank ceremonial coffee, ate the cookies I hastily brought out, stared at me silently, and soon departed. Almost immediately, another family group arrived, and then another, until the whole settlement had seen me. Our crew returned right on the heels of the last Indian visitors. I was running a short-order diner! Only Denison didn't eat. He went immediately to bed in the back bunk when he came in, silent, withdrawn, with that frozen look that I came to associate with his severe ulcer attacks.

While I was clearing away the dishes from supper, Jimmy Watson stretched wearily out on the bench and said, "I work so hard up here that when I go home I don't feel like doing anything at all for about two months."

I asked if he ever thought about danger when he was working. "Sure I do," he replied. "It's *really* dangerous work, and I'm often scared. A couple of years ago I hit a big rock on the Ice Road driving a truck the size of Thirty-six. I woke up lying underneath the dashboard." He lit a cigarette; its tip a red period to the square glow from the Lazy Susan heater that sizzled faintly in the dark on its stand at his elbow. "The first time I drove across Marian Lake I was in Thirty-four, with a Cat loaded on my trailer," Jimmy said. "Two miles from shore I happened to look in my mirror and saw that my trailer was going down. I hollered into my radio for the camper to come and pull me out, and then I jumped into the goddamned water with my mukluks on. I was quite excited, and didn't know that where I was it was only four feet deep and I was already on the bottom. John had heard me but wouldn't answer, he was so disgusted that the truck was wasting all this time. He stormed out to see what was wrong, got out of his camper and walked around me, threw up his hands and said, 'Pull it out!' It took four days to pull Thirty-four out because it had struck mud on the bottom and had froze in. We had to break the ice and loosen the mud by dropping two or three charges of dynamite." He laughed. "After two or three days, you are really disgusted, especially when the temperature is forty below, but when we blasted, the truck came out real real easy." He closed his eyes, took a long drag on his cigarette, and then sat up and asked if I would join him in a cup of tea. I got out two tin cups, and while we were drinking our tea he said, "Another time I was in Thirty-four, and there was a fellow in a truck hauling lumber with me, Red

Stirko, and a guy named Peter Goddard, who was my swamper. He was supposed to help me put on chains, maybe cook supper, that kind of thing, but he just sat in the back of the truck and read *Playboy* magazine. I was furious but he's a damned good pilot now, and he taught me to fly, so looking back, it doesn't matter. We had a camp way up the line, at Hottah Lake, and I was scouting, walking in a currenty place in a narrow channel where I thought I could take the trucks through. Well, there was no ice there at all, and I fell through into the current. It was deep as my neck there, and I went *way* down. We built a fire to dry me out. I took all my clothes off at thirty below zero and it was cold as hell. I burnt my goddamn underwear holding it on a stick over the fire when I was standing on spruce boughs to keep my feet from freezing, but that's beside the point."

He paused, thinking. "I tell you, if it hadn't been for Peter and Red Stirko being with me, I'd never have made it," he said. "They had matches, for one thing, and mine were soaking wet because I had to swim about ten feet. Jesus, it was cold! I got everything sort of half dry and we got back in our trucks. I was going to plow straight through to Great Bear Lake, but Stirko's truck went off the road, and with seventy thousand pounds of lumber on his trailer I didn't have enough weight on my truck to pull him out. I had to go back and get a Cat, and while we were pushing and pulling on Stirko's truck my transmission broke, so I had to shut my motor off. I radioed for John to send out a transmission and we sat there for a week, waiting. It felt like a month, because we ran out of propane gas so we had no heat, and I had to build a lean-to shelter out of spruce boughs to keep warm. While I was waiting for John, I also built a little sleigh, because that transmission was going to weigh two hundred pounds, and we were half a mile from where the plane would land. John flew in with Hettrick, carrying the transmission, dumped it on the sleigh, came up and looked at the truck, and said, 'See you, boys. Have fun.' Honest to God. That's all he said, before he took off. Mind you, he was paying for the plane by the hour, but he didn't even stay to have coffee. He just came in from the sky and dropped the transmission in our laps." Jimmy shook his head, laughing. "Honestly, though, I don't know how he stands up, he's got trucks spread out all over the country after the road's open, and he's responsible for them. I guess he knew we could get going by ourselves."

He continued laughing and shaking his head. "John's got a certain way of asking you to do things so you can't refuse," he continued. "I remember once we were coming south after the northern operations were finished for that year, driving vehicles loaded with equipment. I was carrying a truck and John's TD-14 International tractor on my highboy and we were crossing the Mackenzie River on the ice bridge at Fort Providence. It was early May, and the load limit that late in the spring was fifteen thousand pounds. Well, the truck itself probably weighed thirty thousand pounds, and I had more like one hundred thousand pounds there altogether, but John said, 'Take her the way she is.' I was sure I'd have to change my underwear after I crossed, and I knew I was a little bit nervous, but subconsciously I was damned scared. After all, when you know you've got way way too much of a load maybe you don't show it, but you know it. Well, I took the dumb thing across the Mackenzie on the ice bridge, and the ice shook a little bit and lots of water came up. It seems a lot longer when you're driving like that but it's only about two miles, and about forty feet deep in the deepest spot. The ice was very spongy and sort of sank, but it was okay. When I got to the other side I had to change loads with another truck driver. He took my load south and the next morning I took his north, forty-two-thousand pounds of groceries. We just switched trailers, because my truck had six-wheel drive and his didn't. During the night, the government pulled the chain across the ice bridge and put a padlock on, so nobody could cross any more that season. Del Curry was at the south side of the bridge with us too, with a gravel truck to drive north, and he took a crescent wrench and undid the bolt that fastened the chain between the posts. We proceeded to go across, with Del first in the gravel truck, just hoping there was enough ice under the overflow water that was all over the road, covering the top and cracks and holes, some of which were four feet deep. You'd fall in the odd hole, but with six-wheel drive you can pull yourself out. Christ, one hole was *really* deep and I remember the van tipping. It had me quite nervous." He started to laugh again. "That's another one of John's things," he said, lowering his voice. "I didn't want to go back to Yellowknife, I wanted to go home, to British Columbia, and this was a time he gave me an alternative. He said, 'Jimmy, if you want to do it, do it. If you don't want to, it means taking all these groceries back to Hay River and spending a couple of thousand dollars flying them in.' "

He looked at me and smiled. "You love it all and hate it all," he said. "I've driven every plow truck John's got. After you drive one motor for a long time it becomes a part of you, like your right arm. You know every inch of it and what it can and can't do. You swear and curse at it, call it all sorts of names, even kick it. At the same time, it's like your woman. Nobody touches it but yourself, and you get damned careful with it. As for this Ice Road," he added, "I could go the whole trail blindfolded." He stopped talking. He was staring at my hands. I instinctively tried to hide them under the table. "You've never done anything like this before, have you?" he asked. "I'll bet you've never cooked for so many men, either." I put my hands up on the table again, laughing. There were dirty Band-Aids wrapped around eight fingertips.

"I can't do anything without cutting a finger or burning it," I said. "I suppose I'm nervous because I don't know how any of you like your food, or even what you like to eat. You are meat-and-potato eaters, and I'm used to preparing salads and fish. I never thought before I came that I'd be cooking."

"It's the same for you as it is for us, I guess," Jimmy replied, smiling. "You'll find yourself doing a *lot* of things you never dreamed of doing, on the Ice Road."

It had gotten dark so long ago, at four in the afternoon, that now it seemed much later than it really was, eight o'clock. I was exhausted and went to bed. The lights from the other vehicles shone faintly through the camper windows, diffused by the added plastic weather stripping into a ruddy flush that half illuminated the camper, making shadows, like the light from a hall into a darkened bedroom. Denison might have been dead for any sound that he made, but I could hear Jimmy breathing from the bunk beyond the kitchen, where he had flopped down next to John. My feet were cold when I got into bed although I still wore my socks, but my sleeping bag was so warm I took off one sweater. I glimpsed the thermometer on the floor. I must have knocked it down when I was making up my bunk. The reading on the wall all day had been seventy-five degrees above zero in the camper, but when I turned my flashlight on the thermometer where it lay on the floor, before I picked it up, it read ten degrees below zero.

Gentle throb of the camper's motor, idling; soft counterpoint to the low hum of engines around us, deep-toned, resonant. We rock gently, vibrating to this night music.

I fell into a deep sleep and when I awoke, Denison was in the kitchen making breakfast. I jumped out of bed, rolled up my sleeping bag, threw it into the back bunk on top of Jimmy's and John's, and said, "What can I do to help?"

John didn't answer, so I took an empty orange juice can from the kitchen counter, opened the door and threw the can into a snowbank. When I closed the door and walked back down the aisle, Denison was facing me at the stove, spatula in hand, furious. "*Every* time you take an empty can and throw it out you open the door and let the cold air in," he said angrily. "Then you go back and get another can and do the same thing again. Does that make sense? Why don't you take them all at once and throw them out, instead of one at a time? Then we might be able to keep some of the heat in here!"

"I was trying to help," I said weakly.

"If you want to help and if you had any sense, which you don't seem to have, you'd stay out of the way until the men are fed," Denison went on, looking angrier than ever. "That's the best way *you* can help. Don't you see how small this place is? Stay in the corner," he directed, pointing towards the far one on the bench around the table. "Then you'll be out of *my* way while I'm getting breakfast, ennahow."

My head was burning up. I quickly climbed into the corner of the bench and sat there with my feet up, puffing on a cigarette to hide my embarrassment.

Jimmy Watson had been outside checking over 36 and he came in just then. "Hi, how did you sleep?" he asked, sitting down beside me. I was speechless. He leaned over the table. "You O.K.?" he asked.

"I'm fine," I whispered.

When Tom, Gilles and Mukluk came in for breakfast I moved across to the opposite bench, with my feet drawn up again out of the way, and listened. The men had worked until three in the morning clearing the portage ahead that Denison and Tom had marked out the previous afternoon. This portage was a long tough one with a hill on it, and Denison wasn't wasting a minute of clear weather. At night, Tom said, truck headlights gave them as good or better visibility than they had in daylight on land among the trees, but scouting a lake at night even with a full moon would be foolhardy.

I cleared away the breakfast dishes after the men left for the portage, and John made breakfast for us, put it on the table, and ate with me. I started to apologize for being in the way, but he opened a can of strawberries, my favorite canned fruit, handed it to me, and changed the subject.

As soon as the dishes were washed we were ready to move on. When Denison set the lighted Lazy Susan in a firm niche in one of the split sections of the steel sink, I mustered up courage to ask what happened to the camper furnace he had been so eager to try out. "Inoperable," he said cheerfully. "I guess it just froze up. It's got to get oxygen from the outer air, and the outside intake area keeps plugging up with snow, so we're in trouble. We *have* to use the Lazy Susan, which burns up oxygen in here. We must be sure to keep the windows open." He reached overhead and cranked open the skylight even further, and stepped back into the living room to push the window out another two inches. "If we didn't keep this Lazy Susan working in back while we're driving, everything would be frozen, all our canned goods. I wish I had my own camper now instead of this rented thing. My camper has a hot-water heater off the engine, just like a regular car heater, and I'd never go again without one in a camper, in no way. You know two things have gone wrong with the heat, don't you?" he said. I shook my head. "Well, we haven't any heat in front in the cab either. The generator shorted, so it's burned out, and there's no power to run the electric motor that keeps the heater going and makes lights. In fact, we have no lights at all now, just enough juice from the battery to keep the truck going. I've borrowed Mukluk's Lazy Susan for heat in front while we're driving. Otherwise our windows will frost up and I won't be able to see where I'm going. The weather's about thirty below and the colder it gets, the quicker we'll frost up. It's too damned cold and rough for me to ride with my head out the window." While he was talking he was packing the loose jars and boxes, all the housekeeping items that would normally rest on an open shelf, into a corrugated box which he braced between propane gas tanks on the floor. I watched, figuring that next time I'd be able to pack it myself. Denison put on his green cap and heavy khaki parka. We were ready to travel.

I came down the camper steps and immediately Denison took them off and put them into the rear slot outside under the floor. Before we got into the front seat, he rolled both cab windows down all the way, and handed me Mukluk's Lazy Susan, with instructions to hold it as close to the windshield as I could without touching it. A round twenty-five-pound tank of propane gas rested on the floor between my feet, connected to the heater by a plastic tube. A blast of forty-below-zero air was coming in through the windows, wide open to provide oxygen. I shivered at the sudden impact of the sharp cold on my right shoulder and pulled up my parka hood around my head.

Even with my parka hood up, I was freezing on my right side, but melting on my left, where I was holding the heavy heater between Denison and myself as close as I could get it to the window without knocking against the radio. I was reminded of a picture in a favorite childhood book of a man scowling on one side of his face and smiling on the other. The temperature differences were so extreme on the right and left sides of my body that I felt as if I had a physical line splitting me down the middle. We were driving in convoy behind Gilles, who was in the Bug; he was following the two big trucks, one of which carried the Cat; behind us, out of sight, was Mukluk in old, slow Fud. We were climbing steadily, lurching from side to side on this rugged stretch of half-built road, the big trucks, streaks of red, moving through the trees ahead of us.

Denison stopped suddenly. He sniffed. I was so single-minded, so concentrated on holding the heater up and trying to keep it steady on this crazy chewed-up trail, that I was only dimly aware that John had jumped from the camper, until the door on my side was flung open and he shouted, "FIRE! The camper's on fire!"

I set the lighted heater carefully down in its holder on the gas tank and ran back in time to see my sleeping bag in flames, flying out the camper door. It soared through the air and landed in the snow beside the road; bright orange-red flames licking the silky green nylon. I was still standing there with my mouth open, staring, when John emerged backwards from the camper down the steps, his face blacked from smoke, spraying from a small hand extinguisher into the camper. It seemed to me that I hadn't a thought in my head; later I realized I was waiting for an explosion.

The camper inside was a mess. The floor, benches, stove, sink, bunks, everything was covered with a white feathery chemical from the extinguisher. The walls and ceiling were coated with black sludge. The little house reeked of smoke; it was a terrible stench. But the fire was out.

Back in the driver's seat, Denison was slumped at the wheel, grey and still. He touched his gloved hand to his forehead as if it pained him. I said weakly, "What luck. There wasn't any wind and no one got hurt."

He was watching in his rear-view mirror for Mukluk to show up in Fud. "That's *right,*" he said. "I never worry about yesterday. When my garage burned to the ground last year in Yellowknife with two big trucks in it and nothing salvaged, I lost fifty thousand dollars in an hour. All long gone. I like to do a job for the job's sake."

Fud wheezed up the hill, clattering and spluttering to a halt beside us. Denison leaned out his open window. "We've had a fire," he shouted to Mukluk above the noise of both motors. "Sleeping bag fell into the heater and things are pretty bad inside the camper." Mukluk waved, shifted gears, and drove ahead, returning shortly with the other trucks. We swung around and proceeded back, single file, to Hislop Lake.

When we came out of the portage, a large eight-by-ten silver-and-red room mounted on four colossal black flotation tires, each three feet across and four feet high, was parked on the lake right in front of us. A vehicular freak. Above the center of three flat windows that formed the windshield was a Cyclops Eye, a big spotlight, burning brightly although it was high noon and the sun was shining. Denison burst out laughing, a welcome sound. "Isn't that a horrible-lookin' sight?" he said. "I call that machine my Beaver and I use it to drag and pack snow. It's a Universal Carrier and it floats. Can't be too careful on ice, so far away from everything! Those flotation tires cost me fifteen hundred dollars each. The Beaver looks like a tin box, real square, but it's covered with aluminum inside and out and was custom built in our Edmonton shop. I told one of my partners, Bob Rand, who did all the work, I wanted a box a guy can sleep, eat and drive in, and he did the rest. Not everybody likes to just bugger back and forth, over and over on the same spot, which is what the Beaver does, pounding the road down with those huge tires. You have to have a funny kind of person on the Beaver, a fellow like George, who's a loner and does a *real* good job. He's just right for it, he actually enjoys puttering around alone. Look at him grinning!" Denison suddenly grinned wildly, imitating him. "We call him Spotlight George, because he drives with his spotlight on *all* the time."

We pulled up beside the Beaver. A heavyset man, bald and weighing about two hundred pounds, who was standing right in front in the center behind the steering wheel, nodded, grinning and waving. We got out and John went into the burned-out camper and returned carrying yesterday's macaroni, a canned ham and a loaf of bread. He handed them up to George, who stood, a welcoming host, at the side entrance of his outlandish vehicle. All trucks are built for long-legged men and the Beaver was no exception, if anything a little worse than most; its door was a good four feet above the Ice Road on which I was standing. Even the camper was too high for me when the steps were not assembled. Sometimes I could put them into place myself, but most of the time they were frozen into their carrying slot underneath, and I wasn't strong enough to release them, no matter how hard I pulled. Desperation was my inspiration to devise a practical and thoroughly undignified method of getting into all high vehicles, preferably when nobody was looking. I carried my notebooks, pencils, gloves, makeup, pocketknife, flashlight, camera, film and Kleenex in a pouch purse on a strap over my arm that left my hands free. If I put this heavily loaded accessory on the ground as a step, I could usually wriggle the rest of the way in on my chest and stomach. I was preparing to do this at the door of the Beaver when George mercifully reached down and pulled me into his aluminum room, lined with comfortable leather benches, a two-burner stove and small table. Shuffling back and forth in his carpet slippers, George produced pots and dishes for the six extra guests who gradually assembled. By two o'clock lunch was over, and the men headed north to continue pounding down the new stretch of road that the camper fire had interrupted. Denison said that Mukluk, he and I were returning to Fort Byers in the two trucks. "Why?" I asked.

"Christ! We've got a broken generator, a broken heater, and a furnace that's broken down, and we've had a fire," Denison exploded. "We're going to fix the camper and make it livable again, fix the heater, and get the parts we need. Isn't that enough?"

I went with Mukluk in Fud. Denison sped off alone in the camper, and all the way down the Ice Road, I expected to round a corner and come upon John either overturned or, at the least, stuck in the snow. Without a passenger to help, he was driving with his left hand while he held the Lazy Susan heater at the windshield with his right hand, too impatient to pause long enough to work out a better mechanical arrangement for such a short trip. He was soon out of sight in the faster vehicle. He was again hauling the Bug, which needed a new transmission, and it danced from side to side at his rear as he picked up speed. He had no lights, either, so he wanted to reach Fort Byers before dark.

Every truck has its own eccentricities, Fud, several times rebuilt, more than most. Her springs were a memory and half the glass in the side windows had been replaced with wood pieces, supplemented by rags stuffed into the chinks. The fumes from the exhaust were pervasive. At the bridge across the bubbling black Emile River, which we reached after dark, steam rose from Fud's radiator and swirled around the headlights, cutting off the view of the road. Mukluk stopped. "Poor old Fud," he said, pulling up his fur-trimmed parka hood preparatory to going outside. "She trusts me to take care of her. It's my duty. Anyway, if I don't, she might leave me stranded in the middle of nowhere!" He reached behind for his tool kit, which was the size and shape of a doctor's kit, got out and climbed up over the high fenders of the truck, pushing up the radiator hood on one side. He bent over the percolating motor, tightened a few nuts and bolts, and went down with a pail to the gurgling river, for water for Fud's thirsty radiator. Cautiously. A man could easily drown if he fell into that swift current; fourteen knots an hour. We stopped several times to give Fud a drink before we bounced off the portage onto the great gleaming black empty space of Marian Lake. It was a dark night, with clouds almost covering a three-quarter moon, but when we were halfway down the lake the clouds parted and the moonbeams shone on the camper, off the road, its nose buried in a snowbank. Through the open camper window, the glow of the propane heater lit up the long mournful face of Denison at the wheel. He had driven the last sixty miles after dark, with a six-volt lantern tied to his front bumper, and had run out of gas. He told us he went off the road when he tried to light a match to check his gas gauge.

Mukluk attached a chain from Fud to the camper and pulled it back on the Ice Road. He gave Denison some gas and we proceeded single file across the rest of Marian Lake to Fort Byers. Fud rattled and shook so under the furious beating of the wind that I expected her to fly apart, dropping us into a heap of rusty parts right on the road. The camper followed behind in our lights, travelling slowly for once; a reassuring presence.

I slept in the garage again, with the smell of the fire in my nostrils and the wreckage of the camper's interior before my eyes. I thought, I am careless and not carrying my weight, a burden that this particular operation cannot afford. Next morning I packed all my belongings and took them with me to the pickup truck which Denison was about to drive into Yellowknife to bring back another generator. I asked if I could go to Yellow-knife with him. By way of answering, he opened the door on the other side, and I got in.

On the way I said, "I'm leaving."

Denison looked straight ahead, but he had a way of curling his upper lip when he was displeased. "I figured you would," he said. "My fault those sleeping bags weren't fastened down, especially when I could see for myself how slippery that nylon covering on yours was. I know better, you don't. You can buy a new sleeping bag in Yellowknife today."

"I'm an awful cook when I cook for your crew. I don't have any confidence," I said. "Besides, I'm in everybody's way."

"You've never done ennathing like this before, have you?" he snapped. "You don't know until you try whether you can do something or not, do you? You can't tell until you try!" Silence. I thought, he's telling me not to go. If he can stand it, so can I. A few minutes later Denison added, "I don't recall ever not being able to do a job I set out to do."

Chapter Three

FIRST TRIP IN:
THE BRIGHT LIGHTS OF TOWN

As soon as we arrived in Yellowknife, and I had taken a bath and put my dirty clothes in the laundromat, I went to buy a sleeping bag at the general store of Weaver and Devore, in the Old Town. The word *yellowknife* was first used by an explorer in the area, Samuel Hearne, in 1771, to describe Indians he met who made weapons and tools of copper, but Yellowknife was founded on gold. Four years after the discovery in 1930 of pitchblende at what is now Port Radium, uranium prospectors coming down the Yellowknife River from Great Bear Lake discovered gold deposits exposed in the ground at the river's mouth and the gold boom began that brought the helter-skelter group of pioneer prospectors, bush pilots and their suppliers together to form the settlement that became Yellowknife. They set up their tents, log cabins and tarpaper shacks on a small island in Yellowknife Bay that is now connected to the mainland by a causeway, and on the narrow rocky peninsula to which it is attached around a large outcropping known to everyone still as the Rock. This part of Yellowknife is now called the Old Town, to distinguish it from the New Town on the flat sandy plain a mile and a half to the south, where the settlement expanded as business grew and more people continued to arrive. Both "towns" extend along the main thoroughfare, Franklin Avenue, named after another early explorer, Sir John Franklin, with a slum area inhabited largely by Indians, Metis and a small colony of hard-drinking diamond drillers in between. The two towns are indistinguishably one, a predominantly white middle-class community. Many older residents continue to live in the quieter Old Town, now largely residential, while the New Town contains the main business and new residential districts, and is alive with cars and trucks. They ceaselessly move up and down the streets bearing their Northwest Territories license plates cut in the form of a prowling polar bear: white, with blue trim and numbers. Once, before I ever went to Yellowknife, I asked a southern Canadian who went up there often what it was like. He replied, "My favorite town. What it's like depends on which way you are coming at it. Either way, it's exciting. If I have been in the High Arctic, it's a swinging place with bright lights and bars, but if I am coming from the South, I know when I arrive there that I am getting into the country."

Yellowknife. The capital of the Territories and its first city: a rough, hard-drinking, warm community of pioneers, a young people's town, because those who can afford to, leave when the climate chills their aching bones; a hospitable, industrious town with an undercurrent of tragedy and disharmony in the unsuccessful mingling of white and native Indian and Metis cultures; where people fight off isolation and the gloom of dark winter months in a round of compulsive activities, and dance into the morning in the Elks' Hall; using the bright long hours of summer sunlight to tee off from the golf course at midnight and to camp outdoors on the lovely lakes that surround them. An isolated speckle in a huge wilderness. A government town. A mining town.

Weaver and Devore, where I had come for my sleeping bag, sells camping equipment, clothing, dry goods and Indian and Eskimo handicrafts, is a self-service market, and a substation of the main post office. It is also the unofficial regional headquarters of the "moccasin telegraph," that mysterious northern communications system that has made its proprietor, Bruce Weaver, one of the most knowledgeable men in Yellowknife. Trappers, prospectors and claim stakers have so much faith in Bruce that they often ask him to get together an order of food and supplies for a given number of days in the bush and don't bother examining their purchases until their plane has dropped the parcels at their destination and it's time to eat.

Bruce Weaver shook his head and tried not to smile at the tragic story of my sleeping bag's demise. He selected a new one for me with a canvas covering so heavy that I could hardly lift it by the handle of the bag it was in, but it was guaranteed to keep a body warm at forty below zero. I wanted to walk, so he said he would send it to the hotel. He came to the door of the store with me, and pointed out a solid-looking house nearby. "My house," he said. "It used to be the manager's at Rayrock Mine. It's thirty by forty feet. John Denison jacked it up, put timbers under it and loaded it on one of his big flat-deck trailers, brought it a hundred and thirty-five miles to Yellowknife by truck, and set it down right here on this cement block." I could appreciate the understatement in Weaver's remarks; I had driven over the Rayrock road myself.

Weaver greeted a tall, frail, elderly man with glasses who was just coming into the store and introduced me to Bill McDonald, whom I knew to be one of Canada's most eminent mining engineers and a Yellowknife resident. McDonald lingered on the steps to talk for a few minutes, calling my attention to a large black raven that was walking along the road. "Yellowknife's town symbol," he said. "A scavenger bird. A pair will sit all day on the top of a building and when they see a dog with a bone one of them will swoop down and annoy him while the other grabs the bone."

I noticed two ravens sitting on the telephone wires across the road, cawing harshly. "Ravens seem to be the only birds around," I said. "I don't see any others."

Mr. McDonald's angular face broke into a slow smile. "I came up here in 1920, and did the first mapping for the government of the Great Slave area and the Barrens around it," he said. "At that time I met a lot of those government men. Biologists and zoologists would ask me to get plants and birds—particularly the skins and eggs of birds—that the scientists couldn't get anyplace else, and I did a lot of bird-banding. An Arctic tern I banded here was picked up two years later near Durban, South Africa. A junco returned here six years in succession until a cat caught it in the Old Town. One comical thing —I used to go down the bay and band eagles, and three different birds were found from the same nest. Now, why would they be from that particular nest, all of them, and not from some other one?" He paused to scratch his head. I said I had heard that prospectors, sometimes as many as a dozen a day, came to see him, bringing their rocks for him to examine. He laughed and did not deny it. "I don't know more than anybody, I've just travelled more," he said. "Mining's a wild life, but this is how I've worked. Say a mining company or an individual took up a group of claims and wanted some information. Well, he had me look his claims over, make a map, take samples, have them assayed, and recommend what to do. I always took along my own tent, cooking utensils, and everything. I would go out and mark the holes and tell the contract drillers where to drill, and then I'd do the geology of the core. I still have lots of inquiries coming in—'Stake me gold.' 'Stake me uranium.' Everybody here—clerks in the stores, taxi drivers, everybody—wants to gamble on a mining stock. They found somebody who staked a moose pasture—land not known to have anything on it but moose at the time of staking, and who made a lot of money with it. They want to do that, too." He paused and took out a little pouch of tobacco and some papers, rolled a cigarette and offered it to me. I declined, so he lit it, took a little puff, and continued: "I went to work for Consolidated Mining and Smelter Company, the Cominco interests that own the Con Gold Mine here in Yellowknife, and in 1936 I came up and outlined the first find. Just one vein, that turned out to be the best. When I found that first vein, I brought in the drill. The heavy drill broke the snow and showed the rock. It showed visible gold. The drill had to go another two hundred yards over to the place we were going to drill, and the shaft was actually sunk more than three hundred feet deep." His face lit up. "Right there, at that first vein," he said, "oh, it was just splashed with visible gold."

Bill McDonald went on into the store and I looked at my watch. I was going to have lunch with two friends, Rae Parker and Kay Vaydik, at the Yellowknife Inn's Coffee Shop, but I had gotten started so early in the day that I still had time to kill. I decided to walk over to the house of Sam Otto, in the Old Town. I had been told that Mr. Otto maintained some sort of a special northern mining museum in his home.

Mr. Otto was a professional prospector. In the stratified world of Yellowknife mining, the first step towards establishing a mine is claim-staking, the primary occupation of most prospectors. Claim-staking is hard work. Unsurveyed land in Canada belongs to the federal government, and most of the land in the Northwest Territories has never been surveyed. Once land is surveyed, surface rights can be bought, but the right to mine underground can only be leased. The possessor of a claim can keep what he removes from below the staked ground, paying a production royalty to the government. A claim is 1,500 feet square, a little more than a quarter of a mile, and the staker, who has been walking on the Barrens with as many as thirty spruce posts on his backpack board, mounds a post with rocks at each of the four corners of his site and fastens a numbered tag to each post. He usually stakes about a dozen claims a day, and must register his claims within thirty to sixty days, depending on how far he is from town, in the Mining Recorder's Office in Yellowknife. Government inspectors visit the staked land to observe what's being done there and if nothing is going on, the claim lapses after a year and can be restaked by someone else. Claim-staking is a favorite weekend preoccupation, and many Yellowknifers vanish regularly into the bush every Friday night, hunting for precious minerals.

The professional claim-staker may be an old-fashioned prospector staking claims to develop for himself, but he is more likely to be staking to resell, or for an absentee group with a promoter and an office in Vancouver or Toronto, or for an established mining company with other mines. Promoters are respectable men in Canadian mining circles, because it requires a great deal of money to start a mine, and they raise the money. There are good promoters and bad ones. A bad promoter listens to all the tips in bars and doesn't know or care what he promotes, including moose pasture, but, if possible, he will follow along after a man who he thinks knows something, and promote claims staked on ground next to a major find, or what he thinks might be a major find.

The prospector or claim-staker is usually afflicted with the local Yellowknife ailment, gold fever. He dreams of bringing in a mine, preferably gold or uranium, but if he is lucky or smart he can make a fairly good living just by selling the claims he stakes and letting someone else take the risk of exploration and development.

Sam Otto was an old-fashioned claim-staker who had been prospecting in the Yellowknife area since 1929, although he had never brought in a gold mine. Short, round, bald, and in his seventies, Mr. Otto opened his door to me with a sunny welcoming smile, and led me into the living room which he had set aside for his museum. He remarked that his house, a low frame structure that he started building in 1936 and had been adding to ever since, was probably the only one of the very early homes left. As he led the way into his combination living room and museum, he apologized for laundry hanging from a drying rack that took up all the center space. "My wife, Myrtle, wants an electric dryer, so she keeps these clothes hanging here for days," he explained. Ducking around sheets, socks, sweaters and long underwear, I found myself surrounded by shelves and cases crammed with rock samples, Indian and Eskimo artifacts, stuffed birds and animals, skulls, birds' eggs, pocket knives, cigarette lighters, and Mr. Otto's own teeth, which he had placed in a glass case in his museum when he acquired a new set for himself at the store. They lay next to the skull of a Metis who was murdered at Great Bear Lake. A boa constrictor of unknown origin was fastened to the ceiling. "We keep everything—that's an old Barrens habit," Mr. Otto said. "I'm proudest of this." He held up a chunk of reddish metal that would make a handsome surrealist sculpture. It was native copper, which he had found "someplace in the Coppermine district just stickin' right out of the rock." He patted it and added, "I've been hoarding my chunk for twenty years. It was forty-five pounds before a piece came off. I'd like to find a chunk of gold as big as that slab. I'd settle for twenty-five or thirty thousand bucks, or just chop off what I needed. We are looking for anything that makes money, but this is gold country." He halted before a wall case devoted to gold-ore nuggets, neatly labelled, from every gold mine, past or present, in the area. At another case, he picked up a black, bubbly rock. "This is bubble pitch —pitchblende that has bubbles that ooze out—and it's the closest you get to radium in its pure state," he said. Reaching under the hanging wash he pulled out a Geiger counter and held the pitchblende close to the machine, which immediately began to tick. "There'll be a lot of helicopters out this summer," he said wistfully. "I've had a heart attack, but until now I was out every summer. Last fall I had the plane pick me up on September twenty-eighth on the Coppermine River. They knew where they'd left me. If you ain't out by the end of September, you could be caught by ice for another six weeks, and it's a long walk to where a plane might be able to land. Sometimes people get left out in the bush, but my wife is the best expediter you can get, and if one plane doesn't pick me up, she makes sure another does." Mr. Otto had a friendly, beaming manner, but when I asked where his claims were, he instantly stiffened and said, "I have claims, but where and what they are I don't answer unless you can go to the States and come back with a stack of money." He relaxed and added, "Everyone knows when you go out where you are going. They don't know the exact location, but they've got a pretty good idea. Some of those guys can tell the value of your rocks without looking through the sack. We don't tell everything, but we want to know everything, and we all end up the same way: lucky to have a grubstake."

When I left Sam Otto's house I started to walk back to the Yellowknife Inn, but almost immediately someone pulled up beside me in a pickup truck and offered me a lift. Although the city limits of Yellowknife are about fifteen miles in any direction from the center of town, in twelve of those miles there is nothing except Giant Gold Mine, an Indian village, and the airport, so the town itself is very compact. As a newcomer, I had been totally confused by distances, or lack of them, because everyone offered me a lift, even if I was merely going from the Yellow-knife Inn to the Hudson's Bay Company department store, a block away. Until I got my bearings, I would settle down for a chat, but before the introductions were finished, the ride would be over. Climbing in and out of cars could easily be the only exercise a visitor might get.

Back at the Inn, I stopped at the counter in the Coffee Shop for a word with the dignified cashier, Rose Curry, the wife of Denison's old friend, Del. As usual, she was wearing shoulder-length earrings she had made with precision pliers that Del had once given her for Christmas. Her earring collection included a pair of five-inch buffalo bones, and a set four inches long made from beer caps. Today she was wearing two miniature thermometers that registered from twenty to seventy degrees above zero, pretty warm weather for Yellowknife. According to the reading on her ears, the Coffee Shop temperature was at a comfortable seventy degrees, Fahrenheit.

I sat down to wait for my friends, glancing first at the menu to see what I would order: clam chowder, since the Chinese chef at the Inn makes the best north of New England, and an open mushroom sandwich, another house specialty, although I was tempted by the local whitefish for which Great Slave Lake is famous. Then I leaned back to watch the action, for although there is a neat rectangular Town Hall on a side street, where the mayor of Yellowknife and his Town Council meet regularly, and a six-story office building where the Territorial Government supervises the business of the Northwest Territories under the watchful eye of the resident Commissioner, many people feel still that the real headquarters of Yellowknife is in the Coffee Shop and bar of the Yellowknife Inn.

A number of residents use the Coffee Shop as an office and some even bring their books and papers to the counters or to the booths along the walls. Really private business can be conducted at the dining tables, but the round stools at the counters provide better visibility, so they are preferred. The Coffee Shop opens for breakfast at six. Construction workers are the first customers, followed by truckers, office workers, and members of the Northwest Territories Council when they are staying at the hotel during the two-to-three week Council sessions held usually in January and in June; but at ten, mining men drift in for the real business of the day—to find out who is drilling for what minerals, and where, and with what results. After a hasty glance to see who is present, they drop casually down in their seats to exchange vital scraps of information in low voices, or they eavesdrop on someone else. Some oldtimers visit the Coffee Shop religiously when they are not in the bush. One, who adheres to a strict schedule, comes in alone at eight, ten, and two o'clock, and reappears at nine in the evening with his entire family. If the weather is bad, the mining men are joined at the counters by pilots of the eight local air-charter services. Government and construction workers crowd in again at noon, but the three-o'clock coffee break brings back the mining people, who have been busy checking out the morning's information, and the bush pilots, if continuing bad weather or darkness keeps them from flying. During the day, an occasional drunk may wander in, but he will be thrown out.

When the schoolchildren flock into the Coffee Shop at three-forty-five, the adult population shifts to the Inn's bar—a dim, commodious cocktail lounge. Mining business, the pulse of Yellowknife, now is in the conversations at the small round tables in the lounge until closing time, at one o'clock in the morning. The prospecting and mining done in the Yellowknife Inn are in the tradition of its founder, the late Vic Ingraham, a former prospector known as Old Cedarfoot. Former employees, recalling the hotelkeeper and his bartender, Jim, who was famous for his ability to fall asleep standing up, will sing out, "The squeak of Vic's legs can be heard from afar, as Sleepy Jim sleeps at the Yellowknife Bar." Ingraham lost both his legs in the thirties, in a fire on a boat on Great Bear Lake, and although he learned to walk well on two wooden legs, he thereafter lived a more settled, if not a quieter life in Yellowknife. He provided quarters for transients in the Old Town, both at the first Yellowknife Hotel and at a twelve-room hotel and beer parlor called the Old Stope—a stope is an excavated area in a mine—which burned to the ground on New Year's Day, 1968. Ingraham built the new Yellowknife Hotel, now the Inn, in 1946, providing bedrooms-with-bath, luxurious accommodations undreamed-of then in the North, on the projected site of the New Town when nothing was there but a few shacks. An all-weather landing strip for aircraft had been put down a year or so earlier, making it possible to reach Yellowknife during break-up and freeze-up—three-week periods when the ice on rivers and lakes is not thick enough or stable enough for a plane to land on or for a vehicle or a man to cross. Proposals to make Yellowknife accessible by land year-round include the construction of a multimillion-dollar bridge across the Mackenzie River (which is spanned by the ice bridge in winter, a ferry in summer, but by nothing in between), and the use of specially designed Hovercraft to sweep across the river on a cushion of air or balloons filled with helium, to carry trucks and cars. Now, during break-up and freeze-up, everything—both people and freight—comes to the capital of the Territories by air.

Rae Parker and Kay Vaydik, the two friends for whom I had been waiting, arrived and while we were eating our lunch I described my experiences on the Ice Road. Denison was an old friend of both of them, but they had never been on his road to Echo Bay. When I began what to me was a sad tale of troubles with cold, primitive living conditions, when I described what life was like in a truck on the Ice Road, they laughed. My unexpected role as dishwasher and cook for half a dozen strange men, my inexperience and slowness to adjust, Denison's impatience, anger and terrible silences and finally, the fire in the camper, produced, not sympathy but laughter. The incineration of my sleeping bag seemed especially hilarious. "What's so funny about that?" I asked plaintively, and they howled with delight. People at neighboring tables were staring at us. I was laughing too. Once started, I couldn't stop. As I wiped my eyes and blew my nose I realized I had passed some kind of a Survival Test. In the North, if you can laugh at yourself you are ahead of the game, or at least holding your own. Either give up or laugh. I had not given up; therefore I had earned the laughter of my friends.

We were just finishing our coffee when a square-jawed, pleasant-looking man passed our table, and my friends invited him to join us. He was Don Stewart, the Mayor of Hay River, the small community about 120 miles south of Yellowknife, on the other side of Great Slave Lake. "I hear you had an extraordinary plane flight recently," Kay said.

Mr. Stewart grinned, and said that yes indeed, he *had* had quite an extraordinary flight. It all began when he and two of his town councillors were returning to Hay River from Yellowknife, where they had been seeking a federal grant for a water sewer. "We had cried long and loud and got a million and a half dollars for our water sewer," Mr. Stewart, a big, easygoing man, began, "and now we were on our way home. There were four of us in a Cessna 185, Town Councillors Ed Studney and Norm McCowan, myself and the pilot, sitting two in the front, two in the back. We left Yellowknife at nine in the morning. It was good weather, but very cold, and over Great Slave Lake we ran into an ice fog—you know, where the moisture actually freezes, with visibility reduced to a quarter of a mile. Normally the trip in the Cessna between Yellowknife and Hay River takes an hour, but after we had been flying two hours while we tried unsuccessfuly to follow the shore line, we had to land. It was very uncomfortable sitting in the aircraft at forty-five degrees below zero, so when we thought conditions had improved, the pilot began to taxi. He had damaged a wheel ski, so instead of rising in the air we were pivoting around on one ski." Stewart sighed. "So Ed Studney got out of the plane to give it a bit of a push to get it moving, and as soon as the pilot had straightened out he took off and left Ed standing there, instead of waiting for him to jump back into the plane. I grabbed that pilot and said, 'For God's sake, pick up that man! In this fog, we may never find him!'

"We missed Studney on the first pass, but on the next turn we fortunately saw Ed jumping straight up and down at least thirty feet in the air—higher than the plane coming in to pick him up. He was wearing his regular business clothes, with just an ordinary parka and overshoes, and had only two matches in his pocket. What scared him most was that in an ice fog sound disappears, and an airplane can't be seen or heard, so he figured his chances of survival were nil in the clothes he was in and without an axe or shovel, and no shelter around. He didn't say a word. He just climbed back in and fastened his seat belt. Then he leaned over and said to the pilot, 'If there's any more goddamned pushing, you'll get out and do it.' We were airborne again, but by this time gas was running short, and we knew we didn't have a prize pilot. The other councillor—McCowan, who is principal of the high school—kept saying, 'Look here, boy, the gas gauge says empty.' The pilot's reply was 'Don't worry, it's broken, and so is the compass.' We spotted a big fishing camp below, with human beings running around, and gas tanks, and a fire, so we landed there. The pilot said he wasn't sure of the battery, so he would fill the plane with gas without turning off the engine. Meanwhile, we went into the cabin to drink coffee. The pilot came in and was spooning sugar into his cup when someone asked, 'Who's flying your airplane?' We rushed to the window, and sure enough, the plane was moving along, picking its way around a snowmobile and the gasoline barrels just as if it had eyes. After zigzagging around a bit, it straightened out and headed for the shack we're in. There were about a dozen people in that cabin, and up to then nobody had moved—we were mesmerized—but if you want to see something funny, watch twelve guys head under a kitchen table at one time. I don't know what we thought we were doing! The pilot was still standing at the window with his mouth open when one ski caught on the shoreline and the plane made a beautiful hundred-and-eighty-degree turn, picked up speed, its tail went into flight position, and it disappeared across the lake into this ice fog. Everybody came to life and ran out, trying to follow this thing they couldn't even see—everybody except the three passengers. We stayed behind, and McCowan, who's rather a pensive type, said, 'Thank God! Thank God! I didn't want to ride in it anyway.' The three of us went into hysterics, rolling on the floor like a bunch of fools, howling with laughter. The others returned in about an hour and a half. They had found the aircraft, which had ground-looped and smashed to pieces twelve miles from shore. We still had sixty-five miles to go to Hay River, so we made arrangements for the snowmobile to drive us there. All hell broke loose when we got home, because when we hadn't appeared my wife had instigated a search, so everyone was out looking for us." Stewart laughed. "The next day, I get a telephone call from the pilot, asking whom he should bill. I said, 'Try God.'"

Chapter Four

SECOND TRIP OUT:
GETTING WET

I returned to Fort Byers with Denison in the evening and slept in the smoky-smelling camper again in the garage. In the morning while I was waiting to go back up the Ice Road I heated water and washed the greasy smoke from the walls of the camper with soapy paper towelling. My spirits soared as the evil-smelling oily black slime that had blanketed the camper interior, constant reminder of disaster, disappeared, and the light beige plywood panelling reappeared like the sun after days of gloomy darkness. The furnace could not be repaired, but we had acquired another generator; one that provided only enough current for the pickup truck's heater and lights with a fraction left over for dim illumination in the ceiling fixture of the camper. The Lazy Susan became part of our permanent equipment, and several fat gas tanks took up half the floor space in the kitchen. The last thing Denison did before we started travelling was to place a large plank across the side of the back bunk to prevent anything from falling out. The Lazy Susan, already lit, was propped again in the steel sink. "A little heat's better than none," John said. "The camper's a deep-freeze without it. It just takes too long to get that frost out and warm everything up, otherwise."

We were again hauling the old blue Bug, with a new transmission. We also were bringing a new crew member, a red-haired Cat skinner from the Saskatchewan prairies, Bob Burns, to drive Denison's big red TD-14 International tractor instead of Gilles, whose real winter job was cooking for the truckers when the Ice Road was open. In summer he was a diamond driller.

We crossed the highway onto the Ice Road and Denison slid a stereo tape of dance music into the recorder. He drove casually with one hand, scanning the road ahead, absorbed in his thoughts.

Burns and I talked. "Bein' a Cat skinner is different to operating a truck," Burns said. "You haven't got no steering wheel, so you steer by pulling the clutch levers and stepping on the brake to slow the track down. Snow is easy to work with because it don't take much power. Just push it with your Cat blade. That's called 'dozing.' "

I asked if he became attached to one Cat the way truckers do to a single vehicle. "You get the feeling *absolutely* that one tractor is yours," he said. "Another Cat might be exactly the same, but it isn't. I don't like to change unless I'm going to somethin' bigger and better." He turned to Denison. "What model International do you have?" he asked.

"Nineteen fifty-six model," Denison replied. "Thirty-five thousand dollars new, but I paid twelve thousand for it seven years ago." We are crossing Marian Lake again. Soft blue light, winter sun shining on the flat snowy lake surface. Why is it so hazy? "Because the sun shines so low up here, that's why," Denison said. "Each day it gets a little higher and then we have a little more sunlight." Dark shadows along the drifts, a shady border to the glistening road. A freshly plowed road! Mukluk left Fort Byers three hours ahead of us, working his way north, plowing, in Fud. When Denison stopped on the lake to call the garage on the radiophone, Henry Ford reported that Mukluk had forgotten his sleeping bag.

"While we've been gone, the men have been carrying on," Denison said, after we had started moving again. "Jimmy scouted ahead without me, so they had enough to do. One day's scouting gives two or three days of road work. They went across Squirrel, Mazenod and Sarah, and we'll find them at Faber Lake. Let's see. We've been gone about forty-eight hours, since the fire. Two nights and this is the second day. We should be there in six hours."

"Lots to think about, including a driver who forgot his sleeping bag," Denison continued. "I'm figurin' out who is going to drive what and I don't want too many people. You've got to feed them and worry about them and they take up a place to sleep. My biggest worry until now has been fuel supply. That's the one thing we have to have. Most of the trucks carry two-hundred-gallon tanks, which would take them a thousand miles on a highway but here that gives you two or three hundred miles. You can run for a week, idling, but if you're working that's good for about twenty-four hours, especially plowing heavy snow. Thirty-six gets three miles to the gallon and sometimes a truck uses ten gallons to go one mile. On a good trip to Echo Bay the trucks regularly make it with two hundred and fifty gallons, but on a bad trip it'll be five hundred. Instead of carrying extra tanks, I keep a cache of three thousand gallons of Diesel and a lot of forty-five-gallon drums of gasoline at my second rest stop at the mine on Hottah Lake. The Cats and my big trucks use Diesel; I like Diesel motors for heavy-duty work because the motors are better and more economical to run, but this camper, Fud and the Beaver have gasoline motors. Oh, I almost forgot. There's my little three-hundred-gallon tanker on wheels that we can pull behind ennathing we have, that's up the way. It's an old army surplus that I got off the DEW line, real handy."

Wild wind on the open lake; a low continued scream that threatens to drown out the quiet dance tune on the tape recorder; a gale that presses against this single frail vehicle crossing the open lake with such force that I wonder: are we driving or being blown to the far shore? Denison looked in his side mirror, and reported that the door of the Bug had flown open. He stopped and Burns ran back, head down, holding fast to the side of the camper, and slammed the Bug door shut. We paused again at the end of the lake, while Denison pushed what looked like a second gearshift on the floor, putting the truck into four-wheel drive which gave each wheel its own driving power on the rough portage. He had been doing this whenever we came off a lake onto land and shifting back before we dropped down on the next lake, but I was just becoming aware, like someone emerging from shock. The wind had died down; we were in the woods, and travelling fast. We raced through the Rayrock portage, across the rushing Emile River, past the skeletal mine buildings. "If we keep on like this, good weather and all, we'll make all kinds of miles," Denison said. He was singing to the music in his off-key fashion. Climbing a long hill, I glimpsed a flash of bright red and green in the snow beside the road. My burned sleeping bag. Will it remain there, to disappear under the snow each winter and emerge like an exotic flower each spring? At the top of the hill, a puff of smoke like a mammoth wad of cotton rose above the trees; it was the exhaust from Mukluk's Fud. He was packing the snow on the road, back and forth, back and forth, hauling two four-by-eight-foot steel drags, one behind the other. They were made to order from Denison's design in Edmonton: the first, a beadwork of heavy chains on a crossbar that dragged through the snow so that snow fell into any holes and knocked out the air, to make a solid base; the other, a big screen with sievelike holes to catch the snow in high spots and shake it down into low places on the road. The beads from the first drag rippled, a pleasant clinking sound, strange musical notes in an Arctic wilderness.

We stopped briefly to make tea for Mukluk, then continued our journey. We were moving through a white corridor lined with trees thirty and forty feet high. Spruce and willow branches covered with snow bent down and reached out for us as we brushed past them. A ptarmigan half-flew, half-ran on feathered feet in front of us. A white rabbit scurried onto the road, hesitated, skittered off into the bush instead. Bob Burns turned and watched until the rabbit disappeared. "Little rabbits have a pretty hard go of it," he observed, as he settled back in his seat. "Everybody's after them. They don't have a friend in the world."

The sun sank in the slate-blue sky; a rosy light spread across the white treetops. The road, never smooth, became even choppier and we bounced to the ceiling when the truck wheels hit a deep spot. "Any time you come to these bad holes, drag snow in and press it down," Denison said to Burns. The going was so tough that I braced my feet against the floor to retain my balance. I held onto the seat. "Throwing snow off the road does this," Denison muttered. "That's why I've got to be here."

The sun below the trees and the bare branches of silver birches were outlined against the darkening sky. Quiet, on the portage. The road was protected from the wind by the trees but the cold penetrated, coming up through the floor around our feet. I asked Burns how he drove a Cat in the open without freezing. "If she's canvassed in, it's so hot in a Cat you can even work without your mitts," he said. "If she's workin' good, she keeps you warm. But as soon as you idle her down and stop workin', it's icy cold, all right."

Denison called out the names of the small lakes we traversed: Squirrel, Mazenod, Sarah, where the camper headlights picked out a forlorn wooden caboose on the ice, pulled from its summer storage on the shore to its winter site on the lake, by one of the big trucks just ahead of us. This would be the first one-hundred-mile stop where the truckers could eat and sleep on the Echo Bay run as soon as the road was in, with Gilles as resident cook.

Faber Lake. Twenty-five miles long. Endless on this black night. A mile out on the lake we drove up to John's battered yellow gas tank on a four-wheeled wagon. It was listing to one side. Tom had been hauling it until it had a flat tire, a minor catastrophe that he had reported by radiophone to Fort Byers while we were still there, so Denison had brought a spare in the Bug. He and Burns changed the tire, hooked the gas tank on behind the Bug and we continued north. We were hauling two vehicles now, the driverless Bug with its motor running, and the gas tank.

We passed the Beaver in the middle of Faber Lake; its big spotlight momentarily blinded us when we were face to face. George was standing at the steering wheel in his illuminated tin kitchen, his round face all smiles. He was heading back south, to work over the portage we had just left. At the north end of Faber, parked at the entrance to the portage beyond it, we came upon the other vehicles, 36, with the Cat on its back, and Tom's 34; shadowy hulks, framed in their red and yellow clearance lights.

We halted beside them. John started dinner instantly: pork cutlets, dehydrated mashed potatoes, canned corn. He wanted everyone to keep working after dark, to make up for lost time caused by the camper fire, and he was a much faster cook than I. Immediately after supper the men departed; Burns first, on the Cat, followed by Gilles Chartrand in the Bug, then Tom Berry and Jimmy Watson in the big trucks, 36 and 34, and Mukluk, who had arrived late in Fud, bringing up the rear. One by one they disappeared around the bend going north. We followed, travelling two miles over a road that was a half-broken trail. Could *any* wheeled vehicle move over terrain as deeply rutted as this? The camper staggered from side to side, with an occasional drunken lurch that unexpectedly threw us forward, motor whining in protest. I held the windshield back with my palms flat against it, to prevent the glass from smacking me in the forehead.

This is the darkest of nights. Inky blackness all around us. Light!

We stop in the sudden glare of a single spotlight. The Cat materializes, coming directly at us. Burns veers and turns, stops alongside us, the Cat's spotlight facing in the same direction as our headlights.

What is happening?

Two headlamps blind us. The Bug rushes at us, turns away; Gilles swings it around and he stops beside the Cat. A roar, a windy gust, a triangle of two more headlights beneath a blinding spotlight, and Jimmy Watson is upon us, crashing through the underbrush as he wheels 36 away and around.

Confusion! I don't understand this coming and going! Some of the vehicles here should be up ahead packing the portage; some should be behind and now are piling in, crowding us in this small grove of trees. Why this gathering? *Trouble* somewhere! Everyone has come to help, although I cannot see what they have come to help for.

Denison sits with his elbow on the steering wheel, his chin in his hand, staring ahead. We are part of a semicircle of brilliant light that illuminates a single area in front of us as dramatically as if it were the stage of a theatre. In the center of that stage, I finally see: pathetic, forlorn, broken Fud, ominously quiet, her lights out, her silver shack lying over on one side on the ground.

Mukluk climbed out of Fud and walked over to the camper. Denison rolled down his window. "S'matter, Mukluk, don't you like your bed no more?" he asked.

"I didn't know I had lost the caboose until the engine got

warm," Mukluk replied, rubbing his unshaven chin unhappily. "When the shack fell off it broke the water lines."

The red gasoline drums that Mukluk had been carrying behind the shack were scattered on the ground. Burns, his orange wool cap pulled down over his ears, drove slowly forward with the Cat to move the barrels out of the way. "Don't bust 'em, that's our spare gas," Denison whispered, leaning over the wheel to watch Burns maneuver. He sat back, relieved. "You can tell Burns is an expert Cat man," he said. "Look at the way he's running that blade. He has to keep working it all the time to hold it level like that!"

Another roar: a red Titan breathing noisily behind us. Tom sped past in 34, halted abruptly alongside Fud. "Look at old Tom go by!" Denison exclaimed. Mukluk, back in the driver's seat in Fud, was talking out his window to Tom. "The men obviously have a plan, so let's see what they do with it," John said. "I like to give a guy a job to do and leave him alone. That's why guys'll work for you. Let them work it out for themselves, eh? So many things we should have now, like a double block! When you think where the hell we're at and where our supplies are, and how independent we have to be!"

Mukluk stepped down on the ground again, and with Jimmy's help, was trying to right Fud's fallen shack, running chains around it, passing them across Tom's flat open trailer, hooking them up on the winch of the Cat. Burns was standing up in the Cat, looking over the top of the canvas, exposed to the cold air from the waist up in his battered khaki parka, oblivious to the weather. He maneuvered the winch, skillfully turning the shack, and began to lift it, slowly, by the chains. "You're going to lose it, you guys," Denison said softly. The shack slipped from the chains and fell over on the ground. John leaned back. "Couldn't see what they had to hold it," he said. "I would put a chain right around on the topside to hold it so it won't tip." He sighed. "The trick is to get that shack back where it belongs without wrecking it, and the higher the chain, the less chance of its falling over. We come up here with junk, so nothing's valuable, but it's costing time!"

The men rearranged the chains over the top. On the third try, they set the shack on the back of Fud again. They came over to the camper then, stamping their feet and pounding their fists together to offset the forty-degree-below cold, while they talked to John. Tom Berry's beard was white from frost. Mukluk's three-day stubble had little icicles hanging from it. Tom said, "Well, Mukluk, I guess you'll be staying with me. Is it okay, John, if I charge him rent?"

John laughed. "Let's take Fud up to Rae Lake where we can work on it, and we'll camp there for the night," he said. "Put the drums back on, tie 'em down, and let's get going." With that, he started off in the camper, and a mile farther, we bumped down on the first of a small group of interconnected bodies of water known variously as Rae Lake or Lakes. "Accidents like that one happen all the time," John said cheerily. "What I really hate is leaving ennathing behind in the bush. Somebody's always driving over it later."

We were the first to arrive on the lake. I sat in the cab of the camper while John tried unsuccessfully to telephone Henry Ford at Fort Byers, and I watched the trucks arrive at our rendezvous. I was fascinated by the spots of bright color breaking through the darkness; the bright yellow-white of headlamps, and the small amber dots of clearance lights coming steadily towards us from the portage road, suddenly dropping as the vehicles bounced from the land to the lake; the cheerful reds, reflected in red shadows on the snow when the trucks came into our circle and backed into position. When I got out I would be walking through corridors of amber and red lights between the parked trucks, accompanied by the comforting low music of thrumming truck motors.

Denison gave up trying to telephone and put the round black microphone back on its hook on the dashboard; yet he was in no hurry to move. He seemed caught up for the moment as

I was in the magic of the approaching trucks, the colored lights, the soft rumbling of engine sounds. We were—all of us together —just one tiny sphere of man-made illumination—orange, yellow-white and red—in the darkness for several hundred miles. Only Fud was outside our circle on the lake where the Cat had dropped her, a shadow, without lights.

I noticed that the big trucks, 36 and 34, had a single blue bulb among the amber ones at the front, and asked John why this was. "Sometimes we put an odd green or blue one in our clearance lights for identification, so our boys will know each other when they pass on the road," he said. "Lots of times when you meet a guy on the road you might want to tell him something, and when you see that blue light you can stop him. We don't use hardly any green, just blue, and we put it in the front. Clearance lights, which are there to outline the load, are always amber facing front and around the sides, but they are red at the back, on both the cab and the trailer. Every snowplow has a spotlight generally right in the middle in front, and there are extra lights besides on three-foot bracket extensions so they'll be over the tops of the snowplows to use as headlights. I'll bet you haven't noticed the lights on the outside mirrors on all the trucks. They're there so you can see where you've been, see what's behind on the side, and see back to your trailers, the side of your van and the truck coming behind. The widest part of the load is the mirror, so we put lights on their edges. That way, when we meet people on a narrow road, we can see how close we can come, and if our men don't hit the mirrors, they don't hit ennathing else. We break a *lot* of mirrors goin' close and slow, especially around the garages, and trees break them in the bush."

Mukluk came in to discuss Fud's problems with Denison, and Jimmy was already asleep, exhausted, in the large back bunk he shared with Denison. I took two mugs of coffee and walked across the ice to Tom Berry's truck, 34, and knocked on the door. He opened his window and leaned out to see who it was.

He opened the door then, took the coffee from me, reached out and pulled me up into the passenger seat of his truck. I settled down breathlessly and said, "Why does everything break down? Is it because John uses such old equipment?"

Tom rubbed his hand up and down on his beard, drank some of the hot coffee I had brought him, and set the cup down on the spotless red surface above his dashboard. He lit a cigarette before he answered. "John uses a lot of old stuff because even if it were new when he bought it, chances are it would break anyway," he said. "Most trucks are built for warmer weather. The average life of a vehicle up here is two years, and then most of the machines are wrecks. It can't be helped. When the temperature gets down past forty below zero, metal crystallizes and breaks. Even the 'dozer blade on that Cat is liable to bust if it hits a rock. Oil's another problem. Cold oil solidifies and shock absorbers can't move, so when the going is rough the metal breaks instead. Oil solidifies in a cold engine, so to lubricate our engines we have them going day and night. Keep an engine running ten minutes without oil and you need a new motor. Same thing with the transmission and differential, and with your gears. If oil isn't warm enough to flow through them, gears running dry cut a track, metal right into metal. Another thing, if your weather stripping on your doors and windows gets froze hard, just closing the door raps metal on metal with no cushion, and the windows crack. Even a vehicle's frame can separate from the running gear. John would rather rebuild a machine when it breaks than start with a new one."

Somebody's headlights shone in my face all night, a diffused gleam through the window plastic that blended harmoniously with the glow from the propane heater. Half-waking during the night in that reddish glow, I thought I was sleeping in front of a wood fire. The ice trembled, vibrating to the humming motors; soft lullaby that put me back to sleep again.

Sleeping in the camper was not like being in a bedroom at home. We never took off any clothes except jackets and sweaters. I crawled into my sleeping bag each night fully clothed in my flannel shirt, wearing duofold long winter underwear underneath, and below that my regular nylon underthings. The only time I ever managed to change into the clean underwear I carried with me was once or twice in the morning right after all the men had departed together. Going to the toilet presents a slight problem to any woman travelling in the Arctic once she has left a settlement, especially above the treeline, and on flat terrain; in this case, frequently the flattest of flat terrains, a lake. Wind, low temperature, the possibility of a sudden whiteout and the danger of falling into ground holes off the road made it unwise ever to venture more than a few feet from a sheltering vehicle. The mitigating factor, however, was that in this cold, dry climate, which required constant applications of cold cream to keep my exposed hands and face from acquiring the texture of a very dry prune, my body was dehydrated. I was always thirsty and drank at least twice as much fluid as I ordinarily required; like the men, I never sat down in the camper without a cup of tea or coffee at my elbow. But I eliminated only a fraction of that enormous intake, usually not more than once daily since it was so much trouble. Each day I waited to go to the toilet, which was of course outdoors in the snow or on the ice road, until the men were all in the camper after I had served them their breakfast. While they were still eating I would pick up my toothbrush, a cup of water, towel and soap (in the beginning rather ostentatiously), and depart. I would leave my washing utensils on the camper steps until I found a place in the snow a few feet from the camper that served as a toilet; at forty to sixty degrees below zero, there is no inclination to wander, looking for the perfect spot. Then I would return to the camper steps, brush my teeth using the water I had brought with me, reserving half the cup to wash my hands, with soap I had also carried outside. The reward for all this was a final scrub of my face with fresh clean snow; there is no joy greater than the sting of that pristine Arctic snow, nothing I can think of more refreshing than the pleasant shock of the cold soft whiteness scrubbed into one's face until one's cheeks feel fiery red, as the first rays of the sun send a hint of rosy light across the dark horizon.

In the very beginning, I toileted and washed as soon as I awoke, while it was still totally dark, but I stopped after I got caught, with the unexpected arrival of Spotlight George, in the Beaver's spotlight. An early conversation with Denison made it clear to me that the men, unaccustomed to the presence of a woman, did not want to be surprised early in the morning in their own ablutions by my unexpected presence, and from then on I was really careful to stay indoors always, early in the morning and at bedtime. When we were travelling it was much simpler. I would tell whoever was driving the camper that I had to go, and we would stop while I went on the road behind the back steps: a rare event, because of dehydration.

Out of curiosity, I once asked Denison how the men felt about having a woman along while they were building the road. He shrugged. "I don't particularly care how they feel," he said. "You are with us, and they put up with you. They don't too much like something new and different, which is always hard, and they have to watch their language, but you are here, and they have lots to do." I said that I hadn't noticed that they were watching their language much—not that I cared, with two sons who had broken me in early on four-letter words. "I honestly don't think the men are watching their language," I protested.

Denison looked at me with that half-pitying glance that I recognized as being reserved for my *really* dumb remarks. "You don't *think* they are watching their language, but they *are*," he said. "They just don't relax as much, but they put up with you, like me."

Another time, when I was asking him what the transmission on a truck was, I said, "I guess my questions must seem pretty stupid to you sometimes."

"You want it true, don't you?" he replied. "You don't know nothin' about anything like that, 'specially equipment."

Denison had been cooking breakfasts, working so silently and fast that he would have the whole meal ready before I had my bed apart, or my sleeping bag packed away, and the table back in place. The morning after Fud lost her shack Denison's ulcers made him so sick to his stomach that I volunteered as chef. It was pitch dark, it was seven o'clock, and I knew he wanted breakfast over with in a hurry. The four men were already seated at the table, politely waiting, watching me. Mukluk had said grace over the canned juice and was making toast on the grill of the Lazy Susan, which was in its stand right beside him. Worse than anything, Denison was leaning on one elbow above me in the back bunk, right above my head, silently observing the scene. I burned the bacon, fried nine eggs, turned them to order, and broke seven. There was a ghastly silence while I served up the messy yellow and white mixtures, two by two, surrounded by black strips of carbonated bacon. On the last egg that I turned, I looked up at Denison in a kind of quiet desperation. He managed a wan smile. "You lose your nerve at the very last minute, every time," he said.

John got up and went off to find the next portage, too ill to eat breakfast, but obsessed to get going. He was driving the Bug with Jimmy sitting beside him, and before he left he showed me on the map where we were, almost halfway between Yellowknife and Great Bear Lake, on Rae Lake, which extends for eighteen miles through an archipelago of tiny islands, with a half-mile of land that separates it from the next lake, Tuche (pronounced Ta-ka). Rae Lake is notorious for uneven ice depths due to narrow rocky passages and uncertain currents between the islands, and previously Denison's road had avoided this lake surface by taking an all-land route around that was extremely rough and hilly. This year he had decided to save three or four miles of rough portage and two or three days of road-making by cutting directly across the lake. The only land construction would be the half-mile connection between Rae and Tuche lakes. John had arranged for the men at the Hislop

Indian village to check the depth of the lake ice and mark out a new portage, the half-mile connecting link between the two lakes. What he and Jimmy were looking for now was snowshoe tracks and other markings that the Indians had left in the bush leading from the old road to the new.

Their morning search was unsuccessful, and after lunch they set off again. This time they took me along. I sat in the back of the Bug on a plank on the floor, below the escape hatch in the ceiling that had once had a sliding door but was covered now by a flimsy rag of a coat. "I don't trust this old pile of junk but there's no point spending ten or twelve thousand dollars for a new one when I use it only this once a year," said Denison, who was feeling considerably better. We were breezing over the ice but there was an ominous clink in the engine. Denison was driving and Jimmy was holding his foot pressed down on the exposed gearshift, which was half-broken, to keep it from jumping off into neutral. We came to the north end of Rae Lake, traversing several potholes, and hit the old portage road with a terrible thud. The new route would utilize the old portage entrance but would turn off sharply towards Tuche Lake, cutting off several miles on land. We kept stopping so that Jimmy could look for snowshoe tracks, and he finally came back and said he had found them in the snow, and also a red marker. He said the new route was so short and so close by that he could actually hear the voices of our men, who had moved forward and were clearing the road in and out of the last Rae Lake pothole. Denison, always eager to scout ahead of the crew, decided to continue across Tuche Lake and beyond before turning back, but a few miles out on the ice, the Bug stopped. "Engine's buggered. The temperature and oil are both down," John said. "We must have burned a bearing." Both men got out and tinkered with the motor. I was convinced by now that they could fix any piece of machinery any place, so I was not surprised when the engine started chugging again right away, but we had to drive slowly so as not to put a strain on it. We turned around and retraced our steps to where Jimmy had found the markings. Through the thick undergrowth we could see the smoke of our trucks and hear the men talking, but between us and them was a deep wooded ravine, a rugged half-mile of terrain through which the new portage would have to be built. Denison stopped the Bug, and Jimmy cut across the ravine on foot to show the men where to break the new road.

The sun was going down and John was impatient. Why didn't Jimmy return? "Why don't we follow Jimmy in the Bug?" I asked.

"The way this old Bug is now, she'd never make it!" Denison said. "We'd have to go right through the trees. The only way we can get to the other trucks is to go back and around to them the way we came, and this Bug's so broke down, I don't think it would make that now, either. My idea is to have Jimmy tell the men where we are, and have them come to *us* on the new trail, clearin' it," He looked at his watch, swore, got out of the Bug and disappeared through the snow into the ravine.

In the crippled Bombardier with its engine still running, for company I had Jimmy Watson's tool kit, an oil and a gasoline drum, an ice auger, a shovel, an axe, and two propane heaters, one of which Denison lit before he left. I was quite warm and since it was dark out, I curled up with a sleeping bag as a pillow and slept. When I awoke, it was after five, so I stepped out of the Bug, wondering if I should follow Denison. The snow was surprisingly deep, up to my waist; in the ravine, it would be up to my neck. How often I had read about novices in the North who froze to death a few yards from shelter! I was turning to get back in the Bug when I saw an electric lantern swinging towards me. Denison emerged from the darkness. He climbed into the driver's seat looking grim. "The Cat's in the water," he said heavily. "It's down four feet in the last pothole, about thirty feet from shore, turned over on its right side. If we had a winch on a truck we could pull it out in a few minutes, but the winch on Thirty-six has a burned-out bearing, and the only other winch that's strong enough is on the Cat itself. The radios are dead, so I'll have to go back to the garage for help. But the first thing I have to do is to get this Bug back to the other vehicles while it's still running. Keep your foot on the gearshift, and let's go!"

I am sitting where Jimmy sat, my foot pressed down on the gearshift, my hand pressed on my knee to keep my foot steady, my other arm bracing me on the seat. The Bug leaps forward with a horrid lurch. I look up into the stream of brightness made by our headlights and gasp. We are driving directly into a large white tree whose thick trunk is coming up to meet us out of the dark. Small brush crackling under our treads and the treetrunk closer and closer. I look at Denison; he is looking straight at the treetrunk but makes no effort to swerve. Swerve where? We are surrounded by trees. "Keep your foot on that gear!" he snaps, without turning his head. So I hold on to the gear and the seat, and the tree comes up to our windshield, separated from my face by the short curved front of the Bug and its little bumper. I am too petrified to make a sound. I can't make a sound. I expect the thick trunk to smash the windshield and wipe me away.

CRACK!

The tree snaps off like a twig! Unbelievable! It falls over, laden with snow, as neatly as if it has been cut with a scissors.

CRACK! CRACK! CRACK!

The trees fall before us as we crash through that woods. A demented force! The old Bug rattles and shakes, quivers with each blow.

CRACK! CRACK! CRACK!

I am getting so used to this madness that I don't even close my eyes any more when we hit. It takes a birch longer to break than a spruce. Am I dreaming? Is this a nightmare?

A yellow patch of light above the trees ahead in the black sky. We leap onto the ice, into a circle of headlights. We are crossing the pothole and the Cat, Denison's large red TD–14

International tractor, is lying on its side, great wounded animal, its right track under water with broken ice floating around it. The canvas, so short a time ago such brave protection for Burns, is flapping nervously in the strong wind. The other vehicles are standing at a respectful distance, shedding light; comforting companions, noble mourners. Denison shouts, "Lift your foot!" and as I do, the gearshift slips into neutral and we come to a shivering stop, the motor idling. My toes are stiff and cold from the air that has been blowing on them through the hole at the base of the gear. How far did we come? Half a mile? Impossible! It must have been miles. It was a matter of minutes. It seemed like my lifetime.

Denison got out and walked around the Cat. The men clustered silently around him, waiting for him to say something. He stood there, looking drawn and sick, and then told the men to bring their vehicles back to where the camper was still sitting, on the first of the Rae Lakes where we had spent the previous night. We drove back in the Bug, with one of the men following in a big truck in case we broke down.

In the camper, Denison tried the radio. No operator's cool voice on the phone, only static. The power steering on 34 was broken so Tom needed to go back anyway. He would try to get Jim Magrum or Hughie Arden to come and pull John's Cat out of the ice. "Either one can do it," John said after Tom had gone. "Hughie's an awful tough man. He used to have the logging contract for Discovery Mine, and once a stick came up over the track of the Cat and went right through his stomach and out his back. Terrible! It was maybe an inch thick, and he couldn't move with it in him, so he pulled it out himself. Luckily it passed by his vital organs and he managed to run the Cat the fifteen miles back to Discovery. He was flown back to Yellowknife and spent a long time in hospital, but ennabody else would have died. As for Magrum, nothing's too tough for him. The telephone-communications people put a tractor through the ice at

Port Radium, and I had the contract to take it out. It was in the spring and so dangerous that you can't really be paid enough for that kind of work, and we did it for six thousand dollars. It could have taken a long time, but Jimmy knew exactly what he was doing, and he pulled it out in one day, with anchors and a winch line. Jimmy did the pulling out and I watched. I learn something from those fellows every time."

The radio was silent all the next day and the day after, Denison was really ill and stopped eating. I thought, I am watching a man worry himself to death. He lay on the back bunk of the camper as still as death, eyes closed; opened them and turned his head only when the men came to report on their work. Without a Cat to clear away trees and rocks, no portage roads could be broken open. Fud's shack had been fastened in position again and her water lines hooked up, so Mukluk and Jimmy Watson with 36 returned to dragging and packing down the portages behind us and plowing the lakes to keep the new road clear of drifts. Bob Burns spent his nights in Fud but his days in the camper, bereft, grieving for his half-drowned Cat, head down, a paperback mystery open and unread in his hand, smoking cigarette after cigarette and drinking coffee. I drove up once with Jimmy in 36, to see the red Cat. It was well frozen into its icy prison and coated with tons of ice above the water line. A sudden drop in temperature a day or so earlier had plunged the thermometer from twenty below to sixty below and after several days the world seemed mighty cold. "You know why that Cat went through the ice?" I heard John say to Jimmy one night. "Because there was such a hell of a temperature change the other day, that's why. It got awful cold awful fast, a temperature change of forty degrees in about five or six hours, and when that happens the ice goes just like glass. The airlines take twenty-four hours before they land a Hercules freight plane on the ice after such a real quick change in temperature, and we should not have worked for at least eight hours, while the ice tightened up. I was too busy to realize what was happening, so I just kept going. I should have shut down for a day until the ice was stabilized, but I wasn't thinkin'."

The second night, Jimmy returned late from work on the portage. The others had already gone back to their trucks after dinner. He and I sat down to a can of mushroom soup and a tin of strawberries, too tired, too depressed for more. We ate by the flickering light of a candle to conserve the fading current. We were also running low on propane gas. Jimmy and I kept our voices down so as not to disturb Denison. I described the crazy ride through the trees two days earlier. "You could never have done that in summer when it's warm," Jimmy said. "The trees snapped off when you hit them because they were frozen. Incidentally, you would never have made it in the Bug for any distance. It was going to break down any minute!"

I asked him how sick he thought John was. I had noticed a sort of fatalistic acceptance of Denison's condition. "Pretty bad, but not so that we have to get a plane to fly him out like some of the other times," Jimmy whispered. "Last year he was flown out three times. He'd be out for a day and then he'd be okay and he'd come back. John'll pick up when things get better. He shouldn't be doing this kind of work, but you can't stop him.

"Year before last, we were around Faber, just one lake closer to town, and we had to wait for an airplane to pick him up. It was before his last operation, and he was sick, real sick; he couldn't swallow, and was choking and vomiting. He was so weak he couldn't stand up. I honestly thought he would die coming home. We came into Yellowknife at night. You're not supposed to land on Yellowknife Bay at night, but we did. We came down without lights or anything, it was darker than *anything*, it was so dark that we missed the runway a little bit and knocked out some of those little spruce trees at the shoreline. But John wouldn't go to the hospital. As soon as he got to town he said he felt much better and that he didn't want to be tied up in any goddamned hospital because it wouldn't do any good.

So in a day or two he was back on the road again." Jimmy turned his empty fruit bowl slowly around with his fingers. "John should have died several times up here," he said, "and that's the truth."

When Jimmy went to bed, although I wasn't sleepy I went to bed also; it was just too much trouble reading by candlelight. Before the fire in the camper, when we still had electric lights, all of us read after dinner or in bed. I lay there listening to Denison breathing steadily in the back bunk, and Jimmy moving around restlessly beside him. Suddenly a flashlight went on and I heard Jimmy say in a loud whisper, "John?" Then louder, "John!"

There was a stirring and John said, "Yup?"

"John," he said. "You've gone to bed with your hat on."

I pulled myself up on one elbow and looked out from my bunk. It was true. Denison was wearing the green cap he had worn all day, lying on his back with the visor over his forehead, covering his eyes.

"John," Jimmy went on, in a normal speaking voice. *"Nobody* goes to bed with their hat on."

"I do," said John.

There was a silence. Jimmy continued to stare at him, holding the flashlight with its beam turned on the green hat. Denison hadn't moved and the visor still shaded his eyes. "But *why?*" Jimmy finally said.

"Dunno. Had it on, I guess. Never took it off."

"Well, why don't you take it off now that I've called your attention to it?"

"Don't want to. I've got it on now."

There was a long silence. Jimmy turned off the flashlight and lay down. The light suddenly went on again. Jimmy was sitting bolt upright, staring at John. There was something very surrealist about this. A small surrealist drama.

"John," he said.

Silence.

Jimmy drew a long sighing breath. "John, I've *never* slept in a bed with *anyone* who was wearing a hat," he said. Another sigh. "I don't know whether I *can.*"

"Sorry about that," John replied. Silence. Nobody moved.

It seemed like a long long time before Jimmy turned off the flashlight and lay down. I listened then to the spluttering heater and the rumbling motors, felt the vibration of the truck, rocking almost imperceptibly. How frail a shelter this camper is! This tiny tin box on wheels, thin metal walls to hold back the shrieking wind, rattling windowpanes—the harsh reminders that, outside, the Furies rage at our presence. Their antagonist, John Denison, the human force, whose will and mind and strength are spent on a road that exists for three months a year and disappears; that slips away in cracking ice, floating jagged slabs, slush melting from the rising sun, into clear blue water. Look down. Look down, passing birds in summer, men in low-flying planes. See the faint green strip beneath the water; relic of that winter path!

What am I watching? A man's struggle to carve out a road in the dead of winter, over land and water that resist every effort to be tamed. Always further north. The ancient Greeks knew Denison before he knew himself. He is Sisyphus, rolling uphill a rock that forever rolls back on him.

I could still hear Jimmy moving about restlessly in the back bunk, and once he flashed the light on briefly, to stare I suppose at Denison in his green cap, lying on his back, his eyes hidden by the visor. I must have fallen asleep before Jimmy did.

I dreamt all the lights were on and that someone was standing in front of me, shouting. I sat up and opened my eyes. No dream. Tom Berry stood in the door, back from Fort Byers, flashing an electric torch that lit up his frosty beard, his wide-open eyes and the whole inside of the camper. It was the first time I had ever seen him agitated. "It's through!" he roared. "I just went through the ice in Thirty-four!"

John was pulling on his boots and struggling into his parka

before Tom stopped shouting. "I heard you drive in, Tom," he said. "I *knew* you were through the ice. I could *feel* it and I heard a crunch. I thought, by Jesus, I'm not going to worry and then I heard some more crunch, crunch, crunch and you yelled."

The men ran out from the other trucks. I started the coffee, but there was no water so I grabbed the thirty-pound ice auger, took it outside and made a futile attempt to dig a hole in the ice. Even though the spoon-shaped scoop on the end of the auger had a knife edge, my stabbing efforts barely grazed the surface of the ice. Mukluk, coming out of his shack, sleepily putting on his parka, took the auger as if it were a feather and scooped a hole, filling my pail with clear, sparkling water.

I put pots of water on the stove, and joined the group outside around the endangered vehicle. Both ends of Tom's proud truck, 34, were standing on the ice, but it sagged deplorably in the middle where the back wheels of the cab and the front wheels of the trailer were partially under water. Thank heaven for the special rescue squad that had arrived with Tom! The expert team summoned to retrieve John's Cat from its watery hole: Hughie Arden; Johnny Soldat, a young Eskimo from Coppermine who lived with the Arden family; and Davy Lorenzen, a light-haired, easy-mannered man in his thirties, who had his own sand and gravel business in summer but worked for Denison in the winter. They had driven out behind Tom in Davy's Diesel tow truck, a modest, black, five-ton Diamond T model, that had two gin poles shaped in an A-form on its back with a winch line going through it for lifting and towing. The Diamond T was standing at a discreet distance on the ice behind the accident, and it was hauling a trailer that carried an amazing giraffelike machine with a long neck full of pulleys and cables for lifting heavy objects, called a cherry picker. Tom had also brought out on his lowboy two other handy items: Hughie's silver caboose, equipped for living, and his yellow Cat.

Burns was already preparing to drive Hughie's Cat off the back of 34's half-sunk trailer, down two planks laid from the back of the lowboy to the ice. The other men started up the Herman Nelson heater that I had last seen in the garage at Fort Byers, which Tom had brought with him, to thaw the back wheels of 34 and prevent them from freezing into the ice. A twenty-foot parachute had been put over this whole back section of the truck and over the heater to hold in the warmth, and for the men to work under. A parachute was an admirable cover for thawing or repair work on the Ice Road because it could be stored in a small bag, and was cheaper and lighter than a bulky canvas.

I went back into the camper, and Denison came right after me, carrying a package of T-bone steaks he had picked off the deepfreeze, the space inside the bumper on the outside of the camper. He immediately started cooking them in a frying pan on the stove. "Do the wheels of those big trucks actually *freeze* into the ice?" I asked.

Without raising his eyes from his cooking Denison said, "Those wheels are frozen in now on Thirty-four, but we'll thaw them out, easy. If we didn't have a Herman Nelson, we'd use a propane torch. If we didn't have that we'd build a fire under the brake drums with twigs. You don't even think about it, that's just somethin' you have to do up here, like checkin' the oil. If your wheels won't go, so, thaw them out."

The men came in to eat, blowing on their red hands, and immediately began a postmortem. "That's only four inches of ice you dropped through, Tom," Hughie said. "The cab's front wheels passed right over that spot but its back wheels were too heavy. It's lucky that they landed on a rock!"

Little rivulets of water were dripping from Tom's melting beard onto his checked jacket. He wiped his beard carefully. "When the truck went through the ice, it went BOOM! and I tried to change gears real quick," Tom said. "Plop! It went down and I thought, I better not jump before I see if it settles first: if I take it out of gear it might stop movin', and on the other hand, when it's in gear like that and it keeps movin', it might keep goin' to the bottom of the lake. So then it comes to an abrupt halt on the rock it's sittin' on now. If it had been deep there it would have torn off the fifth wheel and broken the trailer connection, but as it was, it just broke the fifth wheel and the airline to the brakes."

As soon as I had washed the dishes I started packing up for travelling, without being told. The radio was still out, more parts were needed right away to get 34 running, and there was no other way to get them than to drive 125 hard miles back to Fort Byers. Tom had brought word that Jimmy Watson's wife was in the hospital to have their first baby, so Jimmy was driving back with us and going on home to British Columbia. I would miss him.

When we started back John drove so fast that we got stuck on the first portage. We were going up a small hill, and the wheels just spun around. Jimmy got out and shovelled snow around them, and Denison rocked the camper, packing the snow under the tires until the ground was level enough to move again. Driving was slow and tough, and after an hour or so, we stopped and waited while John got out and was sick in the snow. After that, he went to bed in back, in the camper. Jimmy drove and we did not stop again until we reached Fort Byers around six in the morning.

The woods are beautiful at night, the trees, the bushes; shadowy forms who gracefully bow as we sweep along; bend their branches, nodding, with their heavy burdens of snow. Snow everywhere, snowladen branches, snowcovered ground. On the lakes, snowy drifts, banked high, gleam in the headlights, form a continuous border to channel the gliding turning humming tires. White earth, black heaven twinkling with stars. The gods of the North shake our bones, scream windy anger at our tiny invasion of—our dot of moving life on—their snowy earth kingdom.

I had brought some cans of fruit juice, a box of cookies and a thermos of hot coffee into the cab of the camper for our all-night drive. When the road was rough, Jimmy drove with both hands on the wheel, hunched forward, tense, watching everything, his eyes darting everywhere. Like his Uncle John, he could also relax where he was sure of the terrain, a feat for any driver less knowledgeable. Then, leaning back in the seat, driving with one hand and sipping coffee from the cup I handed him, he talked.

"I was havin' a nightmare when Tom broke in tonight," Jimmy said. "I dreamt that the earth was being towed around by a space ship and we were swingin' and tossin'! So many things that happen up here are like nightmares. Last year it blowed in on Hottah Lake, which is fifty miles long and the biggest lake on the Ice Road before Great Bear, and I was three and a half days with Jim Magrum sittin' there in a Bombardier without heat, in sixty-below temperature with a forty-mile-an-hour wind blowin', which you can figure with your wind-chill factor puts the temperature at about a hundred and twenty below."

"How did you manage?" I asked.

"It's too bad Jim Magrum couldn't come with John this time, because he can really find his way around!" Jimmy said. He's the kind of guy I admire, and we've had a lot of experiences together, good and bad. I know I got on Jim's nerves quite often, but he put up with me. The time in the Bombardier we were just workin' the Ice Road and Jim was teaching me how to scout it. He's a fantastic guy with a sense of direction, and after he taught me I knew like the back of my hand where to go. We were just goin' onto Hottah Lake when gas overflowed into the motor and the motor burnt up. All the wiring burnt and while it was burning I managed to get on the radio to Hay River and tell whoever answered there our position, and ask him to call John and tell him we were in trouble and needed someone to pick us up, because we had no heat. Well, we stayed the night in that Bug because it all happened about 11:00 P.M. Where we were, there were very few trees for protection and the Bug filled

John Denison, in the cab of the African Queen. He has just told me the truck we are in has fallen through the ice on Great Bear Lake!

One of the big snowplow trucks widening the Ice Road after it is in place. It's an endless battle against wind to keep it open.

Chilly winter scene at Port Radium, with Great Bear Lake in the foreground. (Carl Engel photo)

My first look at "Fort" Byers: fuel storage tanks and a bunk-cookhouse. At the turnoff, where the 520-kilometer Ice Road begins.

A truck rendezvous on the Ice Road. Lots of hard water beneath!

Roadbuilding. First, the scout, a Bombardier "bug"; then the plow truck, 36; followed by Truck 34, carrying the Cat, to roll the surface.

Portrait of my favorite truck, No. 36, the African Queen; complete with lowboy trailer, caboose, and custom-designed snowplow.

Trucks arriving at the mine with freight, over the newly opened Ice Road. Our camper in the foreground.

The camper; my home, my office, and the crew's kitchen, where I presided as the reluctant cook while the Ice Road was being built.

Echo Bay mine buildings. That's our camper again (left), waiting, while the trucks unload and get repaired.

Denison cooking breakfast. Periodically he decided that his unpaid cook was too slow getting the men out on the road, and took over.

Trucks crossing one of the nineteen lakes the Ice Road traverses, carrying lumber and a pickup truck for the mine at Port Radium.

John Denison (left), returning from a talk with the driver of the tractor, who is about to open a portage between two lakes.

Hughie Arden's Cat, making a portage at the north end of the Ice Road. The lake that Hughie has just left is behind him.

On a portage, we stopped behind a dog team that looked driverless, until an Indian hunter popped up in the carry-all and pulled over.

The Beaver: a wonderful, clumsy, amphibious room on wheels with a kitchen, bunks, and big flotation tires that pack down snow.

Truck 34, carrying the Cat on its lowboy, stopping for a lunch break at Hottah Lake camp.

The spruce-bough lean-to Jimmy Watson built on a portage to keep warm, when 34 broke down and he waited a week for a new transmission.

Hughie Arden and Burns under a parachute, welding a broken link on Arden's Cat, in 60-below temperature, in a pothole near Hottah Lake.

The left front end of Hughie's Cat, under water, three feet below the icy surface of Hardisty Lake. It took an hour to winch it out.

The cherry picker, a giraffe-like machine for lifting heavy objects; this time three vehicles that went through the ice at Rae Lake.

Denison getting fresh water and testing the thickness of the ice with an ice auger. Depth needed: 18 inches; preferably, three feet.

Denison gassing up the camper from the gas and diesel oil storage trailer parked three-quarters of the way up the Ice Road.

Our camper and truck 43, a twenty-year-old workhorse affectionately called Fud (from F.W.D.4, for Four Wheel Drive) at the gas cache.

Poor old Fud. Its right wheel has disappeared under the ice! An early contributor to the epidemic of disasters on Hardisty Lake.

Prospector Sam Otto, with a friend, Norm Burgess, in Otto's Yellowknife "museum," holding up native copper he found near Coppermine.

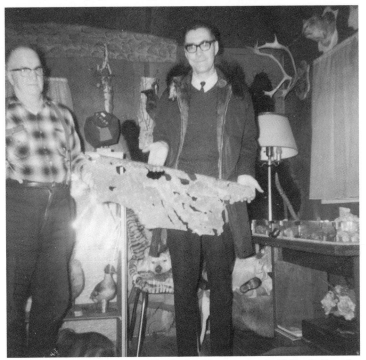

Headquarters of the Northwest Territories Government, in Yellowknife, when I was there. I warmed up and washed in Yellowknife.

Jim and June Magrum, who trapped in the Barrens for years, taking their children with them. Jim was killed in a plane crash later.

Denison opening a can of butter in the caboose that served as a rest camp at Faber Lake. Note Denison's gaunt look. He was ill by then.

Pouring gold into a brick mold at Cominco's Con Mine, in Yellowknife. Each brick, weighing 50 to 70 pounds, is worth a fortune.

I jumped into a cab in Yellowknife, and said, "Take me to a gold mine." This is what I saw as we drove up to Con Mine.

Perseverando: What all the struggle is for. A freight convoy on its way to the mine, after we opened the Ice Road for the season.

full of snow, tiny crystals of ice like a powder through the cracks or even the slightest hole in our machine. It was so cold the propane bottle froze up and the heater wouldn't light, but anyway we wouldn't want to risk having it on in there when we were sleeping. We lay in our sleeping bags and tried to keep warm, but we felt so numb we could hardly move. Jim wouldn't let me sleep because when you sleep your metabolism slows down and you can freeze really easy."

"What happened the next day?" I asked.

"The next morning as soon as it was light, the two of us decided I should walk to John's Hottah Lake camp, which was six miles away, and get a fire lit so we'd have a warm place to stay," he said. "I put on my face mask and went across, but when I got to the camp and tried to get fuel to light the stove, the fuel had jelled and wouldn't light. I got some paper lit, but it was really torture because it was so cold I couldn't hold a match in my fingers. I turned around and started back, because as you know day is like night and it had already started getting dark. The ice was thin on either side of the Bug, so I did what Magrum had told me to, I picked a star where I thought it was, and walked straight for it. Meanwhile, Jim was in the Bombardier trying to warm flashlight batteries enough with his hands to thaw them and he had been quite worried about me. We stayed the night again in the Bug, but he wouldn't let me sleep then, either, so the next day we threw our sleeping bags out into a snowbank, just to break the monotony, and stayed for a while outside, and then moved back into the Bug." He stopped and pointed to the thermos of hot coffee, and I poured him another cup. "Boy, that tastes good!" he said. "Talkin' about that time and how cold it was makes me feel cold all over again!"

"I can imagine," I said. "So then what happened?"

"The third day we heard the airplane come," he said. "It flew over the top of us and missed, but I guess about an hour later it backtracked, and finally spotted us. We had made markers, of course, and we were waving our hands and hollerin'. You kind of get bushed, really overwhelmed by happiness that they have come to get you. It wasn't so bad that third day anyway, because it got warmer out and we ate some cans of potted meat. When the airplane lands, though, you feel so important, to think that someone would come to get you, and it sure makes you feel lonely when the pilot misses and flies over and doesn't stop."

"What did you think about all that time before you were picked up?" I asked. "I mean, besides how cold it was and when you would be rescued."

"Oh, mostly about getting married, which I did soon after," Jimmy replied. "Magrum has six kids, so he worried about money. We thought we were goin' to die, so we spent most of our time makin' our wills with each other in case one of us survived."

In midmorning we arrived at Fort Byers. I decided to continue with John and Jimmy to Yellowknife so I could sit in a warm bath. The last seventy miles, from Fort Byers to Yellowknife, were grimly silent. Denison, awake and driving, was so withdrawn that, although he was visible, I felt as if he were enveloped in a heavy dark blanket, with nothing showing but his long nose.

Chapter Five

SECOND TRIP IN:
GOLD

I said farewell to Jimmy over a bowl of New England clam chowder in the Coffee Shop at the Inn, took my bath and paid what seemed now like a ritual visit to the laundromat, walking around several cables on the street. In winter the sidewalks and sides of buildings all over Yellowknife are strung with heavy black wires; they hang from the upper windows of two-story structures on Franklin Avenue, and are wound around lamp-posts, in door frames, and across sidewalks. Automobile owners plug these wires, connected to electrical units, into devices that charge their car batteries, and into heating units that keep the automobile blocks and oil pans from freezing overnight. For short visits in subzero weather, people leave their car engines on just as we did on the Ice Road, and for the same reason: once off, it might not be so easy to get them to start again. The entrance to a building where a large crowd is gathered is always encircled by clouds of steam and the low hum of dozens of motors.

Undecided what to do after I dropped off my laundry, I crossed the street and spied a taxi at the stand by the hotel entrance. I jumped in and said to the driver, "Take me to a gold mine."

There are two working gold mines inside the city limits of Yellowknife; the bigger one, Giant Mine, three-and-a-half miles from the center of town, and Con Mine, on the shore of Yellow-knife Bay, half a mile and a three-minute taxi ride from the Inn. A good part of Yellowknife is over the Con Mine. "In my house, I can hear the dynamite charges going off in the Con Mine, pop, pop, pop," Kay Vaydik once said. I told this to John and he added, "When they are tunneling under the town, diggin' the ore out, why I can hear the blasts, walkin' down the street."

The driver took me to Con Mine, and at its entrance we passed a sign proclaiming that Con was the first gold mine in the Northwest Territories and had commenced production in 1938. All I could see of the mine as I came in was a group of small white buildings with green trim over which the tall timbers of the mine shaft's head frame towered like the top of an eleva-tor shaft, which is essentially what it is. I found the office of the manager, Alec Richardson, and explained to him that I was travelling with John Denison and his crew while they built the Ice Road to Port Radium; that I had this one afternoon free; and had always wanted to see a gold mine. "You're travelling with *whom, where?*" he exclaimed, looking at me in astonishment. "The Ice Road? To Echo Bay? *Really?*" He stared at me with the same incredulous expression I had seen for a moment on the face of Romeo Dusseault, the cook at Fort Byers, when I first met him. "I went on the truck with John part way up the Ice Road last year *after* it was open," Richardson said. "I found it a fairly hairy experience."

"Did you?" I asked faintly.

"Yes, I did," he said firmly. "I thought to myself, if this truck breaks down, it's going to be fairly chilly. It's pretty hairy to travel in that convoy, I can tell you. I suppose you know they've lost a couple of trucks."

"Yes, I do," I said.

"I've known John a long time," Richardson said, as we walked out of his office towards the mine mill. "The first time I came to work at the Con Mine was from nineteen forty-six to forty-nine. I was in the beer parlor of the Old Stope Hotel with a friend and came out with a bottle of beer under my coat, which was illegal. I accidentally dropped the beer on the ground, and the largest hand I ever saw and the largest cop I ever saw suddenly materialized and John Denison—he was in the R.C.M.P. then—said, 'Young fella, you better get yourself home!' Twenty years later, I came back to Yellowknife and I was walking down the street and I felt a heavy hand on my shoulder. A voice behind me said, 'What are you doing here, young fella?' and there was John. He hadn't changed, except he's so much thinner. He's driving himself too hard."

On the way across the mine yard to the mill Richardson explained that one-third of the machinery in the mine mill had a single purpose: to crush the big chunks of mined gold ore— already crushed once before being brought up from somewhere in the thirty miles of underground tunnels and stopes of the mine—to grains that could be run through a screen whose mesh was the thickness of a human hair. "To produce enough gold for a signet ring would require mining a ton of rock," Richardson said. "For one penny, three hundred and sixty thousand penny-size pieces of quartz ore—that's gold ore—would have to be processed."

The gold ore looked like dirty, wet rock to me, but Richardson said it yielded almost six-tenths of an ounce of gold per ton of ore, and thus was high-grade ore for a Canadian mine. The inside of the mill was a seeming madhouse of massive tanks, huge revolving barrels of steel balls, great crushing plates, conveyor belts, wheels, a roar of noise, and the sour smells of sulphur, arsenic and cyanide. Soft, sticky brownish-grey dust covered everything. The pulverized ore, Richardson explained, was finally subjected to a flotation process that separated the valuable metals from the waste, or tailings. Five hundred tons of ore was reduced to one hundred tons, and the rest was diverted into a tailings pond. The one hundred tons of gold concentrate was then clarified in a cyanide solution and entered the final filter press, which looked to me like a standing steam radiator with white sheets between the ridges. The gold at this point was black, like wet soot.

"After two weeks in this filter," Richardson said, shouting above the milling racket, "the concentrate is ready to be refined into bullion. This process, in which the gold finally begins to look like gold, takes place in a small shed kept locked. Pickup trucks carry the wet black precipitate over to the shed in pans holding four hundred and sixty-five pounds each."

I was lucky. I had come just in time to see the pouring of the gold, which is done once or twice a month. We came into the small pouring shed as Con's refiner was removing a tray of concentrate from the large safe where it had been stored, and feeding it into a small oil-fired furnace that pivoted on a stand. While we waited, the ore was cooked at a temperature of 2,000 degrees. At that heat, gold settles at the bottom and impurities float to the top. When the refiner tipped the boiler to pour, out came impure slag first, a lovely molten orange. The slag was wheeled away, and the refiner tipped the furnace a second time. Lemon-yellow molten gold flowed into a mold the shape and size of an ordinary building brick.

When the brick, containing seventy-five percent gold and from ten to twenty percent silver, with scatterings of zinc, copper and lead in it, is cool, it is wrapped in canvas, strapped with steel bindings, and sent by registered mail from the Yellowknife post office to the mint, where the silver and the other impurities are removed. Each brick weighed from fifty to seventy pounds and was worth in excess of fifty thousand dollars, probably nearer one hundred thousand dollars at the fluctuating high price of gold. "I have a standing offer that anyone who can carry a gold brick the half mile to town in their two hands can have it," Richardson shouted. "One fellow got from the mine to the warehouse with it and gave me a bad time for a minute, but then he put it down in a hurry. That was a couple of hundred feet. Quite a few women have tried, but they can hardly get out of the office door."

"What would you do if anyone looked as if they'd make it?" I yelled.

"I'd trip them before they got there," he shouted. "Mind you, I wouldn't like to say anyone in the world couldn't do it, but it's doubtful. That's very concentrated weight, in a small volume."

When we got outside, I asked, "Is it true that Yellowknife has a highway paved with gold?"

He laughed. "Yes, in a way," he said. "When the Mackenzie Highway extension was continued northeast of town, they used a large pile of gold-ore tailings from Con for fill, and gold-bearing ore is also used for some downtown sidewalks. I myself once helped make the surface of a tennis court with reject samples from the Assay Office. When that gold ore was crushed it was a fine aggregate and made a real nice, just dandy surface."

On leaving, I shared a taxi with two men, to one of whom Richardson said as he was closing the cab door, "Tell her about Yellowknife. You're an oldtimer and know what's going on." The first stop was the airport, four miles in the opposite direction from town, so we had plenty of time.

"There are no normal people here and it's a very cosmopolitan town," the older gentleman began with enthusiasm. "When my wife gives a dinner party our guests are likely to include an Irishman, a Finn, three Germans, a Swede and a Belgian. We have had six population waves in Yellowknife, the last the arrival of the federal government. We call all the people who came between nineteen hundred thirty-eight and nineteen hundred forty-six bona-fide oldtimers, and they regard people like me, who came to stay a little later, as sort of second-string oldtimers, but not newcomers anymore. During the Second World War, Yellowknife had a depression; it lacked manpower, materials, and everything else. This is gold country, though, and in nineteen forty-four word got around that gold had been discovered at what is now Giant Mine. Boom! Five or six thousand people crowded around the Rock or camped in the bush that summer, including me, and a plane took off from the bay every minute. Diamond drills were working all over the place, and everybody you met held a piece of gold in his hand. There were tents everywhere. You had to step over the people sleeping on the ground in paper cartons."

The other man, sitting in the front seat with the driver, had turned and was listening attentively. My companion in the back seat continued, "The population dropped off in nineteen forty-seven, when the fly-by-nighters moved to greener pastures—to Uranium City, in northern Saskatchewan, and to Ontario and Quebec. After that came the quiet years, from nineteen forty-eight to nineteen fifty-four. Giant Mine went into production in forty-eight, business improved and consolidated, and people became more entrenched. For three years, we had a mild uranium boom with Rayrock Mine, but it shut down in fifty-nine. The Byrne family, who are based here and in Toronto, developed a small gold mine called Discovery, sixty miles north. That has now closed because the ore has been mined out. A major gold exploration in sixty-two, Tundra Mine, two hundred and forty miles northeast by land in the middle of the Barrens, was in operation four years and increased our pace of business because we fed the people in the bush, but it lies dormant now. The Barrens, all the land beyond the tree line, in winter is just one big white mass—an easy place to get lost in, because it has so few geographical features that it's hard to map-read."

We arrived at the airport, and the other man got out and ran for his plane. My companion waved absentmindedly and went on, "Mining interest shifted to lead and zinc on Great Slave's south shore in nineteen sixty-five, and a lot of Yellowknife claim-stakers and prospectors went across the lake. The federal government brought a railroad in there, and Pine Point Mine opened. It got its investment of twenty-two million dollars back in its first year of operation. It's owned by the same company that has the Con Mine—Cominco Limited. At Pine Point, they just shovelled the ore into railroad cars and sent it out on two trains a week, eight hundred thousand dollars each time, and as the saying goes, laughed all the way to the bank. The expense was practically nothing. The Pine Point breakthrough showed how money can be made."

At the end of the airport road, we passed a large plane with a big tank body under the cockpit, mounted on a concrete pedestal. "That's the famous Bristol airplane that one of our best bush pilots, an oldtimer named Don Braun—we call him the Barren Land Fox—landed on an ice floe nineteen miles from the North Pole in 1967, without any landing strip, to bring supplies to government scientists," he said. "Max Ward, our local boy-who-made-good with a charter aircraft service he started here, and that now operates all over the west, sold it to the town for one dollar."

Our taxi turned towards town, and we passed a good-looking stone-and-frame structure that looked like a motel. "The Correctional Institution," he continued. "It's the first formal prison in the Territories, but nobody calls it a jail. We don't have many real criminals of the hardened type yet within the Territories. Most of our law problems stem from alcohol and the intrusion of white culture on our native populations. Our judges try to give suspended sentences of not more than two years, less a day, so our natives, won't have to go Outside to a provincial penitentiary and become hardened criminals. Anyway, confinement does something to a native. We usually refer to the Correctional Institution as the Crowbar Motel, or the Y.C.I. for Yellowknife Collegiate Institute. It was constructed in nineteen sixty-seven, the same year that Yellowknife was proclaimed the capital of the Northwest Territories. That's when the territorial government began moving from Ottawa to Yellowknife, and three years later we were made a city by proclamation. The population has doubled since all the civil servants have arrived, and they are still coming. The newest group came in to establish a command base to maintain Canada's sovereignty of the Arctic Ocean and seas and the Arctic Islands. Who needs that? As if they weren't enough, because of the excitement over oil and gas exploration, the Feds are all over the place with environmentalists, who have gone into competition with our Territorial Government to see who can check up first on the poor man who wants to light a bonfire or build a little road. We need controls, but not all those environmentalists crawling all over us. Everyone wants to get on the bandwagon."

We had arrived at the hotel. I told my companion how much I had enjoyed the ride, thanked him, and went to my room, where I packed my little black bag with clean underwear, dressed again in my duofolds and layers of sweaters and socks for the return to the Ice Road, and went down to the lobby to sit and wait for Denison to pick me up. However sick he might be, I knew he would be going back, but I had no idea when.

If you sit in the lobby of the Yellowknife Inn long enough, you are likely to see everyone you know. My friend Kay Vaydik's prospector husband, Chuck, strolled by and stopped when he saw me. "Hello! What's wrong with you?" Chuck exclaimed. "You look terrible!"

"I am," I said. I listed the catastrophes that had occurred so far on the Ice Road. "The harder I try to be helpful, the more I'm annoying everybody," I said. "Especially Denison. I am *definitely* in the way."

"What!" Chuck cried. "You're trying to be helpful? That's the worst thing you can do!" He pulled up a chair and sat down. "Tell me about it," he said.

I had an overwhelming desire to talk. "The second morning on the road I got up and offered to help," I burst out. "What do you think Denison said? 'There's only room for one person to work in here, isn't that right?' he said, 'and I know where everything is, and put it out in the same spot each time, and put it back in the same spot when I'm finished using it.' Well, he *was* right, of course. I hadn't realized that everything had to have its special place in such small quarters, and that if I didn't put things back exactly where they had been it would take him time to locate them again. I wasn't thinking, and on that Ice Road, you can't afford not to think. Then there was the matter of my sleeping bag," I continued. "You know that it fell into the Lazy Susan and started a fire that almost burned the camper up?"

"I heard about that," Chuck said.

"Well, mine was the only sleeping bag with a slippery nylon cover, the rest are all canvas. I felt really awful about that."

"Anything else?" Chuck asked.

"Yes," I said. "After John told me to put things back where I found them, he said, 'If you had any sense at all, which you don't seem to have, you'd sit down in that corner and stay out of the way, especially until the men are fed. That's the best way *you* can help.' I'm not saying he was wrong, but that hurt."

Vaydik laughed. Laughed! Why did everyone laugh? It had been one of the most humiliating moments of my life. I should have known enough to get out of the way without being told.

"Then what?" he asked.

"I don't know what's happened, but somehow I'm doing a lot of the cooking now. I do the cooking unless we're in a hurry. I'm slow getting the food on the table and mostly I do all the dishes. Sometimes when Denison wants to get going, he dries. I'm supposed to be recording the road-building process, but I hardly have time to take notes I'm so busy, and anyway I'm too tired. I wouldn't mind, only I'm uneasy all the time because I'm in the way." Chuck was staring at my bandaged fingers, grinning. I looked down at my hands. I had boiled the dishpan water on the stove with all the dirty dishes in it last night before I realized the stove was still on, and it had taken my last two whole fingertips to find out how hot the water was. Now all ten of my fingers wore Band-Aids. "I'm very embarrassed about my fingers," I said. "Denison noticed them when I was getting out of the camper here this morning, and groaned."

I was close to tears. "I'm really quite a good cook at home, but you'd never know it up here," I wailed. "You should see the food I'm dishing up! I can hardly eat it myself! I hate not finishing what I start, but honestly, I should be leaving, instead of waiting now to go back on that Ice Road."

"DON'T LEAVE!" Chuck shouted. Several people in the lobby looked at us curiously. He patted my shoulder and said, "It's the same in any bush operation. Believe me. If you're new at it, in the beginning you get cross and disjointed and think you can't make it. Your sleeping bag is never warm enough, you never undress, and you are spending all your time struggling with the cold, so everything's a problem. In fact, the smallest problems seem like major tragedies."

I drew a deep breath. "Yes," I said.

"This happens to every man the first time he camps in the bush, so why shouldn't it happen to you?" Chuck said. "It's a change in a man's standards. He begins to live more and more like an animal." I nodded. "He warms the dishwater on the stove and begins to use the same dishwater twice."

"Yes," I said.

"When you start cleaning your dishes with paper towelling and *no* dishwater, then you are *really* into it," he added.

"I know what you mean," I said. "I do that quite often."

Chuck looked at me a bit anxiously. "You need to eat a lot of fat or cholesterol in the bush. Are you doing that?"

"I eat lots of canned butter," I said eagerly. "It's better than the fresh butter we get at home."

"Good!" he said. "Now I'll tell you what's going on. Everyone in a bush camp will always take advantage of the newcomer who wants to be helpful. It's always the new guy who gets the water and washes the dishes, and after a few days he wises up and stops. Everybody complains and says, 'Hey, how come you're not getting the water? How come supper isn't ready? How come you're not doing the dishes? The important thing is, DON'T BE HELPFUL! That's the worst thing you can do! Just keep to what you *have* to do, what you came to do mostly, and don't let anybody take advantage of you!"

I thought about this. "Yesterday I suggested that whoever felt I was too slow should do the cooking."

"What happened?"

"No volunteers."

Chuck nodded his head approvingly and smiled. "Very good!" he exclaimed. "You're wising up! You're getting adjusted. You're toughening up more than you know. You'll make it to Echo Bay if John makes it. He's sick and may look as if he's going to die, but he's not going to stop until he gets to Port Radium. He never does. One of these days he *may* die on that Ice Road because he's too sick to do this kind of work, but he's the only guy who would have had the nerve to do it in the first place. So, just remember what I said and you'll get along. DON'T BE HELPFUL!"

Chapter Six

THIRD TRIP OUT:
POOR OLD FUD

We left Yellowknife in late afternoon, bringing a replacement for Jimmy Watson on 36 with us, a veteran of John's Ice Road operations named Lewis Mackenzie; a pleasant, black-haired man in his thirties who drove a truck for Denison in the winter and was a diamond driller in the summer. We stopped at Fort Byers long enough for a quick supper and to pick up as many loaves as I could commandeer of Romeo Dusseault's homemade bread. It was the staple of Denison's meager diet when he ate at all—he would not touch store bread—and I hoarded it in the back of the refrigerator.

We travelled mostly at night, when Denison was driving; he

preferred it. I loved it all; despite the jolting, the uncertainty, the wild antics of the leaping, rolling camper, that ride up the Ice Road remained thrilling and gorgeous, day or night. Tonight had a velvety quality; crossing lakes the scene was bucolic: broad white fields with a yellow friendly moon smiling above the horizon. I half expected to hear the hoot of a train whistle; for a moment I was crossing Ohio fields by rail on a long-ago Christmas visit to my grandparents.

Jimmy Watson had left the African Queen, 36, at the Rae Lakes. We arrived back there in the middle of the night, and the pothole where the recent accidents had occurred was alive with lights and people. Tom's truck, 34, had been freed from the ice in our absence and was facing south at the entrance to the portage, ready to leave in the morning for the long journey back to the garage. It would be hauling Denison's red Cat, coated with ice, now loaded on its trailer. The International, inside its transparent casing of ice, at least a foot thick, was much larger than life and very red, as if it were inside a huge magnifying glass. "That Cat normally weighs twelve tons but it must weigh forty now," Hughie said, a note of awe in his voice as we stood gazing at it. "It will take a week to thaw it out."

The men had been working all day and night since we left and their exhausted faces and red-rimmed eyes showed the strain. When we arrived everyone crowded into Hughie's silver caboose, a snug green room with bunks at both ends, a Coleman stove on a table in between, pots and pans hanging from the walls, a gas lamp swinging from the ceiling. Hughie's pants and hat were green too. I sat on the edge of a bunk, and the friendly mongrel dog he had brought along wagged his tail and licked my cold fingers. Watching his dog, Hughie's somber expression lightened and a smile drifted fleetingly across his face. "We picked up your Cat and dropped it back in the water six times before we got it out because the lake surface wouldn't hold, John," Hughie said quietly. "We had to keep lifting it ahead until we found ice close to shore thick enough to hold it."

The caboose door opened and Davy Lorenzen entered, proudly holding aloft an eight-pound whitefish which he had just bought for fifty cents from a passing Indian. He disappeared outside again, but returned immediately. "I put my fish in the deep-freeze," he said. "I've set it in a snowdrift with a red marker on top. I hope I'll remember to take it home when I leave." Davy sat down and lit a cigarette. "We got Tom's truck out first, John, with the cherry picker," he said. "It came out real good, at ten o'clock yesterday morning. We kept pullin' it and droppin' it like a Yo-Yo. We told Tom we ought to drop soapsuds into that water and wash it off, the way it was goin' up and down. As soon as we got Tom's truck out for good we picked the ice off with a power saw and Tom got in and drove it into the bush. We only pulled once to get the lowboy from Tom's truck out, straight backwards, but we had to use the Herman Nelson to get its wheels unfroze from the brake drums. We didn't get that TD–14 Cat of yours out, John, until three-thirty this afternoon. We had to put a cable from the front of Hughie's Cat to Thirty-six and my Diamond T truck, and chain Tom's truck to my bumper, and use all four of them together as an anchor on the shore. When we started, I was just using my Diamond T as an anchor and it rose right up in the air when we started winching! I can tell you, it was quite a job gettin' your Cat out and skiddin' it onto the lowboy! It was some load to pull from the water with all that ice on it!"

John nodded. He was perched on the edge of the opposite bunk, his long body bent over, in his customary thinking position, elbow on his knee, chin resting on his hand.

"Mukluk's old Fud isn't going to last much longer, John," Hughie said.

"I'd ruther wreck Fud on a rock than one of the big ones," John said heavily. "Leave the cherry picker here when you go, Hughie. Leave it here."

Tom departed at seven the next morning. The big International tractor sitting on top of his trailer, on 34, in daylight was a prehistoric mammoth embedded in ice. Hughie, Johnny Soldat, his young Eskimo helper, and Davy Lorenzen left right behind him, in Davy's truck. Davy was carrying the Bug, which had added a broken steering wheel to its list of ailments, and he was pulling the empty fuel tanker behind him. Just before he left, Davy dashed out and hunted through the snowbanks for the fish he had stored in one of them. Too late. Bob Burns had absentmindedly bulldozed it into oblivion. We had a fresh supply of propane gas tanks, leftovers from the trucks going back, and Tom had given us his canned food. Our cupboards sagged with them. Hughie had left his yellow Cat behind to replace John's red one.

After they had gone, I counted heads. There were five of us: Mukluk, Bob Burns, Lewis Mackenzie, Denison, myself. While we were away, Spotlight George had come along the Ice Road in the Beaver and taken Gilles back to Sarah Lake to open the kitchen and rest stop for the truckers in the caboose there. The Ice Road's regular freight run would begin as soon as we reached the Echo Bay Mine and called Fort Byers.

We started travelling north again, cautiously, slowly. Burns was "walking" the Cat, followed by Fud and 36, pulling the drags. John had regained his good humor and, superficially, some of his health: he had started eating soup, canned fruit and homemade bread, in small servings. He put a Tiajuana Brass Ensemble dance tape on the camper's recorder. "Nice day for a drive, eh?" he said. "I hated to see the Bug go back. I really need it for scouting. From now on I'd like to make twenty-five miles a day, ennaway, and we still have two hundred to go. I've already lost five days that'll cost us five thousand dollars.

The temperature had risen from forty below to a semi-tropical twenty-six below zero. John stopped every ten feet on Tuche Lake to check the depth of the ice, digging into it with a needle bar, a heavy steel rod six feet long with a three-sided spear on its lancelike tip. In most places the ice was thirty inches thick, but at a narrows between two small islands it was only fourteen. What a lovely day! Brilliant blue sky with white clouds floating overhead; small multicolored stripes on either side of the bright sun, incomplete rainbows called sun dogs. I look at my watch. Eleven o'clock. Make the most of this gorgeous day; it will be gone by three. We wandered around on the lake, looking for the portage entrance. Animal tracks everywhere and we passed the bones and guts of caribou, sprinkled in bloody array on the snow: Indian hunters had been here ahead of us on their sleds.

When we all stopped for Denison to make his noon call to the garage, Bob Burns and I got out to stretch our legs in the snow. There were tracks in every direction criss-crossing one another, and while we walked in a small circle around the vehicles Burns showed me the difference between the half-moon prints of caribou, whose shorter legs and lighter steps do not drop so far into the deep snow, and the heavy cloven hooves of the high-stepping moose, who sink way down. There were fox tracks too, small doglike prints the size of silver dollars, one directly ahead of another, and the wee dragging imprints of ptarmigan, the beautiful white partridgelike birds whose toe-marks look like a butterfly.

At lunch, Lewis Mackenzie remarked that driving on the Ice Road was far less of a strain for him than driving on a southern highway. "You can't go off in deep ditches or hit anybody around here," he said, "and there's not all that traffic." But he had bad news. The winch on 36 had broken again. Denison was resting when Lewis arrived with this depressing information. John half rose on his elbow, then lay down again and closed his eyes for a moment, opened them and said, "Well, we just can't carry all the spare parts we need. Do you remember the first year we went to Tundra, Lewis? We came out of there with one truck dragging five others that had broken down."

"Yes, and you were so sick we thought we'd be bringin' you back too, in a box," Lewis replied.

Denison got up after lunch to drive. We moved rapidly

along in the good weather, crossing several of the small un-named lakes Denison called potholes, until we arrived at Har-disty Lake, thirty miles long, one of the larger lakes in the chain. "Wish I had my Bug, the one in cold storage, here. I sure could use it," John said wistfully when we bumped from the land onto the lake. "Jimmy Magrum was my foreman when it went in, and he knows exactly where it is, but the son of a gun won't tell me. He keeps offering to split whatever we salvage if I'll go get it with him because he wants the tools and the radio. I have the rig to do it, but I just haven't the time now to go back. As long as it stays under water there won't be any oxidation—if the motor was off. Maybe we'll get it in the spring."

The Cat and 36 turned back to work on the portage we had just traversed, and Fud led us across the lake, plowing the new road. The sun spread an orange light on the drifts ahead as Billy Mukluk drove ten miles an hour through the two-foot snow blanket on the lake, stirring up a shower of flakes that encircled him in white mist. Ahead, small islands surrounded by black rocks jutted above the flat snowy surface. Our trucks were head-ing down the center of the lake towards a point between the islands, and every few feet Mukluk and John got out to check ice depths with auger and needle bar, and to consult with a map.

Denison had not reached the garage on the mobile radio at noon, so we stopped while he tried again. Whenever he used the telephone, the cab of the camper became icy cold, because he had to shut off the engine so that it would not interfere with reception. But there was no reception on Hardisty Lake, not even static. I could not help thinking about how far out of communication we were: how far from help, when the tele-phone was dead; then, how sick John was, how little he ate. Considering the physical demands of his job, and the cold, how long could he go on this way? "Does anything frighten you?" I asked. "Being sick the way you are, for instance?"

"I'm used to that," he said. "Mostly, bad ice frightens me."

The solid back of steady old Fud was right in front of us,

directly in our line of vision, clumping along like a determined old dowager, dressed in a silver caboose trimmed with a line of red fuel drums tied on her rear end. Poor old Fud. Nobody ever thinks of her except as "Poor old Fud." What a sturdy companion she is!

Fud stops.

Suddenly!

We stop.

Fud's right wheel is disappearing under the ice!

I don't believe it.

It happened so quickly. Mukluk leapt out of Fud, leaving the door swinging open. He landed on both feet on the ice, hatchet in hand, backed off several yards away, and stared at his crippled friend.

Denison was the first to speak. "See why we send the little truck first?" he said bitterly. "Now we've lost it! If you want to see things happen, stick around!"

Fud does not disappear under the ice. She lists perilously to the right, seems to sigh; one lurch, but she does not disappear. In fact, she seems to have stopped sinking.

Mukluk moves carefully around to the open door of Fud and gingerly reaches in to lift out his ice auger. Denison picks up his needle bar from the floor under our feet and we get out and meet Mukluk half way between the two trucks on the ice. "Poor old Fud," Mukluk says hoarsely, "I couldn't find a hole deep enough to bury her, John." They test the ice; four inches thick directly ahead of Fud, ten inches thick one hundred feet behind her, where the camper is standing.

In the camper Denison dispensed comfort with coffee to a silent Mukluk at the table. "Hardisty's a bad lake, Billy," he said. "It's spread all over the goddamn place. You went through at a spot where the water swirls because of the islands. You're on a rock and you've got plenty of ice around, but five feet further there isn't any, so look at it this way: we're lucky. It won't be too bad. We may lose half a day, but it could have been the big truck." He pulled on his gloves and stood up. "It's in a square hole and we can back Thirty-six up to it with the Cat on the lowboy, and use the Cat's winch to get it out."

Mukluk drove the camper back to the portage to get Lewis and Burns, to bring back 36 with the Cat. While we were waiting for them, Denison continued walking forward on Hardisty Lake, testing the ice. It was lonesome not to have immediate shelter right at hand, even though I had elected to stay on the lake while Mukluk went back with the camper. I busied myself walking around Fud, keeping a cautious distance from the forlorn half-sunken vehicle. The temperature had dropped suddenly, but it was refreshing to be outside, moving around. Mukluk returned, alone. John was kneeling on the ice, testing it. He stood up when Mukluk drove up beside him, but Mukluk looked away. Mukluk gave a great sigh. "Lewis has broken down, John," he said in his soft voice. "The clutch slips on Thirty-six. His truck can still move, but it can't pull a load."

Denison silently climbed in the camper, picked up the telephone mike, and started the familiar chant. "SX One-five-two-one-three. SX One-five-two-one-four. Do you read me?" Pause. "Over."

No radio reception. Not a sound. Nothing. There is no sound as loud as nothing when you are sitting in a truck on a lake full of bad ice in forty-below-zero weather in an absolutely empty wilderness. I didn't need any direction. I had the camper packed for travelling by the time Denison had given up trying to reach Yellowknife, Fort Byers or Hay River by telephone.

We left Fud in her icy bed in the frosty chill of Hardisty Lake and drove back to the portage. "Try to get Thirty-six back to the garage under its own steam, Lewis," Denison said when we drove up beside the big red truck. "If you're too long getting back, we'll come looking."

We shot off down the partly finished Ice Road, leaving Lewis, and Burns with him, in 36 far behind, taking Mukluk with us. We passed several Indians in the carry-alls of their sleds, who were sound asleep until Denison drew up right behind them and raced the camper motor in their ears. Once, through the trees, I spotted the pointed canvas tent of an Indian out caribou hunting. By four we were at Sarah Lake, and Denison pulled up to the little caboose, where smoke was curling from a small pipe in the roof. Gilles had seen us coming on the lake, and was standing at the door to greet us. We were his first guests. He brought out T-bone steaks, cooked them to perfection, and served them up with canned peas and apricots. Even Denison ate a little; Gilles was a really good cook. When we started off again in the camper it was after dark. Time had become such a blur in my mind that I thought it was the middle of the evening. I glanced at my watch.

Five o'clock. A black mink scampered across the road in the beam of our headlamps, and later the lights exposed a huge grey wolf of storybook ferocity lurking at the side of the road: shining green eyes, face grey as putty, long pointed open jaw and huge jagged teeth. He vanished so quickly that I might have thought I was dreaming if Denison hadn't pointed. The trees made long dark shadows on the white snow, and during the night we passed many Indians out hunting. The eyes of their dogs were visible long before we saw the sleds or men; little double pairs of luminous green lights moving through the blackness in a curved, symmetrical line.

For a while I dozed, waking at the sudden jolt when we dropped from land to lake and at the whining of gears when we climbed back on the land. On ice, travel was smooth and the steady whirr of heavy turning wheels a pleasant melody. Cold and through-your-clothes-cold on the lakes, where there was no blanket of snow-covered trees. "When someone else is driving and I'm sleeping back in the bunk where I can't see, I can wake any time and know from the way the truck is riding exactly where I am," John said. "It feels just enough different on each portage."

We travelled so fast and the journey was so rough, that

when I opened the door of the camper in the garage at Fort Byers all I could see at first were cans of food all over the floor and benches. The bottoms of the overhead cupboards in the living-room area had fallen through on the trip down, and I had to pick up the cans and stack them on the bench before I could make up my bed and get into it.

I had a new neighbor in the garage: Denison's huge Cat, the TD-14, defrosting on top of 34's lowboy trailer that Tom had hauled in only hours before us. A great block of red iron and grey canvas, covered with tons and tons of foot-thick ice. I fell asleep to the sound of water dripping on the garage floor; not the dripping sound of a faucet, but a waterfall, from a new kind of mountain.

Lewis arrived shortly after dawn, exhausted, and went straight to bed. He had driven in 36 all night without a clutch over that dangerous, rough, half-packed-down Ice Road, ten miles an hour, bobtailing—the truckers' expression for driving the cab of a truck without its trailer. Hughie's Cat had been left : ʰe protection of the trees on the portage between Séguin and Hardisty lakes, and for all anyone knew, poor old Fud might by this time be in watery "cold storage" at the bottom of Hardisty. There was no caboose on 36, so both Lewis and Burns had been living with Mukluk in Fud before the disaster; Lewis dropped Burns off to stay at the caboose on Sarah Lake, with Gilles, until construction of the Ice Road was resumed. Temporarily, we were out of business.

Chapter Seven

THIRD TRIP IN: TUNDRA

When Denison drove into Yellowknife right after breakfast to organize his rescue operations for Fud, I went with him. I had a schedule of my own that left no time, nor was I in the mood for the luxuries of bathing, laundry, or any hilarious review of current disasters. Denison was totally preoccupied with rescue logistics, and I found his silence relaxing. "What's the earliest you'd be leaving Yellowknife?" I asked, breaking into the quiet, as we drove down Franklin Avenue.

"Not before three," he said.

"I'd like to talk to people who were with you when you first started building ice roads," I said, "but I don't want to keep you waiting."

"Don't worry about that," he said. "I wouldn't wait."

"Oh," I said.

He seemed to feel a need for a fuller explanation. "I'd have to go," he said. "Sorry about that."

"Would two o'clock be absolutely safe?" I asked.

"Yup," he said.

We parked at the freight office in the yard between two of the huge red Byers trailer vans that were unloading Yellowknife's groceries and other deliveries after their regular thousand-mile haul from Edmonton. I got out of the camper before Denison had turned the motor off, and walked back towards Franklin Avenue. I heard Denison's voice and I turned around. He had his head out the camper window and he called after me, "Go see Stu Demelt, Joe Major and Hughie Parnall."

It was eight-thirty in the morning. I walked down a side street to the neat little building that was the office of Norm Byrne, for whose family John Denison first started building ice roads to their mines around Yellowknife: to Rayrock, the uranium mine whose picturesque skeleton we passed on the Ice Road; to the two small gold mines now closed, Discovery, sixty miles north of town, and Tundra, almost two hundred miles further northeast on the same road into the Barrens, where no man had ever driven a truck before.

Although I came in hesitantly, because I knew Mr. Byrne had been quite ill, he welcomed me cordially. His secretary brought me a cup of coffee, and while I was drinking it Byrne, a severe-looking man with glasses whom I had been told was very formal and businesslike, surprised me by relaxing into reminiscence. "I've known John since the mid-forties when he was one of three members of the Mounted Police stationed in Yellowknife," he said. "He was about thirty then, two hundred and forty pounds, really outstanding in appearance. When he got out of the R.C.M.P. in nineteen forty-seven he came into my office looking for work. We did everything on a handshake, without a contract. John proved you can go anywhere in a truck. To tell you the truth, he was the only man in this country who would have taken on such an assignment. He's an awful man for work, never idle, and it *is* hard work! If he didn't have the good will of every man who works for him he would never be able to drive those fellows the way he does to operate in the places he does. We opened Rayrock in the early fifties and closed it in nineteen fifty-nine. Rayrock probably had the highest-grade uranium in Canada, but it went into the side of a hill and there wasn't much of it. We had to end with half our contract to supply the government with uranium unfulfilled, so we sold the rest of the contract to another very lively mine which produces still under the Rayrock name." I must have looked puzzled, for he added, "Mining companies don't die, they just go pushing on looking for other things. We never had a summer road to Discovery. The Cat trains broke the first roads there, but John introduced the truck, driving it straight from Edmonton to the mine. We couldn't have had a mine at Tundra without John's road, in no way. You have to have heavy machinery to develop a mine, and you couldn't fly that stuff in. To have kept Tundra supplied by air with oil would have required ten Hercules freight planes flying twenty-four hours a day for a month or so every year. Impossible! Ice roads are still the quickest, easiest and cheapest way of opening a mine, ten times cheaper than any other way of doing it, and Tundra could become viable again very quickly.

"Transportation costs are what makes the difference between mining in the north and in the south," he went on. "The air strip at Tundra was four miles from the mine, but our trucks could load lumber we purchased in Vancouver to build camps and plant buildings and drive it two thousand miles directly to the building site. Then John hauled the houses from Rayrock to Discovery, and the big machinery from Rayrock—the mill, the plant, the compressors, the engines—right up through that bush country, on the Barrens, and in to Tundra. Really tough going, because he had to plow out the roads, and in the Barrens the winds are so terrible that roads disappear a half-hour after you make them. Sometimes the trucks would arrive with their loads so frozen that they would have to remain in Tundra's heated garages for three days to thaw out."

Byrne was looking tired, so I stood up to leave. "Glad you stopped in," he said. He got up and walked me to the door. "By the way, has John ever told you about the time he drove an oil truck into Tundra himself?" I said no, and Byrne laughed. "I don't suppose he'll ever live it down," he said. "Ask him about it."

"I certainly will," I said.

It was still early, only nine-fifteen. My next stop was at the Town Garage to see Stu Demelt, who scouted the first Ice Road for Denison to Echo Bay. His current job involved maintenance of the city's heavy-duty vehicles, which, I could see at a glance around the garage, included types that were as familiar to me now as old friends: Cats and snowplows. Demelt, a huge, hulking figure with a lantern jaw and countenance as rugged and full of hills and crevices as the terrain he encountered on the Ice Road, at first was reluctant to talk to me. I told him I had only this one day so far as I knew before I vanished again into the bush on the road to Port Radium, and that I was trying to gain perspective on what I was observing. He motioned me to a seat in his small office and sat down heavily in a chair by the desk.

"The first trip to Echo Bay was a one-trip operation to haul out big generating units from Eldorado Mine," he said. He leaned forward, tense, his big body pressed against the desk. "I think the company lost about thirty-five thousand dollars on that trip because it cost so much more to go in than John had figgered on. It took six weeks altogether. One thing that cost, there was so much snow and we had to have aircraft every three days. Half the thanks has to go to Chuck McAvoy on the scouting for givin' me such a wonderful look at the route from low altitude, to find a way of gettin' through." He laughed. "Once for a joke he dropped me to four feet on Great Bear Lake and said, 'Shove in a needle bar and see wot's wot with the ice!' If it hadn't been for Chuck, the scoutin' would have been twice the trouble."

"When you are up in that plane, what are you looking for?" I asked.

"On a lake, you look for as much open area as you can find and keep away from the current which is created in a narrows; any narrows in any big lake creates water movement which creates bad ice," he replied. "On a portage you look for as smooth goin' as possible, one with light timber, and keep away from rocks and muskeg and big boggy bumps."

He shifted his weight and looked at me. "You haven't got to Hottah yet, the last big lake before Great Bear, but that's where the highboy with the Cat on its back went through the overflow," he said. "It started to go to the bottom, so I got on that Cat and drove it off the trailer and somehow we managed to pull the truck out before it went under." He started drawing squares and circles on an old envelope while he talked. "When we loaded up the trucks at Echo Bay for the return trip, the loads were so tremenjous that everyone said the ice wouldn't hold. Each man was responsible for the man behind him. He couldn't leave the ice without he could sight the guy behind so nobody got left. No one at that time had ever run loads as heavy as thirty to thirty-five ton on heavy Kenworthy trucks over ice. Goin' back across Hardisty, the ice started to break from the heavy loads. We unloaded the Cat, which had already broken an axle on the highboy that was carryin' it, and we plowed a new road outside the broken ice. At Hislop Lake, where the Indian village is, going in to Echo Bay we had scouted in a hurry and come up on the bad side. If we stopped to correct this on our way out we figgered we'd lose another day, so we just sweated it out, countin' the trucks when they finally made it across, with the ten- and twelve-foot-high Diesel motors. On that trip back, I would start at the front of the convoy and work my way to the rear, lookin' for trouble, and at night I would go to bed worryin', will we break through the ice or roll over? I would take the trip ten times in my mind 'afore I could get to sleep."

He began to fill in the squares and circles he had been drawing with criss-cross pencil marks. "If we had known that our road was goin' to develop into a reg'lar route, I would have spent more time scoutin' and we would have done better," he continued. "That road had a lot of bearin' on the Echo Bay Mine comin' in the next year: the cuts were all there and the route marked when it started production. Before we left, I bought maps and checked out a route with the most water and the least bad ice, and I avoided Rae Lakes as much as possible. I'm afeared of islands and narrows and runnin' rivers, where the ice is so often thin. I don't have a fear of ice but I have a turrible respect for it and on that first trip I was never relaxed. My father was a trapper and trader around Yellowknife since 1926 and I've trapped around here since I was nine, so I'm used to all these conditions and have had years of experience testin' ice. You can be four feet from open water and on good ice, and you can walk ahead twenty feet and find only two inches or run out of ice altogether."

"Do you often go on the Echo Bay Road now?" I inquired.

Demelt looked at me steadily for about a minute before he answered. "I never been on it since then and I don't miss it neither," he said. "It was a real interestin' experience but while you are on that road, you're never home free."

I said hastily, "I heard you also scouted the road to Tundra in the Barrens, before you ever went near Echo Bay."

Demelt had started to rise, but he sat down again. "That's right," he said, "and everythin' that gives you trouble on the Echo Bay Road is double trouble in the Barrens. There were just three of us who did the scoutin' for Tundra. We had a Bombardier for goin' ahead, a Cat to do the work and a snowplow to open the road, and John in town, comin' out to check with us once't in a while to see that we hadn't dropped through the ice without mentionin' it. The reg'lar trucks came later. It was routine as long as we was going through timberland, but out in the Barrens was somethin' else. The lakes in the Barrens had real shallow edges with all kinds of rocks that smashed the plow so we had to rebuild it there. Then we got lost in a blizzard and had to sit it out overnight in the open on MacKay Lake, which is the big lake before Tundra, and when the weather cleared we had to cross it and had an *awful* time. Tundra is on the northwest side of the lake, all uphill, with snow drifts ten and twelve foot deep that had to be 'dozed out and packed. The worst thing was the cold and the wind, which created problems you never heard of. You'd have a good wide road on the lakes and twenty minutes later, no road at all, and if there was a storm you allus had to start all over. The snow would be frozen into four-foot-high ridges along the sides of the road, and then fresh snow would fall inside the ridges and be trapped there and be a lot harder to plow out than if we just started a road in a fresh place. We'd be spread a mile wide with roads and unless it was a big lake we'd run out of space and land up on the rocks. Eventually you couldn't go any place. In the Barrens the snow is so fine that if you had a match hole or a nail hole in a tent you'd have a snowdrift across the whole tent to the height of the hole. The snow went right through the holes in the floor of the truck, and built up on the insides of the walls on the floor and on your mitts, so every hour or so you had to stop, shake your hands and clean the snow out of the cab." He stopped and scratched the top of his head.

"Your whole operation depended on your heat, and if your motor stopped you just had to have a propane heater or a Herman Nelson to keep warm so you could make repairs," he added. "In the bush you can make a fire and be comfortable, but any time you are in the Barrens, one mistake can be your last. When we finally got to Tundra the first time with all the trucks, the mine manager came to the door and took our picture. 'I want to get a snap of you,' he said, 'because you'll never be able to keep comin.' But we did."

I looked around the garage. "This seems awfully quiet by comparison," I said. "Don't you miss the excitement?"

"Miss it?" He looked surprised. "I don't miss it a bit!" he said, "I don't like bein' a guinea pig. I began to wonder whether my reflexes were goin' to slow down and whether I was goin' to be able to jump far enough or if the next time across I would go through the ice."

I got up to go. Demelt held up his hand and I waited. "I'll tell you somethin'," he said. "Everyone said we couldn't do Tundra or Bear Lake and we proved that we could. If I were offered a chance't to build that road to Coppermine John's thinkin' of doin', provin' we could do somethin' again that all the people say can't be done, I'd jump at it."

When I left Stu Demelt at ten-thirty, I took a cab to the Flats at the edge of the Old Town, where Demelt said I would find Joe Major and Hughie Parnall in Major's welding shop. At the end of a lane, I let myself through a wire gate, threading my way past machinery and vehicles in the yard, and entered a small building. All work stopped in the shop with my arrival, the only comforting sound in my ears the sizzle of a welding torch that was sending out sparks because its operator, bent over a piece of iron, had not seen or heard me come in. A middle-aged, squarely heavy man with grey-flecked black curling hair and a red face stepped forward, scrutinizing me with narrowed eyes.

"I'm looking for Joe Major," I said hesitantly.

"That's me," he said in a gravelly blustery voice. And waited.

"I'm travelling with the men building the Ice Road to Echo Bay this year," I began timidly, and I saw his eyebrows arch. "I thought maybe you and Mr. Parnall . . . if he's here . . . would tell me about that first trip . . . maybe I'd understand better what's going on now if . . ." My voice trailed off under the weight of that direct scrutiny. Mr. Major looked me up and down. He said, "I haven't time right now. I'm very busy."

"This is my only chance to talk to you, because I have to go right back," I said quickly. "I came in this morning with John Denison, and he suggested I see you." At Denison's name, Joe Major hesitated, then brusquely nodded his head in the direction of a little room at the back. He went up to the welder and tapped him on the shoulder. The welder, who proved to be Hughie Parnall, followed Joe Major into the office, and we all sat down, Major at a battered desk with an old brown dog at his feet. Parnall was a small, bent-over sprite, with very blue eyes and red hair.

"You first," Joe Major said curtly to Parnall.

Parnall began hesitantly. "When I met John, he had just got out of the R.C.M.P. and was freighting on a barge," he said. "He was allus a good-natured fella, but bullheaded, because when he decides to do somethin' he's going to do it. When I first knew him in forty-seven he had a barge on Marian Lake, and he got stuck. In some places it's a lot too deep to walk, but that didn't bother Big John. He bailed out and walked into the lake enna-way and kept walkin'—most of the way through shallow water —right into Fort Rae. That's ten or twelve mile away and the nearest settlement. To get back though, to what you want to know. I'm a mechanic, carryin' my toolbox all the time, and I worked in Edmonton for Byers, and that's where I built the first snowplow for John. We remodelled a farm tractor plow to John's design, and I set it up on an old truck and drove it to Tundra that first time. You wouldn't think of pullin' out of town with that old equipment now, but John had no choice. That's all the trucks he could get with the kind of money he had. He just had to be stupid and determined and damned good to do what he did. That first time to Tundra there were some pretty rough places, but I think it was worth the effort. I really think it was. They couldn't have kept that mine going without us." He was speaking so softly, I had to bend over to hear him.

"The Barrens are just wild, virgin country, with no markings," Joe Major interrupted in his gruff voice. He spoke in an odd, jerky way, coming down hard on each word. "Normal weather in the Barrens is high wind," he said, "but on the Tundra run, in a blizzard we couldn't see to drive and for two or three days we would sit on MacKay Lake, which was the bad one. All bundled together in our trucks. Waitin' for the weather to clear. A Barrens Land blizzard! High winds, and swirling snow, and that's *it*. Keep the trucks running and hope to God they won't stop. Diesels stop when the fuel filters plug up and the gas trucks just plain freeze. Wot's more, if you sit there long enough, you run out of fuel. On the regular Tundra run, I once upset my pickup on a lake forty or fifty miles beyond Discovery Mine. I was all by myself, battery smashed, no motor running, and the temperature minus forty. So I walked back."

"You *what?*" I exclaimed. I was remembering the winds on the lakes, the whiteouts, the snow, the stupefying cold. Above all, the cold.

Joe looked at me, eyebrows raised. "I had no choice," he said. "I was picked up after thirty miles, if I remember rightly. One of the tanker drivers picked me up."

"How was it, building the first road to Echo Bay?" I asked.

Hughie raised his head. "I was with Stu Demelt when he scouted Echo Bay. Everything went all right until we got to Sarah Lake. Stu was on the Cat ahead, pullin' the caboose we lived in, and I stopped to gas up my plow truck with the fuel truck, which was Number Eleven, right behind me. I started goin' ahead again, plowin' heavy snow, and we had a sudden whiteout. I couldn't see ennathing in my mirror so I stopped, and as soon as I stopped there was this big crash. Number Eleven had been followin' right behind me but because of the whiteout I couldn't see it and the driver couldn't see me. His truck hit the timbers on my trailer and *they* hit me right in the back, pushed my whole cab in. I was jammed under the steering wheel and couldn't get out even after they got my door open until they jacked things around. I knew I was hurt, and John got a plane and flew me back to town. I had one or two cracked ribs and that was the end of the Ice Road for me that winter."

"I did the Bear Lake run," Joe Major cut in eagerly. He had been reliving events as Hughie spoke. "I was a mechanic-welder then for Byers, in a cold dark shed here in town. It was *so* small there wasn't no room for nothin', not even one truck. The nose of a truck would just go in and the back end stuck out the door. The wages were damned cheap too. I never drove a truck cross-country, but when I hired on with old John, I started drivin' a plow truck. No highway stuff, but when Hughie got hurt, I flew out with John and lived with Demelt in his Bug for a few days while I fixed his Cat, which had broke down, and then the truck that hit Hughie, which was all smashed up. After that, I was told to overhaul *all* the equipment, which I did. Stu's Bug, where we stayed, was an early-model Bombardier with a plywood body and doors that didn't close too well; a boy could throw a cat through a door any time it was closed. I let the engine run and lived off the heater in that Bug, just got in every night and pulled my eiderdown up the best way I knew how, among the gas drums, toolboxes, grease and pails and God knows wot else inside. After several days of this I said to Demelt, 'Well, I'm ready to go back to town now.' "

Joe Major sat back and laughed. "Stu said, 'Like hell you are, get in the plow and drive,' so I proceeded to head for Echo Bay, with Demelt in the lead and the rest of us behind. I lived in relative comfort from then on in the caboose, which was warm, and I had a good bed to lay on. We carried frozen meats that we fixed in a hurry and we all took turns cookin'. As I recall, Demelt made a pretty fair batch of flapjacks." He puffed on his cigarette, sitting on the edge of his chair in his excitement.

"We generally knew from a map where we were goin' and if a place looked good to drive across for a portage, we'd just go," he continued. "When Denison was along he wouldn't bother waitin' for daylight; he'd just start lookin' for the portage in the dark, drive drive drive, half the night, until we were so bloody tired we'd make camp, and waste time gettin' goin' in the morning. Demelt had the same idea, until we broke him of it. We made him shut down at dusk and have a good sleep, and then there was time to service the equipment in the morning and start drivin'. Breakfast was over by six, and we were on the road. The whole thing took longer than anticipated, a damned good six weeks, and we had a lot of tire trouble. At one point, all the trucks were runnin' on singles, and little trees 'dozed off in a new portage punctured those. We repaired the tires as best we could and when we got as far as Hottah Lake, before Great Bear, a new bunch of tires was flown in. After the new rubber, things went pretty good."

Joe Major was still sitting on the edge of the chair, nervously waving his cigarette; Hughie was leaning forward, taking in every word, watching Joe Major's face. "At the north end on Hottah Lake I was plowin' and I noticed there was ground water flyin' off the plow, which meant bad ice," Joe went on. "I tried to flag Demelt but he didn't see me. The Cat was tied down on the back of Number Eleven, and before we knew it, Number Eleven's highboy broke through, close to shore, and water was up over the tracks of the Cat. Well, there was only one thing to do. The engine was stickin' out above water and still runnin', so we undid the hook that held the Cat to the highboy, and Demelt sat down on the seat of that Cat and drove it off the highboy, with ice on either side of him. Then we ran a cable back and pulled the highboy onto the shore and dried everything out." He shook another cigarette from the package and lit it. "Everybody was takin' chances every day.

"After we dried old Demelt out, our next big thing was the portage between Yen and Gunbarrel lakes," Major said. "That was the worst, very steep, with huge boulders. Demelt dropped a track on the Cat at Gunbarrel and then he lost a sprocket that drove the Cat. Until we got another sprocket the Cat would only steer to one side, so Demelt had to make circle after circle to get that goddamned machine pointed in the right direction. Repairin' the Cat was a fair undertaking, with temperatures forty, fifty below and no parachute for protection, although we did have crowbars and chains and a come-along, which is a small winch. Gunbarrel was certainly the meanest place in the whole goddamned works, it was so steep, so rough." He shifted around in his chair. "You'll see for yourself, when you get there," he said.

"Once't we got on Great Bear Lake the sailin' was pretty good," he added, "although the truck I was drivin' threw a rod. We limped into camp at Echo Bay, coaxin' that truck along and finally pulled it up on shore. One of the guys at the mine met us. We had somethin' to eat. The trip was over." He stopped abruptly.

He sat with his hands on his knees, absentmindedly patting his dog. "I've been thinkin' about John's role," he added. "He was the figurehead, the manager. It was his plan, his idea, and he was lookin' after everybody movin'. He was quite sure he could haul that stuff back from Echo Bay with a truck and he damned well proved it could be done." He paused. "With modern equipment, it might not have been so heartbreakin' . . . well, heartscarin', but with the equipment he had he done extremely well. He had fellows like Parnall here and Demelt and myself, and well, he had foolish damn determination, and that was it. Transport is the big tie-up everywhere, and Christ, an ice road is simple, eh? Eventually, airplanes will haul just as much as a truck a hell of a lot faster, but a winter road is very important to haul equipment at a marginal rate. Even Denison doesn't have enough money to get me to go on a trip like that again," he said firmly. "I couldn't, although the experience was worth it." He stood up. "We had no choice at the time. Well, in a lifetime, a man always pulls off somethin', some caper," he said abruptly. He nodded to me, a quick sharp bob of his head, walked out to his shop and picked up the tools he had dropped when I came in. Parnall gave me a quick nod too, and ducked out the door and over to his work bench.

I left, walking slowly to Franklin Avenue. I was good and tired, and not very far in the Old Town from Jim and June Magrum, who lived in the house next to Sam Otto and his museum. This might be my only opportunity to see them.

Jim Magrum thinks of himself as a trapper, but he has made enough money claim-staking to buy himself a modern one-story house with a stone fireplace, handcarved furniture from Vancouver in the living room, a car and a couple of the small motorcycle-type vehicles with tracks and skis called Skidoos. When I came in both Magrums were sitting at the table, finishing lunch, and I joined them for a cup of coffee. None of the six Magrum children were at home, but an Eskimo family from Coppermine who had dropped by to say hello a month before and were still camped in the living room, wandered in from time to time, to heat a baby bottle or prepare food on the stove.

I gave the Magrums the latest Echo Bay Ice Road news. Magrum, a husky man of medium height a little younger than Denison, laughed when I told him about the continuing calamities. Speaking in his slow drawl, he said, "John'll take a chance't where other men won't. He'll push things through when nobody else can, and do it hisself if somebody won't do it for him. If he had a crew of all John Denisons he wouldn't have to worry."

"John feels pretty much the same about you," I said. "He told me you were one of the people he couldn't get along without in this country. He said you have a real knack for finding your way around on the portages, especially at night."

"Once I've been there, I remember," Jim replied. "I spent a couple of winters on the Cat trains, scoutin' for them. John took the freight-hauling business away from the Cat trains because it took them a month to haul a hundred tons of freight to Echo Bay that you can do in twenty-four hours with trucks, and some of the old portages I can remember, some I can't. You try and follow a map as best you can, but when we were children we *had* to remember, when we had no maps, because if you didn't remember you wouldn't find your way back, eh? Maybe there's a big rock some place that has a funny shape to it, or a hill, or a lake or a bush. But if I were to walk five blocks in Edmonton, I'd be lost. When you are looking for the best portage for a truck to go through you try to find the levellest ground, that's all.

"You've got to remember that I've been up here trappin' most of my life," he continued. "A white man has to have been up here before nineteen thirty-eight to be able to get a trapper's license, and there aren't too many of us left. My children can have the same privilege unless the regulations change. I mixed up my learning between my father, Eskimos and Indians—Indians mostly. My father was a farmer in Saskatchewan, where I was born, and he had always hunted and trapped. He got the northern urge and brought us three young-uns, my brothers and myself, with him. We trapped in the Barrens a long time at a place called Courageous Lake, a couple of hundred miles northeast of Yellowknife and then I got married and couldn't make enough money trappin' for six children. That's how I started freighting out of Yellowknife to different mines with Cats; and I've done a bit of construction and worked for John, and done some claim-staking too."

I said I had heard he had had a bit of luck, claim-staking.

"I was just lucky to get in with the right person at the right time," Jim said. "A lot of oldtimers are around here all their lives and only the odd one ever makes it. What happened, I was dickering with a promoter about some sleighs I had hauled to his camp and I said, 'Do you know any open ground in this country?' and he pulled out a map and showed me where to go.

"Not anybody can do staking," Jim explained. "You've got to map it all out before you start, provided nobody else is in there; otherwise you have to map as you go. Some guys landed in the middle of some land already staked and had to walk ten claims in either direction, but I was lucky—I knew where I was going. Two summers ago, though, a fellow on a boat on Great Slave Lake saw some of our rock samples and sneaked in, in the middle of the night and did some staking we had figured on doing ourselves." His voice got very soft. "I couldn't do anything about it outside of giving him a whippin'," he said. "And maybe I'm goin' to."

He absentmindedly rubbed his back. "Those darn heavy pickets, they're the worst thing," he said.

Jim's wife, June, had been moving around the kitchen making more coffee. She came back and sat down. She was a good-looking, dark-haired woman in her forties, with an easy laugh and a forceful manner, and while she poured a cup of coffee for each of us, she said, "I loved it, in the Barrens. We spent four winters out there when Jim went back to trappin' for white fox and I brought four of our boys to the Barrens, two right after they were born."

Jim laughed. "The first meat they ever eat was dried wolf meat. It's good. When the oldest was a baby, I gave him what I thought was dried caribou, and it turned out to be wolf."

"I liked it out there," June said dreamily. "You got lots of time to yourself. I'll go back any time, after the kids are grown. While they're going to school it's a long time to stay away from them."

"We've got camps all over the Barrens," Jim said, "but I just couldn't make enough money, trappin'. I don't know what's so fascinating about trappin', but it just gets in your blood." He suddenly turned to me and said, "I'll bet you never seen a wolf-paw jacket." I said I never had, and June disappeared and came back with her arms full of fur jackets. She put them on, one at a time, and turned around slowly, to give me a style show; they were made of soft, smooth short fur, with an off-white cast that looked not unlike ermine. "Each of them has a hundred-and-sixty-five hind paws of wolves in 'em," Magrum said. "Hell, the Queen of England couldn't buy these furs!" After June had put on the last of the wolf-paw jackets, she disappeared again and came back wearing a stunning short red-fox jacket. Then she and Jim stood side by side, modelling fringed chamois-colored moose-hide jackets. June said that her neighbour, Myrtle Otto, had an even bigger fur wardrobe; three cocktail collars and three stoles, of white, blue and cross fox, a full-length wolf-paw jacket, a three-quarter lynx coat, a Barren Lands squirrel parka, and a rare white-caribou parka.

"Did any of your children ever get sick when you were out in the Barrens?" I asked. "I was wondering what you'd do if they got sick."

"That happened," June said, looking serious. She turned to Jim, and waited expectantly.

Magrum went and got a can of beer. "The main thing was, we had a two-way radio and it wouldn't work," he began, opening the can and taking a long swallow. "There was her and I and my old man and two little kids, my youngest, who were then two and one. The other ones were in school in town, staying in a hostel. We were trappin' white fox in the Barrens to sell for auction. This young guy got sick and we thought it was appendicitis. We tried to get through on the radio for two days, and then I decided one night I'd better take off to get a plane and get him to hospital. It was June twenty-first, which is all day for twenty-four hours, ennaway, but there was still ice floating on the big lakes. I had to pack a rubber raft with me and blow it up every time I wanted to use it, and that took more energy than walkin'. I was just thinkin' about the extra weight, packin' it, but I didn't realize that blowin' takes so much out of a guy. You wouldn't blow up a raft to go twenty feet, though. A lot of these little creeks were wide open at that time, and I had to wade in up to my waist. I would fall down and once't I was swept away, and just managed a few strokes, to grab the other shore. Well, I had a fifty-pound pack, and what I ate mostly was this here Pablum baby food. I would pour cold water and lots of honey on that, you get lots of energy that way, but the last five miles my feet gave out, right in the arches. I guess there wasn't enough lubrication in the joints there. I wasn't tired, my feet just played out on me. I walked forty-two hours nonstop, I didn't stop to sleep or get warm, from our trappin' camp to Tundra Mine, and the minute I got there I got on the radio and phoned town for a plane to come out. Two hours later the plane had picked up the kid and her and the baby and the old man and then it stopped at Tundra and picked me up too. When we got to town, and she wheeled this little guy into the hospital, it turned out it wasn't appendicitis, but some stomach infection. After I got home my feet swoll up and I didn't walk for two weeks. And that's all there is to it."

"How many miles did you walk, nonstop?" I asked.

"We measured it out afterwards," Magrum said. "It was a hundred and twenty miles." He took another swig of beer.

"Did you ever go through the ice?" I asked. Magrum scratched his head.

"One time on a Cat when they were working on the Snare River power dam near Rayrock, and needed two Cats to build the power line," Magrum said. He got himself another can of beer, opened it, and took a deep swallow. "It was before Christmas and the ice was thin," he said. "There was no road from the Indian settlement at Fort Rae to the Hydro at Snare River, and there was one lake, Russell Lake, I had to cross to get there. I tested the ice, which was fourteen inches, with a dog team, and we figured there was enough ice, ennaway, for the Cat, if I stood on the runnin' board. I figured, I'm pretty fast, and if the Cat goes down I can allus jump. But I was under water before I knew what had happened, and you can't get away from a Cat. When somethin' makes a hole in the water like a Cat does, it creates a suction that pulls you right under, and there's no use fightin'. A guy better sit still and go with her instead of strugglin'. Once she stops fallin', the displaced water pushes up and then you'll boil up with it. It's just a long time to hold your breath, forty feet to go down, and a long ways back up, and you don't have time to take a long deep breath before you're gone under. Well then, after I come up, I caught hold of the sides of the ice at the hole, pulled myself up, and crawled out. I had the smaller Cat behind with a sleigh that carried my grub, tent and fuel. It was colder changin' clothes on that Cat right in the middle of the lake than bein' under water! When I got back to Fort Rae, the priest met me at the Hudson's Bay store and said he had heard what happened to me. He told me he had said a prayer for me the night before, and I said, 'That must have been what saved me.' He took me to the rectory then, and brought out a bottle fifty years old, covered with dust. I said I wouldn't drink alone so he had one too. The next day we went across with the small Cat twenty feet to the side of where the other went down, and delivered it to the Hydro. They were disappointed because we didn't have the two Cats. So a couple of days later we went back and dropped a cable down with a big grappling hook and pulled the Cat that got wet back up through the ice. And that's the end of the story."

"Denison would certainly like to get that Bombardier of his up off the bottom of Hardisty Lake," I said. "Don't you trust him?"

Magrum grinned, and June rolled her eyes. "That Bug is still there and nobody knows where it is but me," Jim said. "It'd be pretty hard to meet a nicer guy than John. I don't know where you'd meet one, and he's allus paid me as much as he can afford, but I want salvage rights on the tools and radio from that Bug. I tried to get it one summer with Lewis, but we didn't have the right riggin'. So I'll wait until John stops hemmin' and hawin' and is good and ready. Then we'll split it. I told John, 'You can see it from the air,' but I sure as hell won't tell him where it is!"

I worried about getting back to Denison's office on time so I was there half an hour early, at one-thirty. Right after me, John came in, looking very cheerful. Everything was arranged for Fud's rescue.

"I feel so much better, I'm actually hungry for a change,"

Denison said. "Come on, I'll buy you a Chinese lunch at the Gold Range Hotel. I like to give them my business because they give me theirs. I do their freighting. Besides, the food is *real* good."

Over Chinese chicken with oranges, I told John how I'd spent my day. "Norm Byrne said to be sure and ask about the time you drove an oil truck to Tundra," I said.

Denison made a face. "Jeez, I guess nobody's goin' to let me forget that one," he said. "Well, Billy Mukluk was supposed to drive a tanker with oil to Tundra and at the last minute he had to go back to Edmonton, so I thought I might as well drive the truck out there myself and see what the men were doing. I drove it into the garage when I got to Tundra mine, and left it to be unloaded and went up and had myself a good sleep. So when I was ready to leave, I asked everyone, 'Are you sure it's been unloaded?' 'Dry as a bone,' they said, all of them. On the way home, I went off the road in one place, and I must have been really stupid and sleepy, because I noticed oil on the snow and thought, 'How come?' and in another place, I couldn't get the truck up the hill, and I said to the guy who was with me, 'You drive this stupid truck up the hill,' and when I got back to town I said to Joe Major, who was working for us, 'Dolly it off, the truck isn't runnin' right,' and one of the fellows said, 'Are you loaded already?' and I said, 'No.' Well, then I found that instead of being unloaded at Tundra I had brought back the whole load, five thousand gallons of oil. The oil was running out the top, there was so much of it, and they had to take it all back to Tundra the next day." He tapped his head with his index finger.

"The trips to Tundra were real tough in those days," he said. "Every day was a bad day. I'm not a driver, that's not my job. I'm the organizer, but that first year I drove the snowplow truck all winter. That road was so goddam rough, and had so many rocks. It was a lot tougher than this road we're building to Echo Bay, about twice as hard. The Barrens are treeless, rocky, flat, windy, really miserable and terrible. Jack Boulding, the manager of Tundra, said to me, 'How come you bring trucks in when I can't keep a road open for three miles to my airport here with two Cats and two four-wheel-drive trucks?"

"What about that?" I asked.

He shrugged, and said matter of factly, "The job was there, so give it a try. I'm allus more interested in the job than the money but my partners aren't. It looked as if it was possible to do it, so I never thought of the negative side. I think about the job and about the cheapest way to compete, and bring it up to a reasonable price, what the traffic will bear. The guys in the office figure out reasons then why it can't be done, but I allus think about how it *can* be done. I had no knowledge of ice roads at that time, but I lived in Dawson Creek, British Columbia, from nineteen fifty-one to fifty-nine, and I hauled a lot of pipeline. I found out you could take a truck any place you could take a Cat, even if you had to tow the truck uphill sometimes. When I went back north again in nineteen fifty-nine they had these houses to move out of Rayrock to Discovery. I figured if a Cat can go to those mines a truck can too, so we did. The way I started freighting for the Byrne mines, they had a mill for Discovery Mine on a barge, and dynamite or some goddam thing on the barge blew up and sank the barge, and they lost the whole mill. They bought another mill in British Columbia, so they asked me to get it to Yellowknife for them, which we did. All I need is a demand for my services, eh? And all I'm interested in is transportation. A pile of gravel means the same to me as a pile of gold or silver, which is everything to the mine, eh? But I'm not interested in the mines, and what they are and what it takes to get them goin'. My job is just movin' freight, and that's what I get paid for."

Denison leaned back, relaxed, stretching his long legs out under the table. "If you think we have haywire equipment now, you should have seen what we started with to Tundra," he said. We *really* had a bunch of old trucks! A six-wheeler, an old tractor, maybe five or six old wrecks besides. I wouldn't try it again with the equipment I had then. It was a lot tougher than this, especially hauling a fifty-three-thousand-gallon fuel-storage tank from the old Negus gold mine in Yellowknife to Tundra. That tank was so big—twenty feet in diameter—that the current had to be cut on one of the main power lines for an hour to let us raise the wire and go under it. I deal with J. C. Byrne, Norm's brother, in Toronto, and he said to me, 'If you can haul that tank to Tundra you can keep it filled up with fuel,' so I said, 'Give me the most you can and I'll see if I can make a dollar.' We made our agreement with a handshake the way we allus do. About a thousand dollars to bring the tank and I needed the work, but do you know why we hauled it? Not for the freight from the tank itself, but for the oil to be hauled later, twenty cents a gallon, or one thousand dollars a trip. It was that road to Tundra that made me think I could make a winter road to Port Radium."

He helped himself to more rice and chicken, started to eat, shook his head and pushed his plate aside. "I don't want to eat too much at one time," he said. "I don't want to push my luck. Oh Jesus, I get sick. Sick, sick, sick. How stupid can you be?"

He picked up the check and glanced at it, then stood up. "You've just eaten a hundred pounds of freight," he said.

"How come?" I asked.

"Well, I charge the Gold Range three-fifty for a hundred pounds of freight, and that's what your lunch cost," he said, "so now I'll be hauling a hundred pounds of freight for nothin'."

Chapter Eight

FOURTH TRIP OUT:
PERSEVERANDO

We left Yellowknife at three, stopped briefly at Fort Byers and started up the Ice Road again after dark, at five in the evening. Denison checked off vehicles on his fingers as we spun along towards Marian Lake; the Bug was out for the season, so the camper would double as the scouting vehicle; Tom Berry had left several hours ahead of us to go back up the Ice Road in 34, loaded with fuel drums and hauling the old tanker; Davy Lorenzen was right behind him in his Diamond T truck, taking Mukluk back with him. Davy would also pick up Burns at Sarah Lake, the cherry picker at the Rae Lakes where it had been left, and finally Hughie's tractor, and take them all to Hardisty,

• **164**

where Fud was. Lewis Mackenzie would return in 36 as soon as the clutch was repaired, and Hughie Arden was going to fly directly to Hardisty Lake in the morning.

Denison was breezy, good-humored; he slid his favorite stereo tape, Herb Alpert's brass ensemble music, into the recorder and tapped the rhythm out with his fingers on the wheel. The Ice Road was improving with each successive trip, but it still had unexpected holes and bumps, hairpin turns, little hills and dangerously steep inclines like the one to and from the Emile River. Furthermore, the temperature had dropped the night before to forty-three below zero.

"Don't your trucks really have brakes when they are driving up and down the Ice Road?" I asked. Hard to believe.

"We don't have any brakes right now on this camper, because it's forty-five below, but I never use brakes ennaway," Denison replied.

"Brakes are nice to have, even if *you* don't use them," I said. "If you got too sick to drive, I could never get us home. I'd have to wait for someone to drive us."

John made a long, sad, mocking face at me. "If you really have to stop you could drive off the road into a deep drift," he said. "I gear down to slow up and in the plow trucks you just drop the plow blade down. You wouldn't have any trouble driving, though. It's easy. You just watch about a mile ahead, and read the signs. There's lots of signs. I can't explain, I just know they're there. Ask any of the drivers. They don't know why they slow down, but they read the signs."

"Well, what?"

"You can tell from the marks on the road when a truck has dragged its tires, and then you'll see a branch or stick that's been put by the side of the road by a driver ahead to mark the bad spot; or you know that another truck has bounced hard in a hole or over a bump, because that knocks snow off the back, which stays in the road in little drops. I know when a corner is coming because of the way the snow is piled, so I slow down long before I get to a corner or a bad place, since I have no brakes. Don't put your brakes on ennaway if you're skidding, put the gas on and straighten out. On the lake, if your truck starts swaying, step easily on the gas to come out of it, but don't stop or you'll go right into a snowbank. All you'd need is a little practice!"

"Did you worry about Lewis Mackenzie driving home in Thirty-six without a clutch?" I asked. "Do you worry about the men when they are out like that alone?"

Denison looked indignant. "Well I guess so!" he exclaimed. "I really care! It's *my* responsibility! If I don't hear from them on the radio by a certain time I'm allus worried about them. When we go and look for them we don't worry about the cost. The worst thing is, when we don't hear from them and can't fly out and find out what's the matter with them because the weather's so bad we can't see to fly. I sure had Lewis on my mind until he was home safe."

We came off Marian Lake onto the Rayrock portage, still a wild rough road, and Denison concentrated on driving. I had lost all sense of time. Nineteen hours of daily darkness made day and night and the days of the week indistinguishable, and it was even harder to keep track of events. I took out a pad and pencil to list our mishaps. We had had three catastrophes requiring trips all the way back to Fort Byers, each time from a point further up the road in its construction: the camper fire; the break through the ice of the big Cat and Tom's truck; and now Fud's fall into Hardisty Lake. Two important vehicles were out of service indefinitely: the Bug and the big Cat. There had been temporary delays like the broken clutch on 36 and Tom's crippled power steering, the accident with Fud's shack, and a string of minor repairs made on the road while we were travelling, these so numerous that I finally put the pad back in my parka pocket. Denison broke into my thoughts. "Have you noticed how smooth the road is becoming?" he asked. I took a really good look ahead into the glare of headlight that illuminated the road. Its surface was smooth as cement, with a white glaze that glistened in the light streaming from the camper headlamps.

"I like driving at night," Denison remarked. "You see holes you don't catch in the daytime unless the sun is shining. This should be a *real* good road if it freezes up right," he said. "Every time we drive it we go in a different track and pack it down a little more."

When the music stopped, Denison removed the tape from the recorder, but instead of inserting another he said, "Seems to me I've been making roads most of my life. Even when I was a boy, my father and I made lots of roads and trails."

"Where was that?" I asked.

"In British Columbia," Denison said. "I was raised there, born in the town of Vernon, on Lake Okanagan. That's really beautiful country. My dad was looking after his mother's farm then, but when I was six, he got a homestead and moved twenty-five miles away, up into the mountains. It took us all day with a horse and wagon to move up there. What about you?"

"Oh, I was born in Cleveland, Ohio, where my mother still lives—my father died there right after his eightieth birthday—and I've been writing all my life," I said. "Since I was twelve, when I began a running novel in my head that I never wrote down. I used to be thinking about that novel while I was riding around on a little horse my father had gotten for me, but I never have written a novel yet. We have a cabin in the country about thirty miles from town that I used to go to a lot with him; that seems to me like a natural forerunner of my trips north. I have one sister—no brothers—and we lived a protected life. I went to college and then to journalism school. After that I wrote a lot for newspapers and magazines, got married to a writer and had two sons who were still in grammar school when I started going North, in 1961. They're grown now and in the theatre. When I came North for the first time, to Ungava Bay in the Eastern Arctic, to attend the second meeting of the first Eskimo cooperative at a place called the George River, we went in by dog sled.

Somehow, riding on a dog sled for six and a half hours down a frozen river to an isolated log cabin, which was where we met with the Eskimos, didn't seem any different from riding along behind my father over the trails in the woods back home in the middle of winter, when I could hear the snow crunching under the horses' hooves, and my hands and feet got cold. Maybe that's why I'm here. Who knows? . . . But tell me about you."

"I'm just a farm boy. Nothing special about that," he said. "There were eight of us in all. I've got five sisters and two brothers and I'm the second oldest, one sister older than me. My dad died a few years back, but my mother is over eighty, and still lives in Vernon." He took a gold ring from his pocket and handed it to me. "The Denison family crest," he said. The word *Perseverando* was etched in below the hand with a finger pointing towards a star. "The Denisons came to Canada in seventeen ninety-two, from England to Toronto, and they were known as the Fighting Denisons," he continued. "There was an Admiral Sir John Denison in the British Navy and there have always been Johns and Herberts and Richards in our family; my own sons are named Richard and John. I have two married daughters in between, Lynne and Donna. Donna has a baby son, named John too. My dad's name broke that pattern; his was Norman Lippincott and we're related to the Lippincotts in the United States. My middle name is Burton, after my father's mother, who was born in Australia. Some of the Denisons stayed in Toronto and became lawyers, but my great-grandfather moved to Winnipeg, and my grandfather came west and homesteaded in Calgary. When my dad was a year old, my grandfather traded what is now the center of the city of Calgary for a team of horses and a wagon, and moved over the Rocky Mountains to British Columbia. That's where my dad grew up and so did I. What else would you like to know?"

"Oh, what it was like, growing up on a farm in the mountains."

He shrugged. "Nothing unusual there," he said. "We

farmed and trapped and logged like everyone else. We lived on this little farm in the hungry thirties, and we had our own trapline, registered in my dad's name. We caught a little bit of everything—lynx, marten, beaver, mink, weasels. Our trapline, was only forty-five miles long, but it was in the mountains, and once I got out there, I loved it. There is nothin' like bein' out in the bush all by yourself. There were no schools at our place so I went to eleven different schools to grade nine, staying with an aunt and uncle in a town called Summerland for two of those school years. I was home for the last two, but I had to travel eight miles to get to the school. I used to take my bike or a horse or walk to school, and it took me thirty-five minutes downhill, and two hours to get back uphill afterwards. That's how steep it was. We lived in a long narrow valley, the Creighton Valley, right in the mountains, and the Creighton Road was really just a wagon track, winding and slanting down and up the sides of deep gullies, with lots of hairpin turns. It was so narrow you'd brush the trees on either side when you went through in a wagon. It was *so* narrow that the postman wrote a letter to the Vernon newspaper, asking that nobody travel on the Creighton Valley Road on Tuesdays and Fridays, because he had to deliver His Majesty's mail. Once he had to back up two miles, because the Anglican minister was coming down. My first freighting job was on the Creighton Valley Road when I was about fifteen. Some guys couldn't get up with a truck, so they hired me with a sleigh and horses.

"The other children were pretty small, so I had to milk ten cows before I left for school in the mornings, and again in the evenings, and do all the other chores besides, like feeding the pigs," he continued. "I got up at four-thirty, and I never got to bed until nine-thirty. My mother used to help me clean the barn after everyone else had gone to bed."

He slowed down as we dropped from a portage onto a lake, rolled down the window for a moment and looked out, then rolled it up again. "We're on the Rae Lakes now," he said. "It was just about here that I brought my mother and my wife a couple of years ago, so they could see what the Ice Road was like," he said. "They really got a kick out of it. My mother said she had never experienced anything quite so wonderful, and the thing she noticed was how still it is. She couldn't get over that, all the snow and not a sound anywhere. We stopped right here for tea, and then we turned and went back."

We were travelling now on the open lake; black night, bright stars. At the end of the Rae Lakes, another portage. Snowy trees spring up to greet us. Welcome. We enter our own narrow corridor of road and travel under an archway of trees that reach down to touch one another above us. Welcome.

"My last year in school, grade nine, we had a seventy-five-dollar government grant and built a little log schoolhouse in our valley," Denison went on. "My dad and I built it, with a slanting split-cedar shake roof and a big window facing the road, really nice, and I was the school janitor. We had eight pupils, but we had to have ten to start a school, so my mother persuaded two of her friends to let her have their children to come and stay with us. The school teacher lived with us too." He began to laugh.

"What's so funny?" I asked.

"I was remembering somethin'," he said. "There's a really beautiful place called Echo Lake, eight miles above where our farm was, in the heart of our mountains on the Creighton Road. My parents moved up there later, when we were all grown, and ran a lodge until my father died, but at the time I'm talkin' about we were still on the farm. We had an old Whippet car, a nineteen twenty-seven model that we bought in the early thirties for a hundred and twenty-five dollars, and I was just a kid then, and drivin' some of the family one day, up to Echo Lake. The steering wheel came off so I said, 'Here. Take this,' and I threw it into the backseat. I drove along all right, just with the spokes, but my sister Sybil, Jimmy's mother, was in the car, and I remember the school teacher's mother was too, and they both about *died.*

That must have been forty years ago, maybe more." He fell silent. "I was just thinkin' how my Dad used to make ice for the ice house at Echo Lake," he said. "He would clear the lake to make it freeze, and it would freeze to two feet deep. You know, I just thought of that."

"Go on," I said.

"You really want to hear more?" he said, looking amazed.

"Yes," I said.

He shifted gears, and we began climbing. "See this little hill?" he said. "When we're travelin' in convoy each one that goes over the hill stops to see if the one behind is up. If he isn't, all he has to do is put on a chain and pull him up." He shifted again as we came to level ground and we sped along. It all seemed so easy.

"Where was I? School, wasn't it? I'll tell you how I learned to drive. I finally had to stop school because we just couldn't manage. I was the oldest boy, and it was too tough for my father when I wasn't there. It was during the depression in the thirties, and he got a job for seventy-five dollars a month working for the irrigation district, which was a big job then. I was fifteen, and we had an old Model T Ford, but up to then he wouldn't let me drive it. When he got the irrigation job he drove me into town, parked the car, took me before the magistrate and applied for my driver's license. 'Can this boy drive?' the magistrate asked, and my father said, 'Yes, he can drive,' so the magistrate said, 'There's no need for a driver's test. If Norman says he can drive, he can drive.' Well, hell, I hadn't driven ten miles, but that's how I learned. I drove us home from town, and I've been driving ever since."

The road was increasingly bumpy in the woods. We were catching up to the new stretch where the snow had not yet been thoroughly dragged, packed and frozen down. I held on to the seat, braced my feet on the floor, and put out a hand to the radio to keep from bumping it. "Then what?" I asked, when we were on level ground, more or less.

"In nineteen thirty-seven, I was twenty-one, and by that time I had worked in packing houses, done some logging, hacked railroad ties with a broad axe, that sort of thing," Denison said. "Then I joined the Royal Canadian Mounted Police. I consider that the R.C.M.P. was where I continued my education, and I got as good a one there as most people get in college. The highlight was when I was chosen to go to the Roosevelt-Churchill Conference in Quebec in nineteen forty-four. After the Quebec Conference, I had to sign up for another five years, but I quit instead and joined the army. I can't explain it, but I spent a year in the army and had a hundred and sixty-five days of leave. I got as far as Newfoundland, where I sat at a switchboard and guarded the transatlantic telephone cable against sabotage. It's about two inches around, and full of wires."

A jolt, and we dropped back on a lake again. White fluffy drifts on either side of the road and where land and lake meet, snow piled in a wide arc, an open vestibule to mark the spot. Animal tracks everyplace, creature whereabouts a well-kept secret. Unseen eyes. Watch us go by. Silence. Silence everywhere. Stillness. Everyone is watching.

"That's enough about me," Denison said.

"You haven't told me how you got to Yellowknife."

"I never talked this long about myself in my life," Denison said, "but it's sort of interestin'. I'm getting a kind of a view of myself, putting it all together this way, eh? When I got out of the army I drove a logging truck in Vernon. I got tired of that so I applied to go back with the R.C.M.P. That was in May, nineteen forty-six, and they said they would engage me if I'd accept duty in the Yukon Territory, or in Yellowknife. I had been thinking about Yellowknife ennaway, so that's where I went, but a year later I bought my way out of the R.C.M.P. You can do that if you've signed up for five years, by paying for every unexpired month of your engagement, and it cost me something over three hundred dollars. When I quit I was making a hundred and twenty-five on the force and working all night in a garage, so I went into the garage full time. I allus liked working around motors. By the time I was fifteen, I had taken our Model T apart and put it together again, long before I could drive it. Being in the R.C.M.P., though, was a wonderful experience, because you did lots besides general police work in Yellowknife. I had my own detachment, was a plain-clothes detective, an Indian agent; we did welfare work, were lawyers, undertakers, doled out food to Indians, fought fires, everything. To tell you the truth, one of the reasons I quit was because I was squeamish when I came to an accident and found a guy half-dead or dying. That sort of thing makes me sick. Another reason was that I wanted to do something on my own."

We were on a portage. The distinctive features of each land section of the Ice Road were beginning to look familiar. There were the wild places, with tangled vines and bushes wrapped with snow; the cathedrals, trees close together, long and narrow evergreens, rising in pointed tips to make church windows in this woods. Mostly, especially at night, still figures stand on snowy stages, frozen into their roles. Patterned snowfall on trees and bushes creating a host of imagined characters: the White Court, crowned kings and queens with an entourage of attendants; turn the corner, a group of dwarfs sit on great white mushrooms; over this next portage and up the next hill, where white hunters, stiff, silent, salute; outstretched arms brandishing long white weapons. Bows and arrows? Rifles? Down the hill, and at the bottom: Valkyries; terrible, large, snowwomen, bosomy. Towering. White knights ride towards us when we swirl past, rocking the bushes. Open the windows of your soul to the night spirits swaying with the wind sashaying into the hidden corners where one's spirit trembles longing to be free. Wild thoughts. Wild wild wild.

Just for fun, because I was pretty sure what he would say, I told John some of what was going through my mind, and asked him what he saw when he was driving. "I don't see nothin' but snow and a place to make a road," he said. "I allus wonder, if it's a tough spot, how can we improve or change it. I'm allus lookin' to see if I can improve it, somehow."

Denison turned the tape recorder on again. Music. Soft, lyrical. This time it was Guy Lombardo.

"How did you get started roadbuilding?" I asked carefully. I wasn't sure he would still talk.

"Yellowknife was having a boom when I came in nineteen forty-six," Denison said. "Very few people in town, but an awful lot of people in the bush. The summer of forty-seven I had a flat-bottomed boat, an old wooden LST with two Chrysler engines, that carried forty ton, and I freighted on Great Slave Lake with it. I hauled lumber and laid telephone cable across Yellowknife Bay, just sat there and reeled the cable out, but it was goddamned cold work. Then I bought an old right-hand-drive army two-ton, four-wheel-drive Marmon truck from a fellow in Hay River, and my brother, Harry, and I drove it to Peace River, in northern Alberta." Denison looked at me expectantly. Expecting what? Not the blank look I gave him. "Oh, you wouldn't know about that," he said, sounding disappointed. "Peace River is four hundred miles from Hay River and there was no road for about one hundred and fifty miles of that and it was winter. Harry and I champed and chewed our way through the bush and when we got to Peace River we stopped to see a friend. 'Where'd you come from?' he asked, and we said, 'Hay River.' He said, 'You can't. It's the middle of winter and there's no road.' So I said, 'Well, we did,' and then Harry and I turned and went back to Hay River by the same route, with a load of machinery and meat. For a while, Harry and I held three jobs between us. We drove the truck twelve hours a day, and a taxi twenty-four hours a day." He looked puzzled. "Let me see, how did we do that?" he said. "I drove the truck from 8:00 A.M. to 8:00 P.M. I generally got to bed between ten and midnight, and got up at three and drove a taxi until 8:00 A.M. Harry did the same in reverse, he drove from 8:00 A.M. to 3:00 A.M., and we never knew how much we made. In one pocket, out the other. In the spring I got another truck which my brother drove and *that's* how I got started in the freighting business," he said. "I've never quit since. One of our first jobs when I formed the D. and S. Trucking Service with Bob Seddon was to deliver a two-ton generator to Giant Mine in Yellowknife. I left Edmonton on a Tuesday, and told my wife, Hannah, that I'd be back on Friday. We crossed the hundred and sixty miles of Great Slave Lake behind a Cat train that was goin' three to four miles an hour with our trucks tied one behind the other. I was drivin' our little four-wheel-drive Marmon, in front, with Bob's three-ton body truck hooked on to my winch line so I could pull him over the tough spots, and *he* was haulin' the sleigh with the generator on it. The temperature was thirty to forty below, and we broke most of our windows when we slammed the doors shut, so we had blankets over them. No antifreeze, because we couldn't buy any. When we wanted somethin' hot to eat we crawled under a tarp and cooked with a blowtorch. We were seven days and nights on the lake, and the whole trip took a month. We stayed two weeks in Yellowknife, which didn't have phones then. So my wife didn't hear ennathing from me for six weeks, until I got home. And I expected to be away four days! I freighted for a while between Edmonton, Yellowknife and points in between, and then I moved to Dawson Creek, where I was a shareholder in a company called Northern Freightways. I was traffic superintendent, sales manager, everything on the road. We were bought out by Consolidated Freightways, just about the biggest outfit in the world. So then, in nineteen fifty-nine I came to Edmonton and joined Byers Transport, and went to Yellowknife to start a northern operations. That's where I met Jerry Byrne, in the winter of fifty-nine, and they had these houses to move out of Rayrock. For a while there, I had houses coming out my ears. The meanest was one I moved from the Snare River Dam ninety miles to Yellowknife, when the dam was converted to remote control operation. A lot of the houses I moved over that terrible bush road were a little off-size, but this one was two stories high—high and topheavy. The deck of our trailer was only eight feet, the overhang almost eighteen. The bathrooms and kitchen and some of the furniture were still inside, and all the stairways and cupboards were on one side, so the load wasn't balanced. That stupid house was so damned tippy that it kept falling over on me. . . . Oh, oh, what's this?"

He slowed down. Directly ahead were a neat set of red backup and yellow clearance lights, bright spots of color in the shadowy black and white darkness ahead: Tom in 34 and Davy, Mukluk and Burns in the Diamond T truck. They should have been at Hardisty Lake long ago. They had left Fort Byers hours before us.

Tom, gloomy, unsmiling, leaned out his window to tell John that the front-wheel axle on 34 was broken. Truck 34, its motor chugging comfortably, was like a vigorous man crippled by a broken leg. The broken part of the axle and wheel was sitting in the snow beside the truck, a mere 150 pounds or so that Tom had had to pry off, lift and carry there.

Everyone came into the camper for tea, which turned into supper. Denison shook his head at the suggestion of a meal, but reached into a cupboard instead for a can of pears, opened it, ate half a pear and made a face. He pushed the can aside. "I'm gettin' lazy. I'd like to quit all this," he said.

"It's a shame we can't tie you up until you get well," Davy remarked.

"No really, I'd like to quit and just repair toasters and bicycles and old ladies' lawn chairs and window screens," John said. "I've got an aunt who lives on Okanagan Lake near Vernon, and when I was visiting there last summer I fixed her broken window, her pump and toaster, all in twenty minutes. There are all kinds of retired people around there with nobody to fix things for them. Christ, I'd make a living, and no worries!"

Davy pulled Tom's truck onto the lake ahead. Tom would wait there for parts to be flown out to him; Hettrick would fly the order back to Yellowknife when he came out with Hughie to Hardisty Lake tomorrow.

Everyone slept. Before dawn we continued north, stopping when we met the Beaver to have breakfast with George, who was shuffling around in his bedroom slippers cooking bacon and eggs. Back at Hardisty Lake, Fud had sunk further, was now half-submerged. "She was thirsty," Mukluk observed sadly, when he saw her again, bent over so far.

Hettrick arrived in his small red-and-white plane with the sun at ten-thirty, and landed on the ice. Before he and Hughie could get out, Denison opened the door, told me to get in and climbed in after me. He directed Hettrick to fly north, saying, "We've finished two hundred miles of road, and there's another hundred and twenty-five to go. I want to see how the rest of it looks from the air before we build any more."

Hughie held the map and showed Hettrick where to go. Denison, behind him, leaned back and closed his eyes. I was sitting on top of the sleeping bags that every bush plane in the North is required to carry, directly behind Denison's seat. "How do you feel?" I asked him. He opened his eyes, put his hand on his stomach, and made a face. "I allus feel sick even when I'm well, in these small planes," he said.

From 3,000 feet above the ground vegetation looks sparse and scratchy; cuts made for previous portages through the trees are visible, in shorter growth. When we swing around to go north, I glance back at the Ice Road: narrow white line, so faint and thin that from this height, someone might have run along there with a pencil on the otherwise unmarked white panorama spread out below us. We fly over an enormous lake. "Great Bear Lake?" I ask, shouting at Denison to make myself heard over the noisy aircraft.

"Hottah Lake," he shouts back. "Fifty miles long. Biggest in the chain until you get to Great Bear."

The plane swoops. Hughie taps my arm, pointing down. Four caribou meander in the snow as if the lake surface was a meadow; a huge-chested male with magnificent antlers, and three smaller females, delicate and feminine. All are a lovely cocoa color, except for their underbellies and the underside of their graceful throats, which are white as the snow in which they stand. Breathtaking! I have goose bumps on the back of my neck. Our plane tilts for a better view and the male glances up, disdainfully turns his back and moves away, holding his stately head in the air. One female moves placidly with him, staying close beside him, but the other two jump nervously about, kicking up snow. I am sorry we have frightened them. We have come down so low that I can see the ridges and ripples on the glazed ice; glare ice, where the snow has blown away.

Caribou tracks everywhere as we proceed north. More caribou sitting in the snow on the lake. One, two, three, four, five, six, seven. I count them as if by doing this I can stamp the scene in my memory. The caribou ignore the plane sweeping over them, but a flock of ptarmigan scamper away, half-flying a few feet from the ground.

At the south end of Hottah, a head frame and a clump of abandoned mine buildings. "The old Indore Uranium Mine," Denison shouts. ". . . didn't last long. This is where I keep a cook, in the middle building, for the season . . . got this fellow coming out, one of the best, on . . . first truck with Bobby Fry . . . probably have to shanghai him out of a bar like the others, not as good cook as Chatrain, but not bad . . . once he's here . . . dries out . . . likely to stay. Men who . . . come to . . . place like this . . . live alone . . . usually alcoholics . . . like it . . . can't get a drink. . . ."

We are flying through a narrow inlet and now the shores open out. At our right, rippling hills sprinkled with black patches of vegetation like the stubbly growth of a man's beard; straight ahead as far as the eye can see, a white ocean, tumbling over the horizon. The radiant glare of the sun lights up windswept black patches of ice directly below, glare ice again. What giant broom has cleaned this spot to make this giant rink?

Denison, peering through his binoculars, shouts. "The Big Lake! Great Bear Lake!"

Denison drops his binoculars around his neck and motions to Hettrick to turn back. We swing around, move back into the chain of lakes, and shortly pass a clump of small shacks, open to the wind, their doors and windows gone; beside them, two planes, half-buried in the snow, their noses and wings protruding. The distinctive placement of the pilot's snubnosed cockpit above the tubular freight-carrying area on the larger plane identifies it as a British Bristol, a twin to the large aircraft mounted at the Yellowknife Airport; the other, a small cabin plane similar to the one we are in. Denison shouts, ". . . Just the shells now . . . went through the ice . . . about six years ago . . . so busted . . . not worth saving . . . I took . . . engines back to Yellowknife . . ."

When we had left Hardisty Lake an hour earlier, Davy was already maneuvering his vehicles into position to pull Fud out of the ice. Back over Hardisty, Denison looked through his binoculars to see how the rescue was progressing. A sharp exclamation of dismay. "Hughie, your tractor's in too!" he shouted. Hughie turned in his seat and looked out the side window. His yellow Cat was over on its side, its left front end about three feet under water.

Our plane bounced when its skis met the ice. Hughie bounded out the door across the ice. He circled the Cat once, then climbed into the Diamond T and conferred with Davy, who had backed his truck as close as he dared to the hunk of yellow iron that jutted through the ice. The weather was brutally cold, sixty below zero, and there was a wind besides. Nobody was staying outdoors a second longer than necessary. Burns and Mukluk, stamping their feet, pounding their fists, followed me into the camper to warm up. Denison, hardly seeming to glance at the ice-bound, half-submerged Cat and Fud, climbed into Davy's truck to confer with Hughie and slammed the door shut. He returned to the camper before Burns and Mukluk had finished their coffee. Nerves taut, high tension wires. Face drawn; obviously sick again. "You'd think there'd be a good break once in a while," he muttered, and went to bed.

Ill as he was, or perhaps because he was so ill, the fury of Denison's spirit affected the others; the sicker he got, the more they strained to finish the Ice Road. He was a tough boss, made outrageous demands by any normal working standards, but the men were in it for more than the job. "He's proved it could be done," was the phrase the men used about Denison even while they grumbled at the lack of sleep, the long hours of hard work, usually adding, "I would do anything for John." They trusted his judgment, relied on his strength, suffered with him. "If you're too tired, sick as he is, he's not afraid to get up and have a go at it," Davy Lorenzen said to me later that day.

It took an hour to pull Hughie's tractor out of Hardisty Lake. Sixty degrees below zero is *cold;* my toes are rigid, fingers numb, my seven layers of clothing as thin as tissue paper; the wind, a knife that cuts through them. I cannot stay outside more than five minutes at a time. I want to see how the men get the tractor out. How do they work outside? They are accustomed to freezing temperatures but they are human and this cold is not for humans. The wolverine fur around my parka hood is supposed to be especially good for protecting the face, because the hairs are long and don't freeze, but my nose feels frozen, as if it will fall off. I have a card Denison gave me entitled "How Cold Is It?" that shows the true temperature when the velocity of the wind is combined with the thermometer reading. There is a sinister green area on the chart that indicates "when the exposed flesh freezes," but the chart reckonings only go as far as forty-five degrees below zero and a forty-five-mile-an-hour wind. The "true" temperature with the wind-chill factor added in at that extreme is one-hundred-and-twelve degrees below zero! Hughie estimates that with the wind blowing at ten miles an hour and the temperature reading sixty below we are contending with cold somewhere in the neighborhood of ninety below zero.

Getting the Cat out of the ice looked deceptively easy. Hughie fastened the Diamond T's winch to the Cat, and Davy started winding it in. Groaning, cracking ice, as the trapped vehicle broke free, and the Cat emerged, swinging on the winch a foot or so above the lake. I held my breath while Burns climbed up and across the winch A-frame and carefully lowered himself into the driver's seat of the Cat while it was still swaying in the air at the end of the winch hook. The winch swung Burns and the Cat over to solid ice, set him down on it, and he started "walking" the Cat.

The men turned immediately to their next task, prying Fud loose from *her* icy bed. At three in the afternoon, Hettrick and Hughie had to leave. The sun was setting and this was not the weather to risk an emergency landing after dark in the bush. The recovery of Fud was hampered by the tons of extra ice on it. Davy's truck was normally about the same weight as Fud, but now the Diamond T was the lighter vehicle. Instead of Fud being lifted free of the ice and water when Davy attached it to the winch on the back of his truck and began winding, the front end of the Diamond T rose five feet in the air. Fud, on the other hand, didn't move. Burns drove cautiously in the Cat across the dangerous ice to the Diamond T, and laid the blade of his Cat on its front fender as an anchor. Light sound of cracking ice; heavy roar of the winch motor. With the combined weight of the Diamond T and the Cat to offset it, Fud came up, just a little, a little more, then up, began to rise, straining, cracking, through the ice, coming slowly, slowly, an inch . . . at . . . a . . . time . . . until it was high enough above the open black hole where it had fallen through to be swung out and above the ice and away. Davy pivoted Fud around and forward, swinging her at the end of the winch line, automotive marionette dangling by a single wire, and set her down on thick ice, behind the camper.

When the men rushed in with this good news to Denison, he rewarded them with a wan smile. Not a minute to be wasted. Hurry, hurry. Out again. Hurry. Chop the ice from Fud's lower extremities before she freezes more! Hurry!

When I came out, Davy was lying on his back underneath Fud, whacking huge chunks of ice from the underside with a hatchet. Mukluk was up above, perched on a fender with a needle bar, breaking up the thick sheet of ice that encased the red radiator hood. Some of the ice taken from Fud was in blocks more than two feet thick. Meanwhile, Burns had lit a propane heater under the engine of the Herman Nelson heater to get *it* started, to warm the frozen motor of Fud enough to get it started eventually too!

The sun had set and the waning grey light filtered through the camper windows. Denison was presumably asleep; the only sound, the gentle perking of coffee on the stove. When Mukluk arrived, sighing with fatigue as he removed his parka, Denison instantly sat up. "Is Fud runnin' yet?," he asked. "I don't hear any snappin', crackin' motor noise!" Mukluk shook his head in the negative and Denison lay down. "Hardisty allus was a bad lake," he said, staring at the ceiling. "Such a shallow, ramblin' thing!"

Davy arrived. "Only one cup of water in Fud's oil pan but an awful lot of ice on her, John," he said. "About one-half of Fud had ice and the front wheel drive is froze up solid. I don't think the radiator's hurt though, and Burns has the Herman Nelson going under the parachute. By tomorrow, we ought to have Fud thawed out and running!"

Everyone went to sleep early. Since Davy's truck had no caboose, he had Jimmy's place in the camper, bunking with Denison. His truck, motor idling, faced the back of the camper, its headlights scanning my face all night. I dreamed I was driving the white frame house I grew up in, sitting on the top step at the front door to steer. I couldn't get the house to stop moving. I awoke, feeling as if I was choking. Instinctively, I jumped from my bunk and flung open the camper door to let in a blast of frigid air and, more important, oxygen. The propane heater was purring cozily. I slept next to the heater, and I had forgotten to open the window nearest me. I dozed off, and when I awoke again, John was in the kitchen, making pancakes. "I had a terrible nightmare last night," he told Davy and me. "I dreamt I was so sick I couldn't work for a whole year!"

With Denison in charge of breakfast, I felt as if I were on a holiday. I went outside right at the door of the camper to brush my teeth, before breakfast, breaking my rule, and scrubbed my face with snow. Mukluk and Burns had slept in Fud, without heat because her motor wasn't running yet, and Mukluk arrived, smiling for the first time since Fud's accident, as I was turning to go inside. "I have to stay with my ship until the very end!" he said cheerily. Over pancakes, he announced that his whiskers had frozen during the night, that it was Sunday and that as a member of the Pentecostal Church he didn't work on Sundays. He laughed, rubbed his grizzled reddish beard, an easy smile lighting his pleasant face and bright blue eyes. "What do you suppose I will do today?" he asked of nobody in particular. "Work on Sunday, of course! But people at home don't know what it's like up here! They can't even imagine it. These spaces. They never believe me when I say I am hauling freight to the Arctic Circle."

Everyone was relaxing this morning, even Denison, who ate one of his own thin, surprisingly delicate pancakes. I would not have dared to cook such thin pancakes for these men. Over coffee, the conversation turned to accidents, a favorite breakfast topic. Someone mentioned Shannon O'Reilly's famous jump through the windshield on the Ice Road the previous year.

"I did the same thing once't myself," Davy Lorenzen said. "I jumped right through the window when I thought my truck was sinkin' and found myself sittin' on a rock in only four feet of water. Know what I thought about? Gettin' the two-thousand-dollar radio out if the truck kept goin' down."

He ran his finger slowly across a jagged scar that started above his eye, went down the side of his cheek and across his mouth, and travelled up the other cheek. It was impossible not to notice it, but strangely enough it accentuated his youthful good looks although it was raw and reddish. "I got this last year when Jimmy Magrum and I were opening the road," Davy said for my benefit, since it was obvious that the others knew all about it. "It was my job to plow the lakes and haul the Cats across them, and Magrum was runnin' the Cat. We were goin' ahead together to find portages, tryin' to get enough of the road marked so that a fellow could keep runnin' that night. The line of our road was crooked so we thought we'd straighten it out with a short cut. I hit a reef with the plow, and the truck stopped so short that there were two holes where our heads went through the windshield. We may have been knocked out, because neither of us knew what had happened. I hollered 'Fire!' and reached for the ignition key and turned off the gas. Why we thought we had caught fire was that the plow truck has headlights above the cab, and we hit that reef so hard that when the truck stopped, the radiator pulled away from the motor with all the hoses, which threw the hot antifreeze into the motor. The steaming antifreeze vapour was rising, and looked like smoke." He stirred his coffee absentmindedly with his spoon and paused to drink some, wiping his mouth with the back of his hand. "Well, I looked over at Jim, and he's bent forward spitting blood, which is all over his mouth, and I guess I was covered with blood too, because I had to have forty-two stitches across this eye and down my cheek and down the side of my other cheek, but he just had cuts and glass in his mouth. After this here happened, we finally see what's wrong in each other, and our main concern is to get back to the other trucks, which were seven miles and seven small lakes away. We lifted the hood and put the radiator hoses back in the motor, wiped the spark plugs, which are in a kind of well, put on the distributor cap and started the truck."

"What time was that?" I asked.

"Two in the morning, and forty below zero," Davy replied, "and we sure couldn't walk those seven miles. The truck stopped, and we had to work on the motor again, and then we saw a light comin' at us through the trees, so we took off on foot, and it was one of our trucks, out lookin' for caribou. He carried us back to Séguin Lake, where the rest of the convoy was. They tried to call for an airplane, but they couldn't get through to Yellowknife until three the next afternoon, and then they sent a plane out to pick us up. By the time I got to the hospital, the doctor said I was already healed, but I did go out to Edmonton in June and get some surgery."

He was still running his finger down his face along the scar. "Another funny thing happened on that trip," he said. "When we were travellin' in the main convoy we picked up an old Indian fellow who was hunting caribou, and gave him a ride. This old fellow had his sleeping bag and all his clothes with him, and he couldn't speak English. I had on a khaki parka, which was covered with blood, and when he saw it he took off and didn't come back. He went into the bush and made a fire, and a dog team behind us picked the old fellow up and took him on to the caribou. It shows, though, that you can't be too careful, plowin'. Even a rock stickin' up an inch out of the ice, if your blade hits it, I don't care if you are going five or twenty-five mile an hour, you will stop dead in your tracks."

Burns shifted uneasily in his seat. "Guess I'll be walkin' the rest of Hardisty with the Cat," he said. "That's eight mile more to the end of the lake."

"Bother you, does it?" Davy asked.

"From time to time now it's been crossin' my mind that I might go in," Burns said. "I figure I'm on borrowed time, *every* time I'm on lake ice in a Cat."

By late afternoon, we were twenty miles beyond Hardisty in the camper, at the beginning of another lake, Malfait, waiting for the trucks pounding down the portage behind us to catch up. The vehicles arrived one by one: Burns on the Cat, Davy, and finally, George in the Beaver. Then—miraculously! Could it be? It was! Fud was coming! Moving slowly along, lopsided because only one headlight was working, plowing the road towards us, slowly slowly in a halo of flying snow. "Poor old Fud," Mukluk said, rolling down his window as he pulled up alongside us. "Now she has only one eye left. May I borrow your electric torch?"

Denison handed Mukluk our torch and he passed us to take his place proudly at the head of the convoy. He stopped to tie the electric torch to his front bumper, then began plowing the new road.

"Fud's amazing the way she keeps going!" I said.

Denison shrugged. "It's a vehicle to me," he said. "Something to work with when there's a job to be done. Like with Fud now, when you hit difficulties, you make up your mind to keep goin' and decide whether something is salvageable. Should I spend a thousand dollars to get a piece of equipment out of the water that is worth only five hundred dollars? Well, it depends on how much I need that vehicle. The first equipment I dropped through the ice was the Bug that went down three hundred and fifty feet in Prosperous Lake. At that moment, it was the only Bombardier in the country. I figured, sure, it would be cheaper to get another Bug, but it was December and there was no road between Edmonton and Yellowknife right then, so there was no way of getting one. Besides, I had no money. As for the personal danger involved in getting a piece of equipment out of the water, you can *never* make enough money to cover that, eh? If you fall through, you can't worry about it. You take all the precautions, and check the ice. If it's thin, you take planks or boards out with you so you can walk or stand on them, so if you *do* fall through you have somethin' to hang onto."

He reached for a bread and butter sandwich on the dashboard and bit from it while he continued talking. "Up north lots of fellows who walk across ice for the first time carry a long pole so that if they go through, the pole will hold on the ice and give them another supporting surface. That's an old, old trick. We've never done it, but some fellows tie a rope around their waist, and if you haven't a rope, you can still use a tire or any damn thing that'll hold you up. You can't plan, you just use whatever's available. We don't take a pole crossing the ice because it's too much trouble, just like a guy not wearing a life-jacket in a boat. We get so used to not falling through that we get overconfident, I guess, but I don't think our winter roads are any more dangerous than driving a truck on a highway with all that traffic. Out here, there's more chance of surviving!"

We had crept up on Fud, and Denison slowed down to let the old truck get a little farther ahead of us. "When we broke the road to Port Radium the first time it was just going to be a one-trip operation," he said. "The Eldorado Mine closed in nineteen fifty-nine and when its big generating units were sold to the Alberta Power Company in Calgary, I was asked if I thought I could bring them out all the way from Port Radium to Calgary. If we hadn't lost money and done the job, more than likely we wouldn't have gotten into that haul in the wintertime. Partly because of our road, Echo Bay Silver Mine went into production the next year, and we've been breaking the Ice Road to Port Radium every winter since, so things generally work out. There's gotta be something to go for to build a road, and the highest-grade silver on the North American continent is at Echo Bay. For us to make money, operations have to be two-way, we've got to have a back haul to get any gravy. We haul in twenty to twenty-five ton per truck and bring about fifteen hundred ton of silver ore out, but at best it's a guess and a gamble what money we'll pick up. Some of the men who drive for us are leased operators who own their own trucks and get paid by the trip, and they have to make ten trips a season to Great Bear Lake to begin to make real money, so we try to see that they get more trips than ten. Others are on salary, working for a bonus. I suppose there are always men who want to try to be first to do things or go where nobody else goes," he added, "so what it comes down to is, that none of us would be here if we didn't like coming."

We had gone twelve miles, to the other end of Malfait Lake. Denison rolled down the window and looked out. "I hope I can find this next portage," he said. "Year before last, I had to go all the way back and get Jim Magrum."

The night crowds us; Denison hurries into the camper and makes a light supper for the men. Without stopping to wash the dishes, we pack for travelling again. With no Bug, the camper does the scouting, and before the men can start working on the next portage, we have to find out where it is. Denison *has* to keep going. It would suit him best if no stops were made to eat or sleep. If he could build his road, drive his men without stopping, the way he runs his machines; the way he runs himself, except that his machine is a human one, partially broken with the demands he has made of it, that he cannot make on the men. They see this in him and admire it, however unreasonable, and give him the best they can.

The men sit in their trucks, the two headlights of the Diamond T, the single eye of Fud's lantern shining in the darkness, and wait, while we drive along the rim of the lake scouting for the portage entrance. We start doing this at eight in the evening. A strange, exotic night; black, without stars, but for the first time we have Northern Lights, white luminous streamers that swish and sigh, great white floating sheets in the open black heavens.

For two hours we drive around and around on the rough ice on the lake, looking for the cut that marked the location of last year's road. A simple maneuver. Yet that slight irregularity in the smooth arrangement of trees and bushes, which would indicate where the old route was, eludes us. It is every place. It is no place. Sixty below zero. Denison has the window down again, for better vision. Fingers of air, colder than cold; the cab is all cold. I pull up my parka hood. We drive parallel to the shore and each time John thinks he sees the portage opening he rolls the window up, turns the camper and drives head-on for the spot, to give it the broadest spectrum of light from our headlamps. How can we miss? But we do. Back again, driving parallel to the shore.

I wonder: How thick is the ice here? The question, once formulated, and admitted, is a shout in my mind but I do not say it out loud. HOW THICK IS THE ICE HERE? HOW THICK IS THE ICE HERE?

Silence.

Safety. Where is safety? Solid ground. Untamed land, reluctant to let us pass. Land. Slipping, sliding, bumping, bouncing, twisting, turning, off the trail, getting stuck portage driving. Mostly getting stuck. But safe. Monstrous paradox! Gentle humming smooth comfortable lake driving. That's the real danger. Sinister. Ready to crack. Cracked. Maybe now. Down through black black black cold cold cold to brown probably soft mud death at the bottom of this lake. Malfait. Badly made. Well named. Look, in that confusing tangle of trees on the shore over there, is that the opening? No? Not there? Or there?

We turn, run parallel to the shore again. If the ice cracks? If we plunge? Black, cold, fighting to rise, helpless, hopeless. A second of recognition, they say. Who is "they"? What will I see? My children's faces? The last moment? What memory? What thought?

The end. Swift? Merciful?

Too soon. I'm not ready. Not yet.

I hear Denison talking, from far far away. "We must have travelled sixty miles in these last two hours," he says. His voice is thin, he sounds weary.

How beautiful danger is! I hate it. I love it. Cold misty night. White burial shrouds in that black sky. Black ice that shines. Called glare ice, because it glares where there is no snow. Polished until it gleams by these brutal winds. Patches of glare ice, patches of snow, long stretches of snow to hide the lake; the black, crystal-cold water. Snow crackles when our tires push on the unplowed crust, make a double line of wheel marks. We are rolling over the snow, crushing it down in our little box of sometimes safety. My stiff fingers touch the slender flat cool black expensive radio. Stiff fingers. I rub the joints, touch the warm wolverine rim of my parka hood, the fur that Jimmy Magrum sold me last year, that June sewed on while I was there one day instead of the white rabbit fur that always shed; I touch my forehead, touch the red frame of the windshield, touch the slippery brown leather seat, touch my eyes, tired from straining to see that space not here not there, but maybe here among the trees.

Sometime Denison must have rolled up the window, because now he is rolling it down again, his head is out the window, the sting of fresh air is good. His face has no expression but his voice is tired. "We might as well wrap it up," he says.

We return to the circle of idling vehicles, cross the line of light made by the double lamps of the Diamond T in front, and pick up Davy Lorenzen. He climbs in the seat beside me. Comforting presence. Davy, with his warm smile, his soft voice, his friendliness, makes me feel secure. He is not smiling now.

Davy has a map spread on his knees. Glances down at the map, up at the sameness of tangled bushes, small trees, at the edge of the lake. Davy points to a space between shrubs. We turn and show the spot with our headlights, moving bright across the black shrub, the ever green of spruce needles. Davy rolls the window down, peers out, rolls it up again, we pass on to another place; and finally give up for the night.

It would have been too late, too dark, anyway, for the men to start work on a strange portage. Denison went back to bed in the camper. Davy and I sat in the cab and watched shooting stars streak across the sky. Davy said, "At first, we fellas didn't like the idea of a woman being here, but we've been watching you. We notice you are always ready to go, so you don't hold things up any. And the cooking! Well, you try hard! It's kind of pleasant having you with us. Different.''

"The funny thing is that even though I don't want any of you to think of me as a woman, I *have* to put on makeup every morning," I said. "Lipstick, eye shadow, eyeliner. I have to put it on, first thing, the way I have to wash my face or brush my teeth to get going.''

"I see you do that," Davy said. "Why?''

"Mukluk was watching me put it on while he drank his coffee this morning, and said he wished I wouldn't," I said. "I wonder myself why I bother.''

We fell silent, watching the Northern Lights. "I think I'm trying to hide," I finally said. "If I'm wearing eye makeup, I feel as if nobody can see me. I'm trying to hide from all of you, Denison especially.''

Davy offered me a cigarette, lit it, lit one for himself and said, "Don't let Daddy Long Legs throw you. I've taken a lot of beatings from John myself but we're good friends. He's a wonderful guy to work for. See how the guys put out for him! Until two in the morning and then get up and start again at five; and he'll have dinner out on the table when you've turned your truck off. He talks back and forth with the men too, and has a way with them that they really like. He has no business bein' out here in the bush now. Everybody knows their job and does as well when he's not here, but John's *got* to be in the bush. It's a good life here in the bush, with good guys, nothin' but beautiful trips. I just wish we could run some of the winters into summer.''

It was a lovely night. The Northern Lights made a gorgeous show of white color in soft bands right down from the top of the sky to the horizon. They had a luminous depth which made you feel that if you could just touch them, they would be like soft gossamer. We sat in the front seat of the camper, with this vision spread out before our eyes on the empty lake, as if ours were the only eyes, we the only audience for a special showing. I finished my cigarette and Davy handed me another. "We knew where you were all the time tonight," Davy said. "This is a big body of water, twelve miles long, and John said, 'Leave your lights on, so I know where you are.' Well, we were watchin' *you* too. If you went around a point you'd disappear and then you'd show up again, poppin' around an island, so we got the lay of the lake by watchin' the lights of the camper. Me and Mukluk was sittin' right there in my truck with the maps in front of us, and we could see exactly where you went, by holdin' the map and watchin' you guys. The camper's a poor thing to go in at night, chasin' around the shore line in deep snow. Not so dangerous as it would be for a plow driver, who's *really* a guinea pig. Look how Magrum and me went through the windshield, plowin' at night!"

He had almost finished his cigarette before he spoke again. "I wonder if you realize how dangerous it was drivin' in the dark on the ice the way you were doin' tonight. You must have been goin' forty mile an hour, twice as fast as we usually drive at night over ice. You could have gone through the ice any time. Did you know that?"

"I did," I heard myself say. "It's the first time in my life I ever rode in a car with my right hand on the handle of a door for two hours."

Lewis Mackenzie arrived for breakfast. He had driven all night in 36, the African Queen. The portage entrance hid until daylight, when it was plainly visible, between two hillocks; admirable, obvious signposts, once you knew. Denison seemed miraculously recovered now that he had a full crew functioning and operations had resumed. The Cat cleaned stumps, trees and rocks from the portage and Fud followed, levelling the road. The Cat had to come and drag Fud up the first hill. Poor Fud. One wheel had stopped working, and she was now a nervous old lady with her skirt pinned up; several bolts had dropped from her plow and it no longer could operate on the hydraulic lift, but was held up by chains that had to be lowered by hand each time it came to a lake to plow. "Fud's only a four-ton truck, not really powerful," Denison remarked, driving slowly along behind her. "I originally bought her from the government for something stupid like five hundred dollars."

We stopped to telephone. Reception was perfect and everyone in the Arctic seemed to have been waiting for this ideal opportunity to make a phone call. While we waited our turn we listened to other conversations on the radiophone; between a teacher on an Arctic island and her supervisor in Yellowknife; two social workers on two different islands in the High Arctic comparing notes on their problems; and between a man putting in an oil rig in the Mackenzie River Delta several hundred miles from us and his partner at Fort Nelson, even farther west, in British Columbia. Usually, people sounded as if they were on an ordinary phone next door, but today the voices echoed as if the speakers were talking through a rain barrel. John recognized the man in the Delta, who had broken down and was asking for parts. When John's turn came, he said to the operator, "I'd like to call Hay River Two-four-four-nine. Denison. Denison. Over." He was calling his partner at their warehouse where his trucks were already loaded up waiting to make the first trip to Port Radium.

When John had finished discussing equipment and fuel distribution with his partner, he added, "We're going now to Beaverlodge Lake. Beaverlodge Lake. Can you hear me?" The answer came back affirmative, with Denison's final words repeated back to him. Denison continued. "Tom still broke down with Thirty-four. Nothing else new. Start the six-wheelers on the first trip with the dynamite for Echo Bay. Dynamite for Echo Bay. They are waiting for it at Port Radium. Waiting for it there. Send a cook to Hottah Lake on the first plow truck through. Send three thousand Diesel to Hottah too. Don't load too heavy. Not too heavy. We are having a few ice problems. A few ice problems." He listened while his partner repeated his directions, signed off with a "Roger!" and we drove on.

We proceeded over the fifteen miles of Beaverlodge Lake

in convoy. Our camper was at the end of the line, so I could see the vehicles moving ahead of me as if I were sitting in the caboose of a freight train, with 36 plowing the road in the lead, looking quite grand. "Nice, eh?" Denison said suddenly. "I get a kick out of it every time I see a damn plow truck up here like this. I like to see the trucks working together. I'll bet that when you go home trucks'll look different and you'll think of all those guys driving them as your friends. After an experience like this, it can't ever be the same again."

It's true. Until I ventured up this Ice Road, a truck was a truck to me; ugly, utilitarian, clumsy, too big, blocking traffic, in my way. Here they were my friends, dramatic personalities, especially the towering warm red plow trucks. A thrilling sight in the light snow falling now. Thin line of trucks against the white landscape, strips of moving color, mostly red, some yellow, some silver: thin thread of vitality moving slowly through this fantastic stillness. Was the world like this when it first began?

Halfway across the lake, Fud, directly ahead of us, stopped. We stopped too, and Denison impatiently drummed his fingers on the steering wheel while Mukluk got out to adjust his plow. John swerved off the road and drew up alongside Mukluk, who smiled cheerfully and said he would be along in a moment; just a matter of tightening a few bolts. Denison drove back on the road ahead of him, and we caught up with the rest of the convoy. Fud soon followed, tagging along about a mile behind.

Denison kept glancing outside at the side mirror on his left. "What are you looking at, all the time?" I asked.

"You always watch behind you," he replied. "Except when a truck is travelling alone, which I don't like. We don't have swampers, a second man on the truck, the way the oil-field men have. An extra person in our regular trucks means a guy can't lay down and rest. When we're traveling in convoy like this we watch out for each other, and each man is responsible for the man behind him. The one in front's all right, because there's someone behind to help him, but the last guy has no one, so the guy in front of him has to make sure he's coming. We call that last man Tail-End Charlie, and the odd time, he doesn't make it. So you stop and hook up a towline and tow him. Once I remember coming up a hill and one of the big trucks behind me didn't make it. The drive shaft wore out because a broken spring was rubbing on the truck frame, and it just went." He looked at me. I had opened my mouth and closed it again. "You want to ask me, but you're scared to. 'What's a drive shaft?' That right?"

I nodded.

"Jeez, I forgot how much you don't know! A drive shaft is the link between the engine and the rear wheels, that turns them. It's about a four-inch steel tube. We had a welding outfit along, so even though it was about forty below as usual, we hauled the truck out on the lake we were about to go over, and pulled the axle housing ahead with a chain. We welded the shaft with a gas welder, right out there in the open. We didn't have the special metal welding rod you need for material, so we used nails for the metal we should have had, and then we chained the axle housing and went on. When we got to the garage, they said, 'Who the hell welded this? It's a terrible thing!' But it got us home."

The gentle falling snow became a thick screen, closing us into a small world. Soon we would be at Hottah Lake, fifty miles long and less than a hundred miles from our destination, Port Radium. We waited at the entrance to the portage that would put us on Hottah Lake, while the Cat went first to clear the way and return to us. We waited. And waited. Denison looked at his watch, frowned, drove up to 36 and told Lewis Mackenzie to find out what was keeping Burns.

Can an inanimate object like a truck show dejection? 36 did. She returned to us from her mission, rocking from side to side on the rough unmade road, descending clumsily from the steep portage to the lake. Bad news again: the swing frame that held the blade together on the Cat had broken. The Cat could move, but it couldn't do any work.

We were still in luck with telephone reception. Denison called Hughie Arden and reached his home in Yellowknife. It was bizarre to be sitting in a truck on a lake at the Arctic Circle surrounded by snow and ice, listening to Mrs. Arden say that Hughie wasn't home, but suggesting where he might be reached. Two more calls and John found him. Hughie would fly out with a new cap for the frame as soon as he could locate one, maybe today.

Denison was away, scouting with Davy in the Diamond T, when Hettrick and Hughie arrived in the Cessna in mid-afternoon, bringing parts for the Cat, bolts for Fud's plow, and stomach pills for Denison. They stayed just long enough to give me the parcels and were gone before Denison returned. When he did, we started immediately travelling north in the camper, heading for Hottah Lake.

We passed Burns, who was already repairing the Cat with the new parts Davy had brought in to him, a quarter of a mile into the bush in the portage. He was working in the open under a parachute, using a portable welder, so we stopped and gave him hot coffee before we continued over a trail where only Davy's truck had been through, scouting just before us. We had a choice; to skid around in Davy's tire ruts, or take a chance on getting stuck going through unbroken, foot-high snow in our lighter, smaller truck, which was close to the ground and top-heavy. Typically, Denison chose to make his own ruts, so we tumbled through the woods, leaping around rocks, swerving to avoid stumps until we darted out on Hottah Lake. Fifty miles of hard ripples and ridges; the crunch of crusty new snow, wind pounding the body of the truck, wind sweeping wild and free across the largest open space short of Great Bear Lake. We were buffeted about like a toy car. Ten miles out, Denison tired of the battle and turned into shore beside a clump of buildings at the water's edge. This was the site of the abandoned Indore uranium mine that we had glimpsed from the air. We stopped in front of a large fuel storage tank, the one Denison had installed there for his truck run. All the other structures were empty dilapidated shacks with gaping windows, open doors banging in the wind, black box shells against the deep blue night that was already catching up with us; except for one building, a rectangular shed that at first looked like the others, but had windows and a padlock on the closed door. This was Denison's second rest stop for the truckers, and as soon as we sent word that we had reached Port Radium, Bobby Fry would bring out the cook to open it up, on his first trip. "Indore Mine was here long before my road," Denison said. "Everything was flown in. It only lasted a year."

The other trucks arrived shortly, and we camped beside the mine buildings for the night. In the morning, I wiped the dirty breakfast dishes with paper towelling while Denison was making his regular morning phone call to Fort Byers, and we started immediately to cross the remaining forty miles of this big lake. We were soon far ahead of the others, skirting in and out of small inlets, around tiny islands, some just a pile of rocks decorated with one lone tree or a clump of bushes. At the north end of Hottah, where the opening into the next portage was partially obscured by a line of small islands, Denison turned the camper with the headlights on to show where we were. The day was slightly overcast, the sun a pale orange, veiled with clouds. The islands and rocks several miles from us across the flat lake created a dancing series of optical illusions; they shimmered hazily, so we were fooled continually into thinking they were the trucks. When the convoy did arrive, we fell in at the end of the line, to let the other vehicles break this roughest of all portage roads so far, a low trail of wet land in and out among the trees. It was beautiful, but treacherous; a narrow lane of old portage through the tall spruce trees, green where the wind had brushed off some of the snow. Beams of sunny light filtered through their branches to light our way.

We slipped and slid through a watery bog in this lovely virgin spruce forest; graceful trees sixty feet tall pointed snowy peaks to the sky. We were stuck a dozen times in a few hundred yards. A dozen times, Denison rocked the camper and freed our wheels. Each jolt was an upheaval. "Better hold the radio steady to keep it from shaking loose," he said grimly. "Do you see why we stick to the lakes as much as we can? Lakes are a blessed relief! Some of the holes we are hitting here are four feet deep under the snow!"

This was a six-mile portage and after we had gone two it felt like a hundred. The trucks ahead were out of sight. We sank into a hole hidden by snow, and no amount of rocking would budge the camper. Denison got out with a shovel, feverishly dug around the wheels, throwing brush into the hole. When the wheels continued spinning he raised the front end of the camper with a jack, pumping up and down on the jack with furious energy, as if the heavy truck was a light car. More brush piled underneath, and he added frozen moss or muskeg, which was everywhere underfoot. Out again, the camper swaying like a rocking horse. I was clinging to the door handle and the dashboard to keep from falling over the driver's wheel. The truck lurched, stopped. It had fallen into a rut so deep on my side that outside my right window the ground was inches from my face. Denison was sitting almost vertically above on my left —or so it seemed—holding onto the steering wheel, looking down at me. He laughed. "Do you think we are going to tip over?" he asked. I nodded, speechless. "I don't like tipping over because I hate getting out the side," he said, quite cheerfully, and began to push on the door at his left, now five feet above the ground. "You have to stand up straight and it's hard then to open the door."

He stood up, I had no idea how, bent over double, pushed his door open, and crawled out. He released the winch chain from its hook on the camper's bumper, and by the time I had crawled backwards on my hands and knees up the seat, squeezing past the steering wheel and out the door, he had fastened the winch line around a tree. Returning to the truck, he turned on the winch motor to wind up the cable.

The camper remained just where it was. It was trapped, motionless in its deep well of a hole, and as the winch chain began winding, the tree to which it was fastened slowly bowed before my fascinated eye and fell to the ground. Denison swore, attached the winch line to a thicker tree and then applied the jack furiously to the front end of the camper as he had before, raising the body several feet this way out of the rut, but still directly over it. He was working so hard that he threw off his parka and worked on in his blue plaid flannel shirtsleeves. Again, he turned on the motor and wound up the winch, hoping with the tree for an anchor to pull the camper forward as the winch line became shorter. This second, thicker tree protested with a series of groans, bent, and with a low, moaning croak, fell into the snow. The back wheel of the camper, meanwhile, had dug a deep hole of its own.

"Impossible," I said.

"What's impossible?"

"To get this camper out. We'll have to wait until the trucks come back and haul us out."

John was studying the new situation. He turned just long enough to frown at me. "You don't think negative like that in this country," he said. "Find out what your troubles are as you go, and keep going. Do you think you could work the winch in the camper, while I direct you?"

Yes, I can. John instructs me on running the winch evenly so I won't tangle the cable and chain as it winds and unwinds on the drum. I am to put my foot down on the clutch and let it out slowly, which will engage the winch and wind up the line. John selects two fair-sized trees close to one another, and wraps the small chain at the end of the winch line around both of them together while I crawl from the bank into the driver's seat. I am so afraid of doing something wrong that I do the only wrong thing possible. When he shouts, "Let out the clutch!" I am so nervous that I jerk my foot up and tangle the winch line. While he leans his weight against the camper so it won't tip over, I put down the clutch and let it out again, this time gradually. The winch line turns on the drum; the camper rises gently from the capturing earth into which its wheels have sunk so deeply. It creeps forward, closer and closer to the trees. Closer. Closer. Will the trees hold? Slender evergreens, spruce with sturdy trunks. Leaning. Leaning. Stop! The camper wheels are on firm ground. I am gripping the driver's wheel for balance, but I no longer need to; we are back on the road. Denison leaves off propping up the camper with his body and removes the winch line from around the trees, and I wind the rest of the cable and chain back on the drum. As fast as he can, John is packing brush and dirt into the holes and ruts in the road, behind and ahead. Done.

I slid over to the passenger side of the camper and Denison got back in the driver's seat. We were free and on our way again. All the camper windows on the right side were broken. A myriad tiny splintered lines in the shatterproof glass. The rear-view mirror had a deep crack, from top to bottom.

This was the messiest of all portages: no level ground, frozen muskeg all the way. We slipped, slid, lurched; sometimes we seemed to be travelling backwards. The more powerful, taller trucks were forward, out of sight, but after several miles I saw white clouds through a cut in the trees: the exhausts from the other vehicles, hanging in the dry cold air. Look out! Another deep rut and we came to a quivering halt. Denison was out with a shovel but not for long. He got back in the camper and honked the horn. The first time I had heard an automobile horn on the Ice Road. It was amazing that it was now working. Ugly dissonance, reminiscent of traffic lights, angry people, asphalt streets. "We'll wait for Davy to come and pull us out," Denison said, in the thin voice I knew meant he was tired. "There's only a mile or two more to this portage." Denison leaned back in the driver's seat, closed his eyes and slept.

I sat quietly waiting, and soon I heard the rumbling sounds of an engine. The Beaver emerged through the trees, square, portly, ponderous. I heard the familiar percolator voice of the Fud. The faces of George and Mukluk through their windshields wavered and danced in my weary vision. Am I so united with this little band that I sense disaster? Denison opened his eyes and sat up. Is that Burns, sitting beside Mukluk in Fud? Why isn't he working the Cat? The trucks halted facing the camper, and Burns climbed down from Fud and came over. He had aged since breakfast. John rolled down his window and propped his chin on his hand, elbow on the wheel. "What now?" he asked.

"The Cat," Burns said, shading his eyes with his hand to avoid looking at Denison. "The tie rod on that track I fixed has parted right at the bottom. That's the first link I ever broke. I can repair it with your portable welder if I can get the parts."

Denison put his hand to his head, as if in sudden pain. "We're broke down," he said. "Within seventy miles of Echo Bay, and we've only got three miles of portage, after this one. Pity of it is, if I can't reach ennabody on the radio, I have to go back."

I made coffee while John tried the radiophone. I was totally tired, myself. Sixty below zero. At that temperature a lot of energy is spent keeping warm! I was thirsty all the time now. I was eating three solid meals a day, but the pounds melted away. Mine was an easy job, riding as a passenger in a small truck, recording what was going on, but I was bone weary: merely getting into and out of heavy socks, sweaters, parka, boots and gloves whenever I went outside or came in again had become an effort; I had to keep alert, ready for anything, watch every move I made when I was walking on ice, climbing in and out of vehicles, preparing food, packing for travel. The danger in being careless, the sure knowledge that if I injured myself it would mean another delay while a plane was called to fetch me, made me apprehensive and tense. I lived under the same strain as the men, cared desperately what happened to the vehicles, was sick at heart when anything broke, which was now almost constantly, wondered if Denison would survive and if I would ever see the Echo Bay Mine again. Port Radium had become the Promised Land. Whatever detachment I had had when I started out was completely gone. Somewhere along the way—at which disaster? at what catastrophe?—I had lost that. Now I wanted to ride the Ice Road all the way to its end as much as anyone involved in its construction, as much as any man. John Denison had infected us all with his singleminded passion to finish the Ice Road to Port Radium.

What were the exact words Joe Major had used to describe this operation to me? They had struck me at the time, leaping out of his sentences to vibrate inside my head. *Heartscaring. Heartbreaking.*

The fire had gone out under the coffeepot on the stove, so I lit another match and put it to the burner, turning up the gas; only the briefest flicker of a flame. I lit a match and it fizzled out. Why bother? I was too lazy, too sleepy, to light another. The daylight was fading fast and it would soon be dark. Why was I so tired? The camper was cosy and warm; the Lazy Susan heater, attached to another gas tank, was hissing pleasantly in its travelling place in the little steel sink. There was a thick crust of snow on the inside of the door, and an inch of ice on the inner plastic of the windows; I could usually tell that it was sixty below outdoors by the amount of frost caked up on the inner window frames.

I heard the growl of the Diamond T backing up to the camper and the clink of a chain as Davy connected his winch to our front bumper. Each vehicle had its own voice. Sometimes I fancied that the trucks were talking to one another. The camper had a quiet car noise, a steady hum; 36 and 34 had the steady roar of Diesel motors, and the Diamond T a lighter roar, but still a roar; Fud was a gas truck, and made a snapping noise, pop, pop, pop; the Beaver and the Bug were like small trucks, quiet like ours, car engines. The drivers could even tell just by listening, what the make and size of an engine was.

Now the Diamond T was shrieking into high gear, there was a jolt, and the camper moved out of the hole it had been in, forward several feet. I grabbed the coffeepot and held onto it until I felt our four oversized tires moving on solid ground. I looked out the camper door as Davy leapt from his truck with an axe and Denison jumped from the camper with a hatchet. Both began furiously hacking ice from the camper wheels. I put on my parka and went out to watch them. Davy, stopping to catch his breath, said, "The camper wheels were caught in a bog under water. The minute they hit the air at sixty below, they've had it. We can't let these wheels freeze up solid."

Denison and Davy came into the camper later just as I lazily lit another match to heat the coffee. When it fizzled out again, Davy struck a match. When it went out, he wheeled around and flung the door open wide. John swore, reached over my head to the skylight, and cranked it wide open. "Too much propane in this goddam camper," he said. "Not enough oxygen. We'll have to be more careful." When the freezing air blew in, my match lighted easily, so did the stove. A breath of the fresh air, and I was wide awake. "We're in luck," Denison said. "I got Henry Ford on the phone at Fort Byers. He's going to order the parts for the Cat from Edmonton. As soon as they come, he'll send them by plane. We don't have to drive back to the garage tonight, after all."

We camped where we were. Spotlight George and Bob Burns arrived for breakfast early the following morning ahead of Mukluk. Since George always cooked breakfast for himself and any boarders in the Beaver, this could only mean one thing: bad news again.

We waited expectantly. Burns cleared his throat several times, looked down at his plate. "Old Fud gave up the ghost last night," he announced. "The front wheel drive is out. It was makin' funny noises all day, so I'm surprised it lasted as long as it did."

John was connecting a new tank of propane gas to the Lazy Susan. He gave it an extra, vicious tug with his wrench before he turned around. "Where's Mukluk?" he asked.

"Mukluk was using the drags late last night on the road," Burns replied. "He's behind you, about two mile."

Davy put down his coffee cup and pulled on his parka and mitts. "I'll pick up Fud by its plow and haul her up to the lake, John," he said, matter of factly. "Then I'll come back and suck the Cat up with the winch so Burns here can get at the track to fix it."

Burns lingered a moment after the others had gone. Looking down at the floor he said, "Do you want to sell Fud, John? I'll buy her from you."

Denison looked at him inquisitively. "How much?"

"Five dollars," Burns said with a sheepish grin.

Denison gave a short laugh. "Would you get Fud out of here?"

"Yes, I'd do that too."

"Nope," John said. "That Fud is a real handy piece of equipment, comin' and goin' the way it does. I'll have her fixed up in a week."

On the way out, Burns stepped aside to let Mukluk in. Billy sat down heavily at the table, pulled off his mitts and examined his right index finger, wiggled it and grimaced with pain. "I think I sprained my finger taking the drag off Fud," he said. "It must be the transmission that broke. The gears are stripped. I was pulling the drag about eleven last night when all of a sudden Fud stopped. She just wouldn't go any more, John." For a second I thought he might cry. He lowered his head and said grace, then sat with fork in hand, breakfast untouched. "So, it was just an abandoned ship," he continued. "I went to sleep right where I was and it was about the best sleep I ever had in that old Fud because it was the first time I ever had a little propane heater and I was nice and warm. Even the floor was so warm that I walked around barefoot. Besides everything else, Fud's got two flat tires, both on one side." He drank his coffee, wiped his stubbled beard with the back of his hand and began eating his eggs as if it was an effort. "May I go home now, John, eh? Maybe, my winter operations cease?"

"This road is shits, half-packed, like half-mixed cement," John said hoarsely. He took off his green cap and rubbed his forehead. "We haven't got it packed down and the top will probably freeze. Listen to that wind! It really blowed in this morning!"

Nobody mentioned the plane coming, but everyone was listening for it. As soon as we heard it overhead, Davy would get in the Diamond T and drive the two miles ahead to Fishtrap Lake, where the plane would land, and bring Hughie back. Our camp in the portage was sheltered from the wind by the woods we were in, but we were parked in an ugly bog. All around us was greenish-yellow slush, overflow that seeped continuously from the moist ground and oozed over the ice. When we made camp there, Denison sent ahead for fresh water to Fishtrap Lake. "This water is nothing but a swamp and too brackish for use," he said. "There are all kinds of overflow, and in this particular spot the water runs a bit, freezes, piles up and freezes into ice that's crappy, full of holes. The trucks break through the first time they go over it, but once it's packed down, it freezes good."

Spotlight George departed alone in the self-contained Beaver and Lewis Mackenzie went ahead in 36 to plow the new road for the twelve miles of Fishtrap Lake, taking Burns with him. Mukluk, who had no vehicle for the moment, and Davy, who was waiting for Hughie, were in the camper with us. Denison was sick again; a little sicker each time he had an ulcer attack. Each fresh catastrophe and delay, each breakdown in operations, compounded his deteriorating condition.

He lay in his bunk, not eating, not drinking either, speaking to no one. His grey skin, with its grey stubble of beard, had two white lines running through it at the corners of his mouth to make him look especially grim. Eyes shut. Chiselled features, absolutely still; that expressionless face-carved-in-stone look. The atmosphere inside the camper was as still and tense as the man who lay above us in the bunk.

For the first time I began to wonder seriously if John was going to die . . . and brushed the thought away, like the first cobweb that settles in a dark corner. Looking back later on that two-day period when we sat in the bog between Hottah and Fishtrap lakes, I always think of us as living statues, sitting in our trucks, not moving. The first day, John went outside several times and threw up, but the second day he was too weak to get up, and we brought him the dishpan. Davy and I begged him to return to Yellowknife with the plane, when it brought Hughie. His reply was always the same: silence. The men came and went, walking softly as if they were in a hospital sickroom, and we spoke in low whispers.

On the second day, towards evening, John was violently ill again. One of the men had brought me a pail of ice from the lake ahead, so I would be sure to have fresh water, and I took Denison's wrench, cracked off a piece of ice with the end of it, went over and stood above him. "Open your mouth," I commanded. "You are completely dehydrated." To my astonishment, he opened his mouth, and I placed the piece of ice between his teeth. I went back to the table and sat down to think about this. A little while later, I handed him a second piece, which he obediently sucked, and an hour later I opened a can of applesauce, and handed him a teaspoon of that. When Davy came in, I whispered what I had done, and he said I would get some kind of a merit award for my courage. Mukluk arrived shortly, and sat down on the bench to read a mystery he had brought over from Fud, and for a while the camper was silent; the only noise, the hissing of the Lazy Susan. I had handed the applesauce can to Denison, and out of the corner of my eye I could see the spoon go from the can to his mouth; stop for a while, then start again.

Davy broke the silence, moving restlessly from his seat at the table beside Mukluk to the bench across the way, lighting a cigarette. From there, he could converse easily with me in the kitchen, where I was preparing dinner. "I like a great big truck; it's more comfortable than this camper, which is so light that when it bounces you can't sit in your seat," Davy said. "Truck driving in the North isn't like highway driving. Outside, I get scared on highways and there's nothin' exciting to be seen on them, nothin' at all. Good or bad, there's somethin' different up here every day. I watch the bush with my eyes gawkin', looking everywhere. There's a lot of life in the bush. At night you just watch the road and can't see nothin' else, but in the daytime you can watch the road *and* the bush, and see the odd track. Now take a highway driver, he won't run into a herd of caribou or pretty near run over a dog team. If he's lucky he'll just see the odd moose, that's all."

Davy suddenly addressed himself to Denison. "John, just before the Beaver left yesterday morning, I went into the bog myself, and I couldn't get out." For the first time in two days, Denison sat up on one elbow and looked interested. "George didn't want to pull me out, but I told him he had to," Davy continued. "You are so afraid of breaking something on that goddamned twelve-thousand-dollar kitchen of yours that you've got him thinkin' the same way." Denison gave a hollow laugh and lay down again, but suddenly he changed his mind, and slowly emerged from his bunk. He sat down, resting his elbows on the table, his chin in his hands.

"The last time I drove a truck on a highway I put it in a rhubarb, drove it right into the ditch, and I got laughed off the road," John said. "I'll bet none of you guys would change places with any of those highway guys."

Davy's face had brightened for an instant, when he saw

John getting up, but now Lorentzen lay down casually on the bench, took off his cap and put it across his chest. He dragged on his cigarette, blew several smoke rings, and watched the smoke spiral to the ceiling. "Bush and highway drivers are two different breeds," Davy said. "Just like among highway drivers, the tankers think the freight haulers are a cut below them, and won't sit in the cafés with them. Well, the highway drivers come in from Outside and think they're goin' to show us bush apes a lot of things. But when one of those highway fellas has somethin' happen to his truck, even though he knows how to repair it he's not used to doin' that, so he just sits and waits for someone to come along and fix it. Their first trip up, these here highway drivers don't even like to cross the Mackenzie River. The ice scares hell out of them, and it's like prodding a cow into an airplane to get them to go out on the ice bridge. They aren't even too confident on the bush trip until they've been at it a while."

Denison laughed. Mukluk looked up and put his book down. "A lot of highway drivers imagine this northern run is a vacation package," John said. "When a guy wants a job he can do ennathing—ennathing until he gets here! *Then* we find out what he can and can't do. Those highway boys arrive in their little Wellington boots and their cotton gloves"—he spoke in a mocking, mincing tone—"just a different breed of drivers, that's all. I remember one new man who drove into overflow ice at Discovery Mine one afternoon. He was so sure he was sinkin' that he left his truck and walked to an island and stayed there all night in front of a little fire, when he could have sat right in his truck." He shook his head. "Beats me. Just because there was a little water on top of the ice. Yet these fellas think we don't know ennathing up here. Maybe we don't, but I learn somethin' new every time I go out in the bush."

I felt a warm glow for the driver who had spent the night outdoors in the Arctic winter sitting on an island. I had the same instinct to get out myself whenever the camper sloshed through ominous outsized puddles in the big lakes. I was apt to keep my hand on the door handle, open the window and nervously peer down to see if our wheels were sinking, but Denison always looked serene. "Overflow on a lake scares *anybody* half to death who has never seen it before," I said crossly. "I wish someone would explain it to me."

"The weight of the truck can cause overflow but mostly it's snow piled up on top of the lakes that does it," John said. "When you get an acre of snow, that's thousands of tons, a lot of weight on a big lake. The water comes up through the cracks in the ice and lays on top of it, and of course the water won't freeze as long as snow falls on top, which acts as insulation. So when you come along in a truck, everything gets wet, but it's just messy the first time. After you come through a couple of times it freezes and makes a real good trail. I must admit though that when you drive on overflow, and your road sags down and there's water on top and you can't tell whether it's all ice or water, it looks pretty goddamned scary."

I could picture it, I was there. "Listen," I said, "How do you know you've got ice underneath? I'd like to know that."

"Well, if you don't fall through, you know it's ice," John said. Everybody laughed but me. "As a rule, if the road is all bent down and the water lays on top, you're safe, but if there's no water, you're not safe, because that means the water's going through. You've got to be a lot more careful and get the hell out of it. This is generally in the spring, when the ice is melting, but it's different every time. Never the same."

"Amazing things happen out here," Davy said. "A couple of years ago we were seven miles short of Great Bear Lake in a storm so bad no one could walk between the trucks. Someone dropped a bolt in a spark-plug hole and had to take the head off the engine on his truck, right in the open, when you could hardly see at all!"

"How did he do it?" I asked.

"Will power," Davy answered. He sat up and addressed

himself to me. "Tell me now, honest, aren't you afraid up here?"

I thought about that. "I really don't think I am, but I don't know why not," I finally replied. "Do I seem to be?"

"Not really," he said. "I guess you don't know any better."

It had been three weeks since Denison had started building the Ice Road, a week since we had been back to Yellowknife. No more bandages on my fingertips. No more complaints about my cooking; the men were too busy. They were just thinking about one thing, finishing the road. I could get a meal together for the crew and pack up immediately afterwards to move on again with a certain speed and expertise; placing all the food and condiments in drawers, and in boxes braced on the floor, while Denison made his scheduled phone calls.

The vehicles had not fared so well as I had. Two, the Bug and John's TD-14 Cat, were disabled and gone for the season, maybe forever, though I doubted that after the way Fud kept breaking down and reappearing; three had been partially under water ("gotten wet" was John's phrase for it), there had been one fire, and numerous, uncountable breakdowns. I missed Jimmy Watson and Tom Berry. Henry Ford relayed the news via the mobile phone that Jimmy had a baby daughter. Tom was still waiting for parts for 34 from Edmonton. Jimmy would return to snowplow the Echo Bay Ice Road when it was open, in 36, and Tom would return whenever his truck, 34, was ready to travel again.

Physically tired, I was spiritually at peace in this strange, existentialist world. I was letting each day come, without thinking ahead at all. On the morning of the third day that we were camped in the bog, we heard the welcome sound of the plane motor. Hettrick was circling overhead, and Denison opened the door of the camper and waved. Davy drove out to the lake and returned with Hughie, Hettrick, and Ike Richardson, Henry Ford's assistant at Fort Byers. While Hughie was outside under the parachute repairing his Cat with Burns, Ike, a big, burly man, sat in the camper with us. Over coffee, he gave us the news: three men fishing on Great Slave Lake in a Bombardier not far from Yellowknife the previous day hit a crack in the ice and went under. Two of them drowned. "You wouldn't think they'd run out of ice on *that* lake!" Denison exclaimed. Ike reported that Denison's new big snowplow truck, No. 37, was on its way to join us with a new driver, Herb Lowen. He would take Tom's place until he returned, and bring the cook for the truck stop at Hottah Lake. The regular trucks were already loaded with freight, including the dynamite, for Echo Bay Mine, and were waiting at Fort Byers for word that we had reached Port Radium; that we had finished the road and opened it for winter freighting.

While Denison and Ike conferred, I went out to watch Burns and Hughie repair the broken link in the track of the Cat, using a portable welder on wheels. The weather had warmed up ten degrees to fifty below zero, and the wind had died down slightly, but the cold still pierced my heavy clothes as if I were walking around in tissue paper. Burns seemed oblivious of the cold. He worked with bare hands beneath the parachute that surrounded his tractor like a tent, stopping only long enough to blow on his hands or rub them on his face as he cut the links off the pins of the track. He worked all day, and I ran back and forth from the camper, watching him work, amazed at his fortitude. Going in and out so often I was careless about putting on my gloves and once absentmindedly grabbed the handle of the door of the camper with my bare hands. My hand stuck to the metal handle and when I yanked my fingers away, I left skin behind and had an abrasion exactly like a burn.

As soon as the Cat was repaired, Hettrick, Hughie and Ike left, as the first salmon streaks that signalled the end of daylight flushed across the sky. Denison packed the camper for travelling, and the plane was still climbing in the sky when he turned the camper around, with Mukluk and me sitting beside him, and started driving south. I had no idea why we were going back and John was too grim to be questioned. When he stood up to leave the camper to go in front to drive, he looked scary, he was so emaciated, and three days' growth of beard had not improved his appearance. I had plenty of time to think, as we barrelled down the road at breakneck speed: he had not eaten more than a few dabs of food, including the applesauce, since our Chinese lunch at the Gold Range a week ago. Was that only a week ago? It was another life.

Thanks to the balloon tires of the Beaver and the heavy wheels of 36, the portage where we had been trapped coming was now relatively level, and wider. Still, twice our vehicle was caught in deep ruts. A short period of judicious rocking put us on our way again. I wondered if John had brought Mukluk along in case we got stuck; I did not think Denison had the strength now to jack up a heavy truck and winch it to trees.

Denison spoke for the first time when we bounced from the portage onto Hottah Lake, indicating why we had come. He told Mukluk to change trucks when we met the new snowplow, 37, and its new driver, Herb Lowen, which he figured would be any time now. We would all turn around then and go back north to Fishtrap Lake, and Mukluk could guide Lowen to our camp. "I don't know what's holdin' him up," John said. "We should have met him by now. It's his first trip north, but he's an experienced driver."

The half-moon shed a grey, cold light on the big lake and from the north end we could see for miles down our long white road. It was alarmingly empty. "He's probably at the Hottah camp having dinner," Denison said. "I told him to drop off the new cook at Sarah Lake and bring Gilles on up here instead. Gilles opened up the Hottah camp for me last year, and he likes it there. When we get to the Indore Mine, Gilles can cook you supper."

"How about you?" I asked.

He made a face, put his hand on his stomach, and shook his

head. He looked terrible. His face was grey, and after such a loss in weight, deeply lined: his normally youthful expression had vanished; he looked grim, aging and terribly sick.

It was so cold on Hottah Lake that even with the heater on and three of us in the front seat giving each other warmth, we were thoroughly chilled. The cold bit through the cab's walls, right into us. The thermometer had dropped down again to sixty below and on the open lake the wind tore savagely at the truck, blowing it back and forth from one side of the road to the other, knocking snow from the drifts. Screaming wind; cold air washing our feet, thrusting with enormous force through holes in the floor, blowing fine powdery snow from the Ice Road below to build in little pyramids around our boots. Mukluk and I, shivering, planned the hot meal we would get: canned corn and string beans with our steak, and for dessert, apricots, and cookies. We had run out of cookies and our bread was green around the edges. How grand to sit down to a hot meal that somebody else had cooked! Mukluk and I planned to have our steaks medium-rare.

The black buildings showing in relief against the night sky were the Indore Mine, we could see the shaft of the head frame. But! Where was the smoke that should be puffing from the stove pipe in the roof of the second building from the left? Surely the truck had come, but where was it? Where?

We drove up to the lifeless shed.

Padlocked.

As bleak, as stark as it had been three days ago when we had camped right here beside the big fuel-storage tank. Empty, silent buildings. No sign of life here. Thoughts raced through my mind. *Something had happened to Lowen! Never been north before! Turned over! Jackknifed! Rhubarbed! Drowned in the Emile River! FELL INTO A LAKE!*

We sat stunned. I thought, we will surely turn back now, John looks so sick. Denison backed the camper into the Ice Road, shifted gears, and we were racing south again, ten miles to the lower end of Hottah Lake. We careened through the next portage, Denison twisting the wheel around in deceptively casual motions. He made it look so easy, driving with a light hand, sometimes only one or two fingers twined around the edge of the wheel.

We slid from side to side. I expected we would land in a snowbank but the road was levelled down better than I could have dreamed possible and Denison was a most skillful driver.

Mukluk was hanging onto his door to keep his balance as the truck swerved from side to side, and I hung onto Mukluk, both of us holding one hand on the radio to avoid hitting it. I was also bracing my body with both feet to keep from bumping Denison's arm. We flew across lakes and portages so fast that I forgot about the cold. *Where was Lowen? Where was the truck?* After Hottah, we crossed Beaverlodge, then Malfait. We were obviously going to find 37, if we had to drive all the way back to Fort Byers. All the way back. Over two hundred miles back.

The grey light adds to the chill. We are flying down the length of Hardisty Lake. Tricky treacherous Hardisty Lake, which has tried to pull Fud and the Cat through the ice to the same watery rest as Denison's Bug that must be sitting—upright, perhaps?—on the lake bottom, in the mud. Has Hardisty snatched the pride of Denison's unorthodox fleet, the new truck, 37, too?

Denison saw it first. He slowed down as we approached the south shore of Hardisty Lake and I searched for the reason. A handsome new red truck was standing on the Ice Road about a mile from shore, facing north, facing us. It was clearly visible in the eerie, cold moonlight, but something was missing. What?

No lights. No lights at all, although smoke puffed from 37's exhaust pipe. So the motor was running. I had eyes for nothing but the truck in this grey illumination and at first didn't see the other vehicle. Goliath and David. A four-passenger sedan, a midget beside 37, was facing in the same direction, north, also with no lights. No smoke from its exhaust, which meant no motor running.

"That's Herb, all right," Denison said.

The truck driver was talking with his head out his side window to the driver of the other car as if they were at a street intersection. When we drove up, bathing both machines in our yellow lights, Lowen got out of 37 and came over to the camper. Denison was waiting for him, chin on hand, elbow resting on the steering wheel. "Hello Herb, what's up?" he said.

"These two men are hunters from Yellowknife and their car has broken down," Lowen said. "Their gas is frozen and their battery's gone dead. My generator's gone, so I have no lights or electricity, myself."

Denison's face had become stony. He nodded curtly to the driver of the small car, got a can of menthol hydrate to melt the ice in the gasoline and another of antifreeze for the radiator from the camper, and handed them without a word to the driver, who had meanwhile gotten out of his car. Still silent, Denison backed the camper in front of the hunter's small Chevrolet, attached a chain to his bumper and towed him forward until his motor started. "I understand there is a truck stop where we can eat around here," the man said. Any of Denison's men, any student of his moods, would have seen the fleeting expression of contempt, the flickering motion of his upper lip, the swift stillness, which signified real fury—he once told me that when he was that angry, he sometimes shook—but it was gone in an instant. "Not open," he said.

When the men had their car turned around headed towards Yellowknife, John sent Mukluk over to invite them into the camper to warm up, and told me to put on some soup and coffee. When the two hunters appeared at the camper door, Denison's glance fell on their hunting costumes and he looked very slightly amused. They were wearing light winter outfits, with ordinary boots. Sixty below. Mindlessly coming out on such a night in such skimpy apparel! Tom Berry was the only person I had ever seen who dared venture outdoors like that. And they had come without even a can of antifreeze!

Around the little table in the camper, conversation limped, collapsed. "What were you planning to do?" I asked, out of curiosity.

"Hunt caribou," one of the men said. "The hunting season's open and we heard that the Ice Road was too. Someone told us there was a place to eat at Hottah Lake."

Denison got up, and turned his back, walking into the kitchen, fiddling with the propane heater tanks. Even his shoulder blades looked outraged. Neither Mukluk nor Lowen nor I felt up to rescuing what remained of this social occasion. The men left, and when I heard their car start in the direction of Yellowknife, I asked Denison if many hunters came out on his road expecting to be fed. Denison said coldly, "A few hunters do this, but not many." He turned to Lowen. "Where's Gilles?" he asked.

"After Burns left, a hunter gave him a lift from Sarah Lake in to Yellowknife. He's in poor shape, but I brought him back with me as far as Fort Byers," Lowen replied. "He was shaking from head to foot, and had eaten only two bowls of soup in the last two days. I left him at the garage to dry out and he's coming on the next truck."

Denison and Mukluk went with Lowen to look at the big truck's broken generator. I warmed more water, washed the dirty dishes. Then I opened the camper door to step outside and dump the dirty dishwater and coffee grounds into deep snow. I did this three times a day and I always set the dishpan and coffeepot carefully down on the camper floor while I turned and descended the steps backwards. If the steps fell off, which they had done several times in very low temperatures, I could control my fall.

This had been a long long day. It was now two in the morning, and I was exhausted. Any long-distance drive on the

Ice Road was physically wearing; I braced myself automatically now, and no longer bounced from one end of the seat to the other, but the effort was tiring, requiring constant attention to the road, almost as if one were driving. I had napped briefly on the trip tonight, packed in between two bodies, but not for long. This had been the wildest, most strenuous drive we had had, even for a passenger.

I was so tired that without thinking, a dangerous luxury on the Ice Road, I opened the door and walked casually down the steps, dishpan in one hand, coffeepot in the other. My right foot on the top step, my left foot on the second.

CRACK!

The stepladder broke away from the camper; I fell with a horrible crash, my back slapping hard on the ice.

The ice spun around. How long I lay there I had no way of knowing; probably not more than a few minutes. Maybe more. A starry blackness swam past my eyes—was it the sky? I lay on my back on the Ice Road, ungloved, bare hands outstretched, dishpan off in one direction, coffeepot in another, too stunned to move. Seasick, sailing, spinning, rocking, on the treacherous hard water of Hardisty Lake. John's Bug. Fud. Hughie's Cat. Now me.

What had I heard about broken backs? If you can move, you're all right. Or maybe if you can't move. I raised my head. My neck was working. My arms. They seemed to move. Now to sit up. This took a little time.

Slowly, carefully, I sit up. I expect to hear something crack in two. *I* expect to crack in two. No, I seem to be all right, except that everything hurts, especially my back and shoulders, and the back of my head. Slowly. Carefully. I stand up, pushing the ground away from under me with my ungloved hands. I reach for the coffeepot, but now with the steps gone, the entrance to the camper is way beyond me, and the steps are too heavy to lift, let alone set back in their slot, if they haven't broken away from their hinges altogether.

I turned the coffeepot upside down on the road and stood on it, then remembered the dishpan, got down painfully, and went over and retrieved it from where it had fallen and spewed dirty dishwater all over the road in back of the camper. The dishpan bottom felt too insubstantial, so I stood again on the coffeepot, and threw the dishpan inside. For a second the coffeepot teetered. Grimly, I held on to the camper floor, and wriggled my way inside. Then I turned around, leaned down painfully, and retrieved the coffee pot.

When I went to close the open camper door with my bare hand, my fingers stuck to the doorknob. Ordinarily this hurt, but this time I didn't feel a thing. Why? Why? How long had I been lying on the Ice Road? There was a pleasant sensation in my fingers of nothingness. At sixty below, less than five minutes of exposure without gloves on the ice would do it; my fingers were a dead white.

There was an extra small pan of water on the back of the stove, cool now, but not icy. Without taking off my parka, I sat down and immersed those frightful pale white frozen fingers of mine into the water. And wept.

It was an agonizing pain: swift, surprising, stabbing pain. I continued to weep while the circulation in my fingers slowly returned, knowing this pain was probably good. Grateful to be alone. My fingers were still immersed in water, turning a reassuring pink, when I heard the men outside.

Someone picked up the steps where they had fallen. Automatically, without thinking again, I poured the water in which my fingers had been soaking down the steel sink, which was empty now because the Lazy Susan was sitting in the aisle of the camper, warming the room. The pipe in the sink!

What a night. My fingers throbbed. My back throbbed. My head throbbed. My neck hurt. And now I had broken the pipe in the sink! I had burdened Denison, in addition to his other problems, with frozen pipes.

I heard Denison being sick outside. Mukluk came back into

the camper alone, and I whispered to him what I had done. While I was packing to travel he poured a fluid down the sink, disappeared outside, and gave me a quick little nod and reassuring smile when he returned. He had done something with alcohol in the elbow of the sink pipe, what, I never found out. I was sure Denison had noticed—he noticed everything, but he never said a word.

We were ready to leave. I was hoping Mukluk would drive the camper, but he was already in 37, holding a small round propane heater up to the windshield, so Lowen would be able to see to drive. No generator meant no defroster, no heater; I was familiar with this condition. With the camper leading, 37 could easily drive without headlights; the grey moonlight in the clear night air lit up the white strip of our road.

Ever since we had caught up with Lowen, Denison had been trying to reach the garage at Fort Byers on the mobile phone, and just before we started back, he finally did. Hettrick would fly out another generator, looking for us below on the lakes until he found us.

What kept Denison going? His eyes were absolutely huge now in his bony face, deep sunk in their sockets. He was so thin and so sick that, obviously, he was travelling solely on some inner strength and power of will: physically no better off than he had been—maybe, probably, worse than when he was lying flat out in the back bunk, motionless, silent.

We had to drive more slowly going back because of the big truck, and when we reached our camp at Fishtrap, he went straight to bed. In the morning, it was apparent that Denison had finally pushed himself too far. For the first time, he was too sick to drive, and Mukluk took the camper across Fishtrap Lake. I inherited Mukluk's task of holding the Lazy Susan heater at the windshield of 37, but it was a much harder job than when I had done it in the camper just before the fire. I sat where Mukluk had been sitting, on a raised place called the "doghouse" that covered the motor, delicately balanced between the driver's and passenger's seat, bracing the propane gas tank connected to the heater with my feet, holding the heater up to the windshield with my left hand, steadying myself on the other side with my right arm. It was a tricky position to maintain even for the short time I did it, less than an hour, on the relatively smooth lake surface mostly. I was not surprised when Lowen told me that yesterday on the seventy-mile trip from Hottah to Fishtrap, on one of the rough portages the heater slipped from Mukluk's grasp and burned the gaping raw hole I noticed in the new brown leather upholstery of the passenger's seat.

In the past two days, when day and night had intermingled, I had again lost track of time. The daylight hours, from ten until four, were so short that most of the work was done in the dark anyway; the men left and returned from our lake campsites at all hours. When a big truck drew up alongside the camper, I would be half-awakened by the added rumbling of another motor to swell the night chorus on the ice, and by the extra tremors as the big vehicle passed by the camper and halted, even before the driver came in to report, as he always did.

Denison directed the road-building operation entirely from his bunk, because he was less actively ill if he lay perfectly still. He forced himself to get up, but only to drive and try the radio, because there was no one else to do either thing unless he took someone off a truck. Once, in case I sometime might have to, I drove the camper. It was the first time I had ever driven a truck, and this one had four gears. I took it across a pothole with Mukluk supervising, when Denison was sleeping inside. We slid over the ice. Afterwards, I went back in the camper to start supper. Denison turned his head as I came in and I said, "*I* was driving the camper across that last pothole."

"I know," Denison said. "I could tell when you shifted gears." Once we stopped at the little yellow gas wagon which we and everyone else occasionally hauled behind our vehicles, to refuel. We were always pulling something behind us and this time it was the drags, so while Denison checked them and the truck engine, I pumped an old-fashioned wobble hand pump to transfer gas from the tanker to the camper. Every time I pushed the handle on the end of the tanker back and forth I pushed a half-gallon of gas into the camper, and the camper needed a lot of gas. I was surprised at the energy this took and I tired out long before I stopped. What an effort the men had to make regularly to do ordinary chores!

Denison was following every detail of road construction, making decisions, but I had not seen him eat anything except pills for two days, and again the only fluid he was drinking was to wash them down. A disadvantage of living at such close quarters as both Davy and I did with Denison, was that willy-nilly, we knew every nuance of his physical condition. He suffered in total silence and I was overwhelmed with relief when the other men arrived in the camper. I had human beings then with whom I could communicate. In this curious world of unlimited space outside, and drastically curtailed space inside the tiny vehicle, I felt that John needed to have the camper to himself, but there was really no place else to go. It was too cold to stay outdoors for more than a few minutes at a time. My best recourse was the cab of the camper, where I would sit with a book, or with one of the men, our cups of coffee resting on the dashboard while we talked.

Sometimes when I returned to the camper, John was lying so still, with his eyes shut, that I wondered if he was breathing. He again ignored Davy's suggestions that he be flown out. His single-minded focus on getting the Ice Road built gave the men a feeling of urgency. They worked almost around the clock, stopping to snatch an hour or two of sleep and food before taking their trucks back out on the road again.

There was general agreement that the best way to get John Denison home alive and make him healthy again was to finish the Ice Road. Soon.

Chapter Nine

THE BIG LAKE

We were at the north end of Fishtrap, facing the strangest of all portages between this and Yen, the next lake; a barrier of sand, a northern phenomenon that never freezes, called an esker. Great light-brown, winding ridge of some mysterious ancient glacial deposit towering above us, extending out of sight. What elemental force placed you here? Sandy, beach-tinted natural dam, warm tan anachronism, broad strip of summer color in all this dazzling white snow and ice! When Denison built his first Ice Road to Echo Bay, he toured four miles to get around this obstacle until his bulldozers knocked off fifteen feet of its forty-foot height and cleaned out the loose gravel to cut a passage through it at just the place where our little band of trucks waited now.

It was nine o'clock in the evening and all the other trucks had turned with their headlights to light up the new plow truck, 37, which had brought the Cat on the lowboy across Fishtrap Lake to its far end. We had arrived in a convoy, then spread out in a semi-circle of lights to illuminate another drama: the main actor, Burns, sitting high up on Hughie's Cat which was at the back end of the lowboy, waiting to descend to the ice. Two slanting boards had been placed from the lowboy to the lake ice to catch the weight of the Cat when its tracks and a fraction more than half its weight moved over the trailer's back and dropped beyond.

Denison and I were sitting in the cab of the camper, providing one of the four sets of footlights for this new stage. Four pairs of truck headlights were shining on 37 and its burden; those of the camper, Davy's Diamond T, 36 (which Lewis Mackenzie was driving) and the Beaver, with its additional spotlight. Spotlight George had rejoined us only that evening.

"I hate to bring a Cat down from a lowboy," John said quietly. "I hate all that bouncing down. There's a very tricky moment when the Cat goes swiftly over the back of the truck and comes down on the ice."

The Cat, with Burns, solemn-faced, at the controls, suddenly swung over the back of the truck. I held my breath while its flat tracks were suspended horizontally in mid-air; the Cat dropped neatly to the safety of the boards, then down on the ice. "I've done that when I've had to, but I'm terrible at it," Denison murmured. "He's *good!*"

The Cat swung around with its big searchlight shining on the esker. It had to be the first vehicle to cross, it was the only one capable of cleaning out the boulders and other large debris deposited there over the past year. Burns skillfully steered his machine up and over the sand barrier, disappearing down the other side. He made several passes back and forth, pounding down the rough road into some semblance of smoothness. The Beaver went next, and I could see, from below, the big wheels levelling the ground one hundred yards away above us. The trucks followed, one at a time, and as each one lurched up the bank, swaying from side to side, threatening to slip back, fighting its way forward, the Cat moved up behind and gave a gentle nudge that sent the vehicle scrambling over the top. Only Fud was missing, waiting alone, abandoned in the portage between Hottah and Fishtrap lakes, where Davy had hauled her so that she would be in the shelter of the trees at the place where we had camped. One of the snowplow trucks would take her on its back to Fort Byers on its return trip.

Safely down from the esker on Yen Lake, we made camp for the night, resuming our positions in a circle facing inwards. I was sleeping in a lighted room; the lights from the other trucks shone through the windows all night. I had forgotten altogether what day of the week it was, or even that there soon would come a time when the road would be done, so it was a shock to learn that at the other end of Yen Lake, four miles away, the next portage would be the last land barrier we would cross before Great Bear Lake. On the other side of this final portage was Gunbarrel Inlet, a narrow entrance channel four miles long and only one mile wide, leading into The Big Lake.

It was fifty below zero, not counting the wind, and all the canned goods I had packed away on the kitchen floor had frozen solid, including one last can of evaporated milk. The trucks worked all night on the esker, levelling the road across it. In the morning we followed the slow-paced Cat across Yen Lake to its north end. The portage we faced now into Great Bear Lake was the shortest one on the Ice Road, about a mile long. It was also the steepest, because the trucks had to climb a rugged slope and then drop down 200 feet between Yen Lake and Gunbarrel Inlet.

Denison had shaved this morning. Was it possible that he expected to reach Port Radium today? I dared not ask. The thinness of his face coming out from behind that grizzled beard shocked me; he was all eyes and bones. Now he restlessly strummed his fingers on the steering wheel while he watched Burns on the Cat mount what appeared to be an almost perpendicular incline. Suddenly the Cat vanished, slipping abruptly over the rim of the hill. "Two days late!" Denison muttered. "I said I'd be in Port Radium two days ago!"

"This looks like a very steep portage," I said. It looked straight up to me; *looking* at it made me jittery.

"This has to be our worst bit of road in the whole system," Denison said. "It's good now compared to what it has been in the past three years when we've had to blast rock to get through. It used to be our biggest bottleneck, and we had to winch every truck up the goddamned thing and down again, which meant keeping a Cat here most of the time. There aren't many trees, but there are an awful lot of rocks, especially at a place you can't see from here where there's a creek and lots of open water runnin'. The snow gets unusually deep in this portage too, about three feet."

The Cat passed back and forth over the portage two or three times. The Beaver followed, hanging over the rim at the peak of the hill, seeming to teeter, as if it were trying to make up its mind which way to go. It disappeared over the other side; a signal for Lewis Mackenzie, the next in line, to start up the hill in the African Queen. The huge truck dipped and twisted, seemed to fall back, then rose in a surge of strength over the top. Denison, suddenly impatient, shifted gears and drove up the perpendicular embankment. Halfway, we were caught in deep snow. The Beaver, which had just returned, climbed up behind us and unsuccessfully tried to push us.

So we waited. The other trucks, 37 and the Diamond T, tried to go by us and got stuck. The Cat, waiting on the side of the hill, at a signal from Denison moved forward. Denison got out and hooked the Cat's winch to our bumper. Back in the camper, he nodded to Burns, who wound up his winch with us hooked on it, pulling us up from the snow-filled hole and out. When we were free and Denison had released us from the winch, Burns moved slowly around the other two trucks, coming in behind to give them a shove that got them going and out of the way. Meanwhile, we were stuck again.

A glance in the camper's rear-view mirror. Smoke, pouring from the space behind the cab! Denison saw it at the same time I did, ran out, picked up an armful of snow, and threw it where the smoke was. The smoke disappeared, and when I got back in the camper, Denison was climbing in on the other side, laughing. It was the first real laugh I had heard from him—I couldn't remember how long since I had heard him laughing like that. "No wonder I've been having so much trouble getting the camper over this hill," he said, looking sheepish, as we moved forward. "I had my brake on. It was my goddam hand emergency brake that caught fire!"

At the top of the hill two red-and-white gasoline drums marked the route. Travelling between them up to the crest, I peered through the camper's windshield over the sheerest drop I had ever seen on anything that could be called a road. On this trip, anything became a road once a vehicle had travelled through it; no terrain was too rough. There was some comfort in seeing 36 at the bottom, placid, intact, motor still running, judging by the white exhaust she was emitting. She must have gotten down somehow to Gunbarrel Inlet; a narrow long space, aptly named. It seemed very far below from where I sat.

Beyond, vast space, white and smooth: Great Bear Lake. We teetered on the top of the portage one more second. I gripped the seat with both hands, held my breath, shut my eyes. We were gliding sliding sideways down the hill to a semi-level area I hadn't seen. I opened my eyes at the sound of running water, open water, on my left, twenty feet away. We crossed this shallow rocky creek, travelled for perhaps a hundred yards on its right around some rapids, made a little turn and came to a place of wide open water, splattered with rocks and boulders.

Stuck again, wheels spinning in the water. The Cat was upon us, attaching a chain to our front bumper, hauling us the short distance up a small ridge. Looking down, again I saw Gunbarrel Inlet, directly below, a quarter of a mile away. No. Too steep. Too steep for this little camper, and then we were tumbling straight down the hill towards the glassy surface of the inlet, pulled as if by some fierce spirit hand to the narrow icy entrance to The Big Lake.

We coasted out on the ice and watched while the others sped down: Davy in his Diamond T truck, with its long gin poles pointing upwards to form a triangle behind the cab; Bob Burns, poised, sure-handed, on the heavy Cat; Herb Lowen, seemingly unfazed by this exotic new landscape, with Mukluk still beside him holding the Lazy Susan heater steady to the windshield. Denison had told Mukluk that he intended to repair Fud and put it back on the Ice Road, plowing, so Mukluk was not to have his wish to end his winter season now. *If* that really *was* his wish.

Everyone left their trucks, motors idling, and joined us in the camper for lunch. We had run out of staples, especially bread, which the men usually toasted on the Lazy Susan, and evaporated milk, which they all used in their coffee and tea. I made a horrible mixture of the last of our hamburgers and mashed potatoes for the men, and a bowl of soup for John. He pushed it away, held his stomach and made a face. He looked up to see us all looking at *him*, sternly, and he laughed, a little embarrassed. Nobody laughed with him. Davy Lorenzen said quietly, "You'd better eat, John. You haven't had anything for three days." Denison hesitated, looking at us. Nobody said anything. Nobody needed to: our anxiety for him was on all our faces. What he saw made him duck his face down and drink his soup.

Suddenly everyone was putting on a coat or parka and saying goodbye to me. Only Herb Lowen and Mukluk in the new handsome plow truck, 37, were going with us to make the Ice Road for the last forty miles to Port Radium. The others were turning back to open an access road to a new silver mine, Terra, eighteen miles in off Fishtrap Lake. Then they would move south, putting the finishing touches to the Ice Road behind us; cementing the snow into ice on the portages, plowing the lakes to keep them open and free of snow. Barring any more accidents, by the end of this day John would be calling Fort Byers from Port Radium, and the trucks from Yellowknife, from Hay River, from Edmonton, would be on their way.

We wiped the dirty dishes with paper towels, packed the camper for travelling, and drove the four miles down Gunbarrel Inlet, only a mile wide between its narrow shores; through the mouth of that Inlet into the great open space of Great Bear Lake. Denison was moving along rapidly at forty miles an hour and Lowen was travelling directly behind us. I could see him plainly in my side-view mirror, because his cabover truck was built like a bus with the driver flat at the front of his efficient-looking vehicle. The Lazy Susan in Mukluk's hand was a round oversized glowing orange at the window, with Mukluk, shadowy, behind it.

It was two in the afternoon when we started across the corner of Great Bear Lake that we must traverse for forty miles before we reached the mine. The sky was grey, the low hills to our right were speckled with black scrubby trees, and there was a thin coating of snow on the ice over which we were gliding. The snow became deeper, so that the camper pushing through it met with crusty resistance, and the ice became rough and bumpy. I must have dozed, because I bounced and swayed and hit the ceiling. I was wide awake suddenly, automatically bracing myself with my hands against the windshield and radio, pressing my feet firmly into the floor. Denison made a swing to the right and motioned out his window for Lowen to do the same. "Sharp ice here," he said to me. "Every year it's different on the Big Lake and we can't ever go the same way. Some years when a wind comes up while the ice is only partly frozen, it makes miles and miles of rough ice with big jagged edges, six inches to three feet high. We try to go around it but that's impossible and we take hours to plow two miles. Then it's real hard work."

"Does the ice ever break the plow?" I asked.

"Sure!" he replied. "The cutting edge of the plow is only half an inch thick and sometimes the ice breaks a chunk off, or it can even snap the whole blade, or break the push rods that fasten the plow to the truck, so we can't plow. If we have a welder with us he welds it up right where we are and if we don't, then we fly the material or welders in. Once, just about here, we ran into *really* rough ice—this is nothing—and it was in one of the early years, before we had a good truck like Thirty-seven. We had two trucks pushing the plow, which was barely hanging together, just pressing on the fenders, with everything gone. It was a complete wreck. God, it was cold too! We were going south, heading home with five or six trucks, and we couldn't move. The snow had blowed up, we had no plow, and *everybody* was tied up. Ennaway, I had Bob Rand, one of my partners, who had made the plow, fly up from Edmonton with a portable welder. He can build ennathing in a shop, but he didn't like workin' outside much. When he landed here he took one look and said, 'I can't fix this out here. I'm going back to Edmonton,' so I said, 'In no way. You have to fix it here.' I went over to the pilot and said, 'Take off, so he can't get on the plane.' The next thing Bob knew, the plane was in the sky and then I said to him, 'The only way you're goin' to get out of here is to fix that plow.' "

John looked out the side in his mirror at 37, which had slowed down in the rough terrain, and he cut our speed to match. "Did he weld it?" I wanted to know.

"Well, sure!" Denison said, looking surprised that I even asked. "We cut up all the tire carriers off the trailers and the bumpers on the backs of the trucks. We just took off any spare iron hanging ennawhere we could find it and he cut it to fit and welded that plow back together again. It took about eight hours, right about here." I looked out the window at this beautiful but bleak terrain and thought about Bob Rand.

"How come you never seem to freeze anything?" I asked. I had been wondering about that ever since I froze my fingers. Two of my frostbitten fingers still gave me a lot of pain and I was sitting on them now, so they would stop aching.

"Oh I freeze quick now, my nose and cheeks and ears, because I froze them so many times," John replied. "But I have no permanent marks from freezing, so I guess Jack Frost doesn't like us guys. Most of the time you're workin' on a warm engine when you're outside and the heat rises. Of course if you're workin' on the bottom the heat doesn't go down, it goes up, so we like to work from the top and on the side. Generally though, you have a Suzy shining at you or a Herman Nelson, and we have a tarp or parachute to stop the wind. We allus have cardboard or plywood along for protection too." He turned and looked at me. "Don't you know nothin' yet?"

I said I guessed I didn't. To change the subject and because the sun was sending streams of golden light through the grey clouds, transforming the scene into one of quiet, cold beauty, I said, "It's beautiful here! Don't you think so?"

"Beautiful?" He bit the word as he said it. "It isn't beautiful to me. I think big trees and nice weather are beautiful, but not snow, ice and rocks. It's just where I come to make a livin'." He was watching Lowen, rolled down his window, waved to him to go further left now, and closed the window again. "I never like to start in on somethin' I don't finish," he said. "One of my biggest problems is that after the price is decided all I care about once I start is gettin' the job done. I stop worryin' about the cost then and this doesn't make my partners too happy sometimes. I got no complaints though and I wouldn't want to change things. I'm a lot happier and better off than a lot of guys I know."

We were now about ten miles out on Great Bear Lake. Denison pointed to a pressure ridge, a wide band of broken ice, several feet high, light blue against the flat snowy ice immediately surrounding it. It ran for miles in a curving line, vanishing somewhere in the middle of the lake. Of all the distinctive features of northern weather that the men who constantly deal with ice dread, they fear the pressure ridge the most, even while it fascinates them; treacherous, deceptive, dangerous, frequently impassable. We followed along inside the curve of this raised band of ice for several miles, until it blocked the way ahead so directly that we could not avoid crossing it. Denison got out, walked over to it, and dug into its craggy ice chips with his foot. He waved Lowen ahead, got back in the camper, and we drove over a low spot, lurching across the bumpy ice. "This is a very small pressure ridge and it's dead," he said. "It's quit moving and the cracks are all froze up."

"How blue it is!" I exclaimed.

"That's because fresh water is directly underneath," John replied. "Ice is a solid, same as metal. It shrinks when the weather is cold, expands when it's warm. Temperature variations change the texture of your ice. On a cold night on these really big lakes, you'll get cracks opening as wide as four feet. On a warm day, you can actually see the expanding ice moving back together again, and if it has expanded beyond the size it was originally, it overlaps and breaks, which leaves real fresh water underneath that spot. Sometimes when the ice overlaps it piles up twenty feet, even higher, and catches you by surprise. That was a pressure ridge we fell into in old Thirty-six last year on this lake, when you flew to Port Radium. Do you remember when we fell into Great Bear Lake?"

I said yes, I did.

"That was a low one. Only it didn't happen to be dead like this one we just went over." Denison's eyes were darting everywhere while he talked. "Jimmy was sitting in the back of a caboose once on Great Bear Lake, further up, when the ice heaved straight up about a mile away from him," Denison continued. "It was in the spring, and he said it was like an earthquake, with everything shakin' and heavin'. There was a great loud bang like a bomb, combined with a heavy thud when the ice cracked. For a second he said he didn't know where to run, until he realized what had happened. Del Curry says the most frustratin' experience he ever had was being on a pressure ridge on Great Slave Lake while it was forming. Guess why? He was asleep. He was in a Bombardier, and had turned around to wait for the man behind him and Del could feel his vehicle shakin' and tremblin', and thought in his sleep that the other guy was just bumpin' him to wake him up. When he opened his eyes, there was a pressure ridge eight feet high right in front of his eyes. All his life he had wanted to see a pressure ridge forming and he had slept right through it, when it did. The trouble with pressure ridges is that they are such a terrible temptation to cross, when they are low. Jimmy Magrum, the son of a gun, he'll go round and round a pressure ridge, but I have a real bad habit of finding the lowest place, breaking it down with a needle bar, throwing some planks down and going through. It looks so easy but if you don't make it you are tipping down into open water the way we did last year in old Thirty-six up at Port Radium."

"Yes."

"That's why I'd ruther have a trailer truck than Cats in the lead in my operation," Denison said. "A Cat drops right down into the open water in a crack, but a truck with a spread of forty feet generally hangs up."

We were travelling through deep hard snow and 37 was plowing a road ahead for us, zigzagging to avoid the rough spots. Denison sped up beside Lowen, and shouted, "If you keep straight ahead, you'll be all right."

John put his foot on the gas again and surged forward ahead of Lowen. "I like to make my road nice and straight," he said. "I like to stay about two miles from shore on this Big Lake to get better perspective of where I'm at. Ennaway, the ice is generally smoother out further. Not that this is rough ice. Some years it's over the top of the plow and over the top of the lowboy."

The sun had come fully out and turned the sky into a clear beautiful blue ceiling, with white white clouds. At this spot, where the wind had swept everything clean as if with a big broom, the lake's surface was a glassy blue-green, with tufts of snow scattered around like powder puffs. There seemed to be a line of these powder puffs popping up from the ice over further to our left on the lake, and John said, "See that? That's the ice cracking. You see it all the time when it's cold on these big lakes. When the ice cracks, it shoots up snow. If we stopped, you could hear it."

"Hear what?" I asked.

"Hear the ice crackin'," he said. "Crack, crack."

We travelled for about an hour until a humming noise sounded above us in the sky. A small red-and-white plane buzzed low and when we waved, it circled and landed on the ice. Hettrick had come once more, carrying two packages, a large one a foot long, and a small one; the new generator for 37 and a box of parts. He handed the boxes to Lowen, waved to us, pointed to his watch, got back in his plane and flew away.

We stood on the ice on Great Bear Lake and watched him leave. It was after four and the sun had slipped almost below the horizon. Looking down into the smooth dark ice under my feet, I did not see the clear blue-green depths that I was expecting, but a million criss-cross lines like a maze, down down down. The sun, so long in coming out, so shortly visible, was a great orange-red sphere, slipping down into an orange strip at the horizon; blue sky slowly turning soft grey with little streaks of salmon pink. "God, but it's beautiful up here!" Denison exclaimed. Shocked, I turned to look at him, but he had slipped swiftly into the camper, after this unseemly display of emotion.

We headed north again. I looked back in my side mirror. Behind us was a long white road, as far as I could see: our Ice Road, bordered with riffles of snow pushed into drifts on either side by the plow. We had come thirty miles on the lake, travelling this narrow trail north that was still big enough for the biggest trucks, a thin line hacked out for 325 miles that reached back all the way to Fort Byers, to Yellowknife, to connect beyond that to southern roads of Canada and highways of the United States.

We were too close to our destination to fix 37's generator now. It was almost five, and although we could see quite well still, Denison turned on our headlights. The lights from Echo Bay Mine were twinkling at us in the darkening sky. They winked, they nodded, they were welcoming us. The whole side of the hill at Port Radium was twinkling with the little lights of other people's lives. We stopped, and the truck beside us stopped too. We had come to a second pressure ridge, higher than the first one by a foot or so, and curving out for miles into the lake.

We backtracked several miles, until we found a hole through the pressure ridge, a reasonably smooth patch of ice. We were further out now on Great Bear Lake, travelling on the left of a little island, doubling on our own tracks, making a second, parallel white road on the other side of the pressure ridge; but we were heading straight for the mine again. As we came closer, I could pick out familiar landmarks; the tank farm, the mill with its long chute to the water's edge, the low narrow bunkhouse, the 128 wooden steps to the top of the hill; the mine manager's house where Mrs. Zigarlik must surely be at her observation post at the window, and would have a warm supper waiting for us. I could not see her, of course, but I knew she was there, with the field glasses that the American professor of botany gave her held up to her eyes. She must have spotted us by now.

I imagined how we looked to Mrs. Zigarlik, who would be standing, round-faced, round-bodied, in her gingham dress at her window, her thin hair combed straight back in a bun, her sharp eyes taking in at once the significance of the bright twin headlights of the camper and the dark headlights of the trailer truck, with the strange glowing orange ball at its windshield, where Mukluk tirelessly held the propane heater aloft. She would have guessed by now that the truck's generator was dead, I am sure of that, would have seen Hettrick's plane land on the ice, and guessed again why he had come. She had long since called her husband's office where the men were placing bets as to the day of our arrival, to tell them what they could already see for themselves: that we had come at last.

Denison halted. Lowen stopped too, looking puzzled. "Our fire's gone out in the Lazy Susan," John said to me.

"How can you tell?"

"I watch for the steam that comes from the vent in the top of the camper in my side mirror, but there's no steam there now," he said. He made no move to get out; neither did he start to go on. He just sat, with his hands limp on the steering wheel.

"Today is the twenty-third of January," he said. "Last year I was here by the twenty-first. Two days late. But that's all behind us now." He paused, then said, "Do you see what we did? Each time we went into town and came out again, we came out further."

"How many miles do you think we drove altogether, on the Ice Road?" I asked.

He was silent while he worked it out in his head. "About a thousand, two hundred and seventy-five miles," he replied. "Are you sorry you came?" he asked suddenly.

"No, of course not. Are you sorry I came?" I asked.

"Nope," he said. "I'd like to see all this written down. The way it really happens."

"I wonder why you do this kind of work, when it makes you so sick," I said. "Everybody thought you might die."

"Well, I'm not goin' to," he said indignantly." If I don't want to I don't have to, do I? Those gravediggers are not goin' to get me because I'm not ready!" He was silent, then said, "I really don't know why I'm doing this, but I guess because I like doing it. Why does a guy do a lot of things? I fell into it, and landed up doing it. Turning left or right sometimes makes a difference. Because I turned this way, I went this way." He searched a little bit further. "Oh, I don't know. Something about the North, maybe. You feel a little more as if you're on your own. You're your own person, somehow."

I could see Lowen and Mukluk looking over at us curiously. But John was not leaving yet. He sat with his chin resting on his hand, elbow on the steering wheel, looking out over the lake towards the mine. "Of course nobody knows what they are doing in this country and we're all dumb buggers to be here. Isn't that right?" he asked. He didn't wait for an answer. "You know, any of these guys could have done what I've done, but they don't seem to be able to, or maybe they don't want to tie it all together," he said. "That's all I do; get the freight, the men, the connections, tie it all together and figure out the costs. Without guys like Hughie Arden or Frank Lorenzen, Davy's father, or Jimmy Magrum, Del Curry and Stu Demelt, without those guys, who went with me on the first road to Tundra where I proved you could build a road over a long distance that far north for freighting and keep it going, I'd never have gotten any of this done. I started up here with no experience and learned from all those guys. Tundra was the real breakthrough because nobody had ever driven trucks into the Barrens before. Now, take Mukluk, Lewis, Davy, Burns, Tom, Jimmy. If I'm lucky, they'll all work for me, and none of them would be here if they didn't want to come. All these guys have helped me. But they wouldn't do it on their own. It works out that way, doesn't it?"

He shifted gears and we moved along towards Port Radium. I could hear the big truck, 37, start up too, I could see it moving again in my mirror, following us where we were lighting the way. Its plow cut a neat broad road behind our tire tracks, flinging snow to both sides in a white cloud from the edges of its wings. The darkness had settled in around us and the twinkling lights of the mine were moving closer, getting brighter. They lit up the white buildings with the green trim, the wooden scaffolding of the stairs up the hill. Lights framed the oblong airstrip over which we were now speeding towards the shore of Echo Bay and the mine buildings beyond.

It was a lovely night, full of moonlight. "We could have come in without lights," John said. "Neither truck really needs lights tonight, but I turned ours on so we could be seen at the mine."

We crossed from the icy surface of Echo Bay to the shore and climbed a little hill. "This was a real good trip," Denison said, as he stopped the camper on the dock where his trucks would start parking to unload freight, in a day or two, maybe even by tomorrow night. "Except for dropping that truck and the accidents, all that falling through the ice and getting wet, opening my road to Echo Bay this year went better than ever before!"